## 《多彩中国节》丛书编委会
### Editorial Committee of the Colorful Chinese Festivals Series

**顾 问**

史蒂文·伍德·施迈德　冯骥才　周明甫

**主 编**

彭新良

**编 委**（按姓名笔画排列）

韦荣慧　田　阡　邢　莉　刘　哲
齐勇锋　阮全友　张　刚　张　跃
张　暖　张曙光　陈　娟　徐　敏
黄忠彩　萧　放　曹雅欣　彭新良

**Consultants**

Steven Wood Schmader　Feng Jicai　Zhou Mingfu

**Chief Editor**

Peng Xinliang

**Editorial Board**

Wei Ronghui　Tian Qian　Xing Li　Liu Zhe

Qi Yongfeng　Ruan Quanyou　Zhang Gang　Zhang Yue

Zhang Nuan　Zhang Shuguang　Chen Juan　Xu Min

Huang Zhongcai　Xiao Fang　Cao Yaxin　Peng Xinliang

丛书主编　彭新良

*Naadam*

汉英对照

# 那达慕

张曙光　著

赵成　刘紫薇　等　译

徐伟红　审校

全国百佳图书出版单位

时代出版传媒股份有限公司

安徽人民出版社

图书在版编目（CIP）数据

那达慕：汉英对照 / 张曙光著；赵成，刘紫薇等译 . -- 合肥：安徽人民出版社，2018.8
（多彩中国节丛书 / 彭新良主编）

ISBN 978-7-212-10031-5

Ⅰ . ①那… Ⅱ . ①张… ②赵…③刘… Ⅲ . ①那达慕大会－风俗习惯－中国－汉、英 Ⅳ . ① K892.312

中国版本图书馆 CIP 数据核字 (2018) 第 005331 号

《多彩中国节》丛书

# 那达慕：汉英对照
NADAMU

彭新良　丛书主编
张曙光　著　　赵成 刘紫薇 等 译　　徐伟红　审校

出 版 人：徐　敏　　　　选题策划：刘　哲　陈　娟
出版统筹：张　旻　袁小燕　　责任编辑：陈　娟　汪　龙　孔　健
责任印制：董　亮　　　　装帧设计：陈　爽　宋文岚

出版发行：时代出版传媒股份有限公司 http://www.press-mart.com
　　　　　安徽人民出版社 http://www.ahpeople.com
地　　址：合肥市政务文化新区翡翠路 1118 号出版传媒广场八楼
邮　　编：230071
电　　话：0551-63533258　0551-63533259（传真）
印　　刷：安徽联众印刷有限公司

开本：880mm×1230mm　1/32　　印张：8.5　　字数：250 千
版次：2018 年 8 月第 1 版　　2018 年 9 月第 1 次印刷

ISBN　978-7-212-10031-5　　　　　　　定价：38.00 元

# 代 序

## 我们共同的日子

个人一年一度最重要的日子是生日,大家一年一度最重要的日子是节日。节日是大家共同的日子。

节日是一种纪念日,内涵多种多样。有民族的、国家的、宗教的,比如国庆节、圣诞节等。有某一类人的,如妇女、儿童、劳动者的,这便是妇女节、儿童节、劳动节等。也有与人们的生活生产密切相关的,这类节日历史悠久,很早就形成了一整套人们约定俗成、代代相传的节日习俗,这是一种传统的节日。传统节日也多种多样。中国是一个多民族国家,有 56 个民族,统称中华民族。传统节日有全民族共有的,也有某个民族特有的。比如春节、中秋节、元宵节、端午节、清明节、重阳节等,就为中华民族所共用和共享;世界文化遗产羌年就为羌族独有和独享。各民族这样的节日很多。

传统节日是在漫长的农耕时代形成的。农耕时代生产与生活、人与自然的关系十分密切。人们或为了感恩于大自然的恩赐,或为了庆祝辛勤劳作换来的收获,或为了激发生命的活力,或为了加强人际的亲情,经过长期相互认同,最终约定俗成,渐渐把一年中某一天确定为节日,并创造了十分完整又严格的节俗,如仪式、庆典、规制、禁忌,乃至特定的游艺、装饰与食品,来把节日这天演化成一个独具内涵、迷人的日子。更重要的是,人们在每一个传统的节日里,还把共同的生活理想、人间愿望与审美追求融入节日的内涵与种种仪式中。因此，它是中华民族世间理想与生活愿望极致的表现。可以说，我们的传统——精神文化传统，往往就是依靠这代代相传的一年一度的节日继承下来的。

然而，自从 20 世纪整个人类进入由农耕文明向工业文明的过渡，农耕时代形成的文化传统开始瓦解。尤其是中国，在近百年由封闭走向开放的过程中，节日文化——特别是城市的节日文化受到现代文明与外来文化的冲击。当下人们已经鲜明地感受到传统节日渐行渐远，并为此产生忧虑。传统节日的淡化必然使其中蕴含的传统精神随之涣散。然而，人们并没有坐等传统的消失，主动和积极地与之应对。这充分显示了当代中国人在文化上的自觉。

近 10 年，随着中国民间文化遗产抢救工程的全面展开，国家非物质文化遗产名录申报工作的有力推动，传统节日受到关注，一些重要的传统节日被列入了国家文化遗产名录。继而，2006 年国家将每年 6 月的第 2 个周六确定为"文化遗产日"，2007 年国务院决定将 3 个中华民族的重要节日——清明节、端午节和中秋节列为法定放假日。这一重大决定，表现了国家对公众的传统文化生活及其传承的重视与尊重，同时也是保护节日文化遗产十分必要的措施。

节日不放假必然直接消解了节日文化，放假则是恢复节日传统的首要条件。但放假不等于远去的节日立即就会回到身边。节日与假日的不同是因为节日有特定的文化内容与文化形式。那么，重温与恢复已经变得陌生的传统节日习俗则是必不可少的了。

千百年来，我们的祖先从生活的愿望出发，为每一个节日都创造出许许多多美丽又动人的习俗。这种愿望是理想主义的，所以节日习俗是理想的；愿望是情感化的，所以节日习俗也是情感化的；愿望是美好的，所以节日习俗是美的。人们用合家团聚的年夜饭迎接新年；把天上的明月化为手中甜甜的月饼，来象征人间的团圆；在严寒刚刚消退、万物复苏的早春，赶到野外去打扫墓地，告慰亡灵，表达心中的缅怀，同时戴花插柳，踏青春游，亲切地拥抱大地山川……这些诗意化的节日习俗，使我们一代代人的心灵获得了美好的安慰与宁静。

对于少数民族来说，他们特有的节日的意义则更加重要。节日还是他们民族集体记忆的载体、共同精神的依托、个性的表现、民族身份之所在。

谁说传统的习俗过时了？如果我们淡忘了这些习俗，就一定要去重温一下传统。重温不是表象地模仿古人的形式，而是用心去体验传统中的精神与情感。

在历史进程中，习俗是在不断变化的，但民族传统的精神实质不应变。这传统就是对美好生活的不懈追求，对大自然的感恩与敬畏，对家庭团圆与世间和谐永恒的企望。

这便是我们节日的主题，也是这套《多彩中国节》丛书编写的根由与目的。

中国 56 个民族是一个大家庭，各民族的节日文化异彩纷呈，既有春节、元宵节、中秋节这样多民族共庆的节日，也有泼水节、火把节、那达慕等少数民族特有的节日。这套丛书选取了中国最有代表性的 10 个传统节日，一节一册，图文并茂，汉英对照，旨在为海内外读者通俗、全面地呈现中国绚丽多彩的节庆文化和民俗文化；放在一起则是中华民族传统节日的一部全书，既有知识性、资料性、工具性，又有可读性和趣味性。10 本精致的小册子，以翔实的文献和生动的传说，将每个节日的源起、流布与习俗，图文并茂、有滋有味地娓娓道来，从这些节日的传统中，可以看出中国人的精神追求和文化脉络。这样一套丛书不仅是对我国传统节日的一次总结，也是对传统节日文化富于创意的弘扬。

　　我读了书稿，心生欣喜，因序之。

冯骥才

（全国政协常委、中国文联原执行副主席）

# Preface

## Our Common Days

The most important day for a person is his or her birthday while the most important days for all are festivals, which are our common days.

Festivals are embedded with rich connotations for remembering. There're ethnic, national, and religious ones, such as National Day and Christmas Day; festivals for a certain group of people, such as Women's Day, Children's Day, and Laborers' Day; and those closely related to people's life and production, which enjoy a long history and feature a complete set of well-established festive traditions passed on from one generation to another. These are so-called traditional festivals, which vary greatly, too.

China, consisting of 56 nationalities, is a multi-ethnic country. People in China are collectively called the Chinese nation. So it's no wonder that some of the traditional festivals are celebrated by all nationalities while others only by certain nationalities, with the representatives of the former ones being the Spring Festival, the Lantern Festival, the Dragon Boat Festival, the Tomb-Sweeping Festival, and the Double Ninth Festival, etc. and that of the latter being the Qiang New Year, a unique festival for Qiang ethnic group. Each of ethnic groups in China has quite a number of their unique traditional festivals.

The traditional festivals have taken shape in the long agrarian times when people were greatly dependent on nature and when life was closely related to production. People gradually saw eye to eye with each other in the long-term practicing sets of rituals, celebrations, taboos as well as games, embellishments, and foods in a strict way and decided to select some days of one year as festivals with a view to expressing their gratitude to nature, celebrating harvesting, stimulating vitality of life, or strengthening bonds between family members and relatives. In this way, festivals have evolved into charming days with unique connotations. More importantly, people have instilled their common aspirations and aesthetic pursuits into festive connotations and rituals. To put it simply, festivals are consummate demonstrations of Chinese people's worldly aspirations and ideals, and Chinese people's spiritual cultures are inherited for generations by them.

Nevertheless, the cultural traditions formed in the agrarian times began to collapse with human beings being in transition from agrarian civilization to industrial one, esp., in China, whose festive cultures were severely hammered by modern civilization and foreign cultures in nearly one hundred years from being closed to opening up to the world. Nowadays, people strongly feel that traditional festivals are drifting away from their lives and are deeply concerned about it owing to the fact that dilution of traditional festivals means the fall of the traditional spirit of Chinese people. Of course, we don't wait and see; instead, we cope with it in a positive way. This fully displays the contemporary Chinese people's cultural consciousness.

In recent ten years, the traditional festivals have been earning more and more attention and some significant ones are included to the list of the National Heritages with the vigorous promotion of China's Folk Heritage Rescue Program and China's intangible cultural heritage application; for example, China set the second Saturday of June as "Cultural Heritage Day" in 2006; the State Council decided to list three significant traditional festivals as legal holidays—the Tomb-Sweeping Festival, the Dragon Boat Festival, and the Mid-Autumn Festival in 2007. These measures show the state gives priority to and pay tribute to the inheritance of public traditional cultures.

Holidays are necessary for spending festivals which will be diluted otherwise; however, holidays don't necessarily bring back traditional festivals. Since festivals, different from holidays, are equipped with special cultural forms and contents, it's essential to recover those traditional festive customs which have become stranger and stranger to contemporary Chinese people.

In the past thousands of years, our ancestors, starting from their aspirations, created many fine and engaging traditions. These aspirations are ideal, emotional, and beautiful, so are the festival traditions. People usher in the New Year by having the meal together on the New Year's Eve, make moon cakes by imitating the moon in the sky, standing for family reunion, or go to sweep the tombs of ancestors or family members for commemorating or comforting in the early spring when the winter just recedes and everything wakes up while taking spring hiking and enjoying spring scenes by the way. These poetic festive customs greatly comfort souls of people for generations.

As for ethnic minority people, their special festivals mean more to them. The festivals carry the collective memory, common spirit, character of their ethnic groups as well as mark their ethnic identities.

Are the traditional festive customs really out-dated? We're compelled to review them if we really forget them. What matters for review is not imitating the forms of the ancient Chinese people's celebrations but experiencing essence and emotions embedded in them with heart and soul.

Traditions have evolved with history's evolving, but the traditional national spirit has never changed. The spirit lies in people's never-ending pursuit for beautiful life, consistent gratitude and awe for nature, constant aspiration for family reunion and world harmony.

This is also the theme of our festivals and the root-cause of compiling the series.

The Chinese nation, featuring its colorful and varieties of festive cultures, boasts the common festivals celebrated by all nationalities, such as the Spring Festival, the Lantern Festival, the Mid-Autumn Festival, and the ethnic festivals, such as the Water Splashing Festival (Thai people), the Torch Festival (Yi people), Naadam (Mongolian nationality). This series, selecting the most typical ten festivals of China, with each festival being in one volume with figures and in both English and Chinese, unfolds the colorful festive and folk cultures in an engaging and all-round way for appealing to foreign readers. If put together, they constitute a complete set of books on Chinese traditional festivals, being instructive and intriguing. The ten brochures elaborate on the origins, distribution, and customs of each festival in an engaging way with figures, tales, and rich literature. Chinese people's spiritual pursuit and cultural veining can be tracked in this series, serving as a summary of Chinese traditional festivals and innovative promotion of them.

I went over the series with delight, and with delight, wrote the preface, too.

Feng Jicai

CPPCC National Committee member

Former Vice-president of the China Federation of Literary and Art Circles

# 目　录

多彩中国节

那达慕

# Contents

# 引　言

　　农历五月至八月，是内蒙古大草原水草丰美的黄金季节，也是蒙古人迎接并感恩苍天赋予的福运吉祥，欢庆、娱乐的时节。只要有蒙古人的地方就有那达慕！在内蒙古各盟旗、新疆、甘肃、青海、云南以及首都北京，人们从四面八方汇聚到一起，沉浸在节日的欢腾与喜悦之中。

　　那达慕，蒙古语意为"游戏""游艺""娱乐"，是蒙古族在游牧生产、生活中发生、发展、演变而来的一项传统的民俗活动。那达慕的历史非常久远，在蒙古族发展的各个历史时期都发挥了重要的作用。那达慕最初通常在祭祀山水、军队出征、凯旋、帝王登基以及大型庆典等场合举行。随着时代发展，逐渐演变成今天的包括多种文化娱乐内容、多种社会功能于一身的民族节庆盛典。当今的那达慕除了传统的"男儿三艺"——摔跤、赛马和射箭外，还有庆典仪式、祭祀祈祷、文艺演出、田径比赛和各类经济文化展览以及订货洽谈、物资交流、聚会欢宴等各类活动内容，是蒙古族文化符号集中表现的舞台。那达慕集合竞技、娱乐、集会、庆祝等多种功能和目的，融会了政治、经济、生产、生活、宗教信仰、象征艺术、社交来往、民族心理等多种文化现象，承担并发挥着满足多重社会、文化需求的功能，表达着蒙古族深层的族群认同、文化信仰和追求。

　　以牧业为主的蒙古族，创造了适应草原生态环境和畜牧的生产生活方式，也形成了有别于农耕文化的草原游牧文化。

　　草原游牧人与农耕民的生活节律存在很大不同。游牧文化的时间概念并不完全以天文周期为依据，而更多以物候的轮换更替为参照。

　　游牧生产更多是以季节为单位，而非时、日。宋代赵珙撰《蒙鞑备录》所记："其俗每以草青为一岁。人有问其岁则曰几草矣，亦尝问彼生月日，笑而答曰，初不知之，亦不能记其春与秋也。"对于游牧民族而言，畜群是其生产生活的根本，"每日跟着畜群跑"，"一切以五畜的需要出发"。游牧民族对草原的依赖性非常强，注重水草的选择，并依季节特性，四季转场，"逐水草而迁徙"是其生活的方式。而这种生活方式下产生了"向夏季游牧地前进的时间""住在夏季游牧驻地的时间""离开夏季游牧驻地的时间"等时间观念。正如一位牧人所讲："我们那时最远到阿巴嘎、阿巴嘎纳尔旗游牧，一走350公里。春、秋几乎都在路上度过。冬季、夏季游牧到自己的故乡，过新年，祭祀自己的敖包。""过去都是游牧的，十几天就得搬家，

○欢乐的那达慕

随着牲畜而游动。哪儿水草好，适合牲畜就往那儿开始游动。10~20里才一户人家。"

按季节来流动的生活方式，确定了游牧民族节日文化的时空边界。空间上，它是流动的、迁移的、离散的；时间上，它是统括的、季节性的、大刻度的。因此，作为游牧生产生活中产生的那达慕强调的是季节性而非日期性。那达慕通常在水草丰美的夏季举行，这是牧业生产的丰收季，牲畜出栏，奶制品上市，在牧业时间的安排上属于相对闲暇期。这时，大大小小的那达慕随着敖包祭祀此起彼伏，官方的、私人的各种形式的那达慕也纷纷开展起来。人们从日常的以家庭为单位的相对独立和单一的生活状态中进入公共的、集体的、狂欢的状态，暂时告别日常的常态，融入身心愉悦的节日当中。那达慕是蒙古族的文化时间，那达慕在草原牧人"年"的时间框架中，具有特定的节日内容和功能。

那达慕持续的时间从一天到三天、五天，甚至七天不等。那达慕的具体日期没有特定的规制，因地域而不同。那达慕的内容、主题、规模、形式、举办者、参加者也呈现出异彩纷呈的局面。不仅如此，同一季节内，相邻地区那达慕举行的频次也不尽相同。以那达慕文化传承保持较为完整的内蒙古锡林郭勒盟东乌珠穆沁旗为例，其传统的敖包那达慕，从每年的四月到八月都在进行。每个嘎查、苏木、家庭都有祭拜的敖包，各种类型敖包的祭祀日期又各不相同，由此形成了那达慕节日簇，贯穿整个夏季。那达慕还与其他庆典活动密切相联，具有很强的伴生性，呈现出多样性和地方性特点。

# Introduction

Every year from Lunar May to August when grasslands grow lush in Inner Mongolia, People will celebrate for the natural blessings. Where there are Mongols, there is Naadam. Whether in Inner Mongolia or Yunnan Province, Mongols from far and near gather together to celebrate the festival, immersing themselves in great jubilation.

Naadam is a Mongolian word which means game, entertainment and recreation, and also a traditional folk activity that emerged, developed and evolved from nomadic life and production. Naadam has played an important role in each historical period of Mongolian development. Originally, it was generally held when people offer sacrifices to nature, troops go on an expedition or return in triumphs, emperors ascend the throne or other grand celebrations. Gradually, it evolved into a grand national festival with many kinds of cultural and recreational activities and carried many social functions. Besides the traditional Three Games of Men( namely Mongolian wrestling, horse racing and archery), other activities, such as rituals and ceremonies, singing and dancing performances, sports and commercial activities are all included in Naadam festival and are the epitomes of the Mongolian culture. Naadam has several functions and objectives such as sports, entertainments, gatherings, and celebrations etc, integrates many cultural symbols including politics, economies, productions, lives, religions, symbolic art, social interactions, national psychology and so on, bears the responsibility to perform the function of satisfying multiple social and cultural needs, and expresses ethnic identity, cultural belief, and deep spiritual pursuits of Mongolian ethnic group.

Mongolian people mainly rely on animal husbandry for livelyhood. And they have adopted a way of production and life that fits grassland circumstances and have formed nomadic grassland culture, differing from farming culture.

Grassland nomads adopt a living pattern quite different from that of farmers. Take the sense of time for an example, instead of judging entirely by astronomical cycle, nomads prefer to use phenological rotation as reference.

Nomads base their production on seasons rather than on hours or days. According to the Memorandum of Mongolian Tartar by Zhao Gong in Song Dynasty (960-1297), it is a custom that "grass turns green and people grow one year older. Therefore people's age is calculated by the glory and gloom of grass. When asked about birth date, they can't answer because they don't know it since the very beginning". For nomadic ethnic groups, herds are the basis of production and life. They drive the herds everyday and everything is based on the needs of herds. It is the normalcy. They base on the grassland strongly, so they have to select grasslands carefully and move from one to another in different seasons. Migration towards water and grassland is a reflection of their lives, which generates the concept of time, such as that of when to move to and leave the summer nomadic encampment, and that of how long to stay there. A shepherd once said: "We've ever reached as for as Abaga, Abaga-nar banner, over 350 kilometers away. In spring and autumn, we almost spend all the time on the way. In winter and summer we move back to celebrate the New Year and hold the ovoo ceremonies. " "In the past, we all live a nomadic life and move every dozen of days. We would move to anywhere there is fertile grassland. Generally speaking, we came across one household every 5 or 10 kilometers or so."

The nomadic lifestyle which features seasonal migration sets a limit to the space and time of festival culture. In terms of space, it reflects that Mongolian people are always on the move, migrating and living separately. In terms of time, it falls on different seasons and they mirror nomadic culture and lifestyle in a broad sense. Therefore, it is the season that Naadam stresses on in nomadic production and life rather than date. Naadam is usually held in summer when the fields are lush with grass and the water is abundant. Summer is also the harvest season of livestock production. With livestock maturing and dairy products coming to the market, summer is a relatively leisure period in animal husbandry. During this period, Naadam of various scales, whether official or private, are held together with ovoo ceremonies. This is a public, collective carnival in which people can temporarily bid farewell to the daily routines and immerse themselves in physical and mental pleasure of the festival. Unique and important for Mongolian culture, Naadam carries specific festive contents and functions in the time frame of "year" for the shepherds.

Naadam lasts for an uncertain period of time ranging from one day to seven days. There is no definite date for Naadam. Contents, themes, scales, forms, hosts and participants can also differ because of geographical differences. In addition, even two neighboring regions may differ in the frequency of Naadam during the same season. For example, in East Ujimqin Banner, Xilingol League and Inner Mongolia where Naadam traditions is well preserved, traditional Ovoo Naadam is celebrated from

A happy meeting between experienced wrestlers and green-hand wrestlers

April to August each year. Also, throughout the dates, each sumu, gachaa and family has its own ovoo to worship on different dates, thus forming a Naadam festival cluster whole summer. Meanwhile, Naadam is also closely associated with other celebrations, showing its diversity and endemicity.

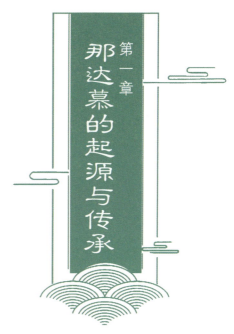

第一章 那达慕的起源与传承

在蒙古语中，"那达慕"一词具体指某一项游戏、运动项目本身，如"额仁郭热本那达慕"，就是指"男儿三艺"，即摔跤（蒙古语称"搏克"）、赛马、射箭三项竞技。但是无论是在蒙古语文献中，还是在内蒙古地区蒙古人的日常生活中，"那达慕"一词一般不会单独出现在蒙古族生活语境中，而是会将它和"耐亦日"（意为：聚会、庆典）一词结合起来，构成"耐亦日·那达慕"复合词，泛指有"那达慕"的"耐亦日"。

从内容、形式以及发生时空条件看，那达慕有三个层面的含义：一是仅指以摔跤、赛马、射箭三项技艺为主的竞技娱乐活动，二是从组织形态上指包含有"那达慕"竞技项目的集会活动，三是从社会功能上指游牧经济下产生的草原节庆。

作为草原节庆，在召开大呼拉尔、庆祝战功、出征、宫廷宴会、皇帝即位、官员升迁、盟旗集会、活佛坐床、敖包祭祀等都举行那达慕。那达慕在共享公共时间、创造共同价值、增强凝聚力方面发挥着重要作用。就其发展传承而言，在不同的时期、地域、功能和效用下，被冠以不同的称谓。

那达慕经历了几百年的发展，不断成熟完善，逐渐成为蒙古族的传统节日。

关于那达慕的起源，主流观点有两个：一是敖包起源说，认为那达慕即敖包祭祀后的娱神活动；另一个是成吉思汗庆典说，认为至少从1206年成吉思汗建立蒙古帝国起便有了那达慕。当然，也有学者认为，那达慕的起源应当追溯到更久远的年代。纳古单夫认为："蒙古族'那达慕'文化，说起它的发轫之初，至少在蒙古人步入文明社会之后，在历史文献上即记述了。当然蒙古人作为中国北方游牧民族的集大成者，他们所承袭的文化，尚须追溯到更古老的时代。仅从匈奴寻源，也要追溯到三千年以前。"

敖包，也作"鄂博"，是蒙古人及相关民族自然崇拜的产物。早期的蒙古人信奉萨满教，在民间记忆中，那达慕的历史

○20世纪30年代的敖包

与蒙古族的宗教信仰历史一样久远。海西希在其《蒙古的宗教》一书中写道："在固定地点堆起的土堆（即鄂博）一般都立于高地、山口、交叉路口等处。它们作为当地的守护神和地神的神祠，享受到了特别的崇拜。因此，在萨满教思想的范畴内，鄂博可以被当作是本地神灵的所在地和汇合处。"

"敖包祭祀后的搏克、赛马就是为了取悦山水及敖包众神，是献给敖包神的'礼物'，这样敖包神就会高兴，能够保佑这方土地的风调雨顺、人畜安康。"事实上，那达慕是敖包祭祀必不可少的一项内容，而敖包祭祀也是那达慕历史发展的重要推动因素。《东观汉记·南匈奴单于传》有单于"岁祭三龙祠，走马，斗橐（骆）驼以为乐事"的记载。《辽史》卷四九也记有契丹人祈雨时亲王及其子孙举行射柳比赛的情景："前期，置百柱天棚。及期，皇帝致奠于先帝御容，乃射柳。皇帝再射，亲王、宰执以次各一射……皇帝、皇后祭东方毕，子弟射柳。"清代《清稗类钞·技勇类》等典籍中更常见有敖包祭祀及其后那达慕的描述。

那达慕本身其实就是敖包祭祀后进行的一种娱神、媚神的仪式活动。那达慕和敖包祭祀是一体的，是一个完整祭祀过程的共同组成。

中国非物质文化遗产网对那达慕是这样表述的："那达慕起源于蒙古汗国建立初期，早在公元1206年，成吉思汗被推举为蒙古大汗时，就举行了盛大的那达慕。"那时，成吉思汗为检阅部队，维护和分配草场，每年7~8月间举行"忽里勒台"（大聚会、会议），将各个部落的首领召集在一起举行那达慕。起初只举行射箭、赛马或摔跤的某一项比赛。

这种始于13世纪，并逐步成型、发展，迄今已有800多年历史的那达慕起源说，现已成为多数人认同的观点。支持这个观点的实证依据是现藏于圣彼得堡艾尔米塔什博物馆的"也孙格石（碑）"，又称"成吉思汗石（碑铭）"。1219—1225 年蒙古帝国在成吉思汗的率领下开始了第一次西征，蒙古军长驱直入，征服花刺子模国，于1225 年凯旋。为庆祝胜利，在蒙古国西境的不哈速只忽举行了盛大的庆典，即那达慕。成吉思汗的弟弟、著名神箭手哈撒儿的儿子也孙格在此次庆典上创下了 335 度（两臂伸展之间的距离为 1 度，约5 尺左右）的射程，并获得成吉思汗降旨刻碑之殊荣，这就是现在的"也孙格石（碑）"。不难看出，当时的庆典中，射箭已是一项竞技娱乐项目。

值得一提的是，今天我们所说"那达慕"的某些内容，虽说古已有之，但就那达慕这种民俗活动直接被冠以"那达慕"称谓并有组织地举办，则是入清以后的事情。对于古代蒙古人而言，"那达慕"并非一个通用的称谓，直至 1947 年内蒙古自治区成立后，"那达慕"一词才开始成为拥有目前我们所共知的特定内涵的专有名词。

1948 年 1 月 1 日呼伦贝尔盟政府成立，在一次有百余人参加的座谈会上，有人提出将甘珠尔庙会改名为呼伦贝尔那达慕。这一建议得到呼伦贝尔党政负责同志的赞同，并将当年 9 月 3 日（农历八月初一）的集会称为甘珠尔庙那达慕大会。甘珠尔庙那达慕属全盟的活动，从 1948 年至 1962 年共举行过 11 次。此后，"那达慕"或"那达慕大会"这一称谓在呼伦贝尔地区传播开来。

锡林郭勒盟那达慕称谓的流行也与呼伦贝尔地区相似。1949 年8 月苏尼特右旗举办了一次"胡硕耐亦日"（旗庆会）。当时的组办者几经推敲，为了与过去王公贵族们的叫法区分开来，决定用"那达慕"来命名那一届"耐亦日"。从此，在锡林郭勒地区，"那达慕"这个称谓也传播开来。

1954 年内蒙古自治区第一届那达慕大会的召开，使得"那达慕"这一称谓在内蒙古自治区乃至其他蒙古族聚集区得以广泛流兴。

二、
那达慕的传承

纵观那达慕历史发展与传承，大体上可以划分为六个发展阶段：12 世纪前的酝酿期、蒙元时期的形成期、明及清初的成熟期、清中期到民国的转型期、中华人民共和国成立后到 20 世纪 80 年代初的传承及模式化发展期、20 世纪 80 年代中期以来的多元发展期。

### （一）酝酿期

从 12 世纪到蒙元时期，那达慕的各单项活动和内容分别独立地得到了娱乐化发展。这时的集会活动中，已有后来发展起来的摔跤、赛马、射箭三项技能的影子。这些活动主要服务于牧民的生产、生活，同时也服务于祭祀活动，是一种具有"巫术"性质的娱神表演，"取悦"天地山水神灵，祈求丰收、人畜安康，具有神秘性和神圣性。

### （二）形成期

蒙元时期为那达慕的形成期。这一时期，那达慕作为一种集竞技、娱乐、集会、庆祝多种功能和目的为一体的民俗事象开始形成，并逐步朝着定型化和程式化方向发展。这一时期，随着蒙古民族统治地位的确立，军事力量的壮大，势力的扩张以及游牧经济的发展，那达慕主要内容的摔跤、赛马、射箭活动有了更为深刻的现实意义和进一步的发展。

○古代蒙古族男子

这一时期，那达慕活动的竞技化程度开始增强，同时其表演、观赏化色彩逐渐提升，从事部分项目的人员开始出现职业化（如摔跤手）。元仁宗时期，延祐六年（1319年）六月戊申，成立了专门管理角力（即摔跤）的官方部门——"校署"，在宫廷中已出现了专门供皇帝消遣和娱乐的职业化的摔跤手。仁宗于"延祐七年六月庚申，赐角抵百二十人钞，各千贯"。由此看，当时不仅有百余人的一个职业队伍，而且还设置了专门的观赏摔跤的场所。此外，从元人笔记以及后期的清朝记载中我们获知，元朝宫廷一度盛行"诈马宴"。所谓"诈马宴"，又称质孙宴，被誉为"蒙古族的第一宴"。"诈马"一种被认为是蒙古语，意为去掉毛发的整畜；另一种被认为是汉语，

"诈"有漂亮、俊俏之意，"诈马"是指装饰华丽的马，"诈马宴"就是要骑乘诈马前往的宴会。质孙（只孙）是蒙古语"颜色"的音译，质孙宴要着一色衣参加。赴宴者所穿的衣服每年都由工匠专制，皇帝颁赐，一日一换，颜色一致。"诈马宴"是集合歌舞、服饰、宴飨、竞技娱乐为一体，并有严格的议程和程式的宫廷较高层级的"耐亦日"（聚会）形式，是届期举行的官方"定制"仪式化的那达慕。

### （三）成熟期

明至清初那达慕得到了长足的发展，臻于成熟，参与那达慕活动人员的职业化特点越发明显，那达慕的娱乐化功能得到增强，并显现出制度化和专业化发展趋势。那达慕的活动组织形式也已基本实现程式化、模式化的形态。

明代，蒙古族统治者退居故土以后，照例举行"那达慕"的"诈马宴"。据明初叶子奇的《草木子》载："北方有诈马筵席，最其筵之盛也。谓王公贵戚子弟竟以衣马华侈相高也。"可见明代"诈马宴"仍在草原上盛行，只是由于蒙古常年的内外战乱，留下的那达慕资料非常少。满清入主中原后，非常重视骑射、角力（摔跤）。皇太极曾下令"子弟辈壮者当令以角弓羽箭习射，幼者当以木弓柳箭习射"，同时以身作则，亲率臣下至演武场较射，还令诸旗下王公贝勒贝子等"各率本旗护军较射"。当时蒙古八旗军是协助清军入关的主力军，自然重视骑射的训练。这一时期成立了专管"男儿三艺"的"善扑营"，将其纳入国家组织和管理的范畴内，促进了三项竞技的发展。还出现了由官方赐予著名摔跤手名号进行奖励的做法，这说明当时摔跤非常普遍和盛行，摔跤手具有较高的社会地位，摔跤作为一种竞技在方方面面都较为成熟。同时，"男儿三艺"被作为各种宴享和招待外藩使臣的重要竞技表演项目。当时那达慕作为展示和宣示藩部势力的一种手段，发挥着一定的政治功能。

## （四）转型期

清中期到民国为那达慕发展的转型期，那达慕作为社会集会的重要组成得到了实质性的扩展，商业贸易成为那达慕的重要内容，"男儿三艺"作为节庆活动的娱乐功能凸现。这一时期，那达慕的主要活动基本上脱离了实用性，尤其是摔跤更是彻底褪去了军事功能而完全演变为娱乐活动。

乾隆年间，每年秋8月木兰围（今河北围场县）时蒙古王公向其敬献酒宴，表演蒙古乐歌、相扑及各样技艺。这种技艺献演和元代诸帝巡幸上都举行诈马宴极其相似。从诗文记载看，与扈从元代皇帝上都巡幸一样，清代也有不少扈从皇帝至避暑山庄的官宦文人写过许多行围即事的诗篇，如纪昀、裘日修、赵翼等均有作品流传。其中赵翼曾亲眼目睹蒙古"布库"（摔跤）的表演，写下了《行围即景·相扑》的长诗，生动地描摹了布库的衣着、对峙双方注目审势的姿态，互相扭结的各种招式以及突施绝技一举获胜的场景。

清政府对蒙古族实行的盟、旗制度，使得那达慕以自然地域为单位，出现了程度不同的地区特点。旗是蒙古地区的基本军事、行政单位，同时也是皇帝赐给旗内各级蒙古封建领主的世袭领地。由此各旗县开始盛行名称不同、目的不同的那达慕。那达慕成为各旗县内部以及旗县之间交往的重要集会和祝庆形式。

《巴林右旗志》记载了从雍正八年（1730年）起，旗内13个寺庙的千余名喇嘛每年集中到大板荟福寺参加一年一度的"六月庙会"。庙会期间，举行喇嘛教的隆重法事典礼，开展群体性的民族文化、

多彩中国节

那达慕

体育和物资交流活动。各旗选派快马、走马、摔跤手、射箭手、棋手参赛，为时一月，热闹非凡。届时还有北京、天津、通辽、赤峰等地的商贩云集于此，商贸活动极为活跃。《阿拉善风俗志》记有乾隆年间，阿拉善第三代王爷罗布桑多尔济迎娶清朝的公主为福晋，成为亲王。为庆大喜，于乾隆三十年（1765年）举办了声势浩大的那达慕，并沿袭了成吉思汗时期与子孙们聚会游乐的传统，将此命名为"乌日森耐亦日"。这次那达慕上聚集了成千上万的牧人，搭建了百顶蒙古包。全旗8个苏木的百姓及衙门的协理、管旗、章京等官员全部承担任务，以苏木为单位组织了"男儿三艺"的训练。最终，从几百对摔跤手中选出32名，从数百名弓箭手中选出120名射手以及从几百匹公马中选出80匹快马参加了比赛。由此可见这次那达慕的规模和规格。这一时期，不仅各个旗县为各种目的举办那达慕，盟旗之间为增强联络和交流也举行"联合"的那达慕。在喀尔喀地区的"七旗""十札萨克"那达慕就是相邻的7个旗和10个盟之间定期举行的那达慕。此外，传统的敖包祭祀那达慕依然盛行，每年定期举办。《清稗类钞·技勇类》《内蒙古纪要》等史料为我们清晰地展现了当时祭祀敖包后那达慕上的摔跤、远程马赛以及走马赛的场面。

　　商业贸易作为那达慕的重要内容和功能，在这一时期得以更好地发展和强化。据日本后藤十三雄的描述："举行甘珠尔庙会、

○民国时期（20世纪30年代）的搏克比赛

查玛会，众多叩拜者云集于此。汉商赶来集市贸易，一夜之间庙宇周围好比出现城镇，非常繁华热闹。"除呼伦贝尔之外，在现锡林郭勒盟多伦诺尔地区，从清康熙时起举行蒙古各盟盟会，成为以喇嘛寺庙为中心的沟通漠南与漠北地区蒙古族集市贸易的枢纽。不论是当时"六月庙会"、甘珠尔庙会还是多伦诺尔集会都是蒙古族对外物资交流，进行商业贸易的重要渠道，成为旅蒙商的"掘金之所"。而那达慕也成为"中国南北物资交流的大商会"。

### （五）模式化发展期

自内蒙古自治区成立到 20 世纪 80 年代初是那达慕模式化发展期，那达慕发展成为具有独立名称的由官方组织的大型综合性集会活动。

这一时期的那达慕已全部直接以"那达慕大会"命名，成为最容易也最适宜集中展演民族文化的舞台。从上世纪 50 年代中后期开始，最具历史传统的敖包祭祀那达慕逐渐减少。那达慕的类型趋于一致，由政府组织的服务于政治、经济目的的庆典类的那达慕大会占据主导地位。

从 1948 年呼伦贝尔盟甘珠尔庙那达慕大会为起始，乌兰察布、伊克昭、巴彦淖尔等各盟相继举行了那达慕大会，并于 1954 年举办了内蒙古自治区首届那达慕大会。这一时期，那达慕大会上除了传统的"男儿三艺"的比赛之外，还有升国旗唱国歌、领导作报告、宣传党的方针政策、举行表彰劳动模范、进行生产竞赛等仪式议程。此外，拔河、篮球赛等现代体育项目也进入那达慕。甚至有些地区，如内蒙古东部的一些旗县，干脆以那达慕名称指代运动会，其中并无传统的"男儿三艺"竞赛，全部是田径及各种球类比赛。这一时期，那达慕的商贸功能仍发挥着一定的作用，物资交流仍是那达慕的重要内容。

## （六）多元发展期

20世纪80年代中期以来那达慕进入了多元发展期，那达慕在内容、规模、类型上都得以扩展，节日形态愈加完整，节日特性愈加突出，节日化趋势更为明显。

首先是那达慕的"民间主导性"越来越凸现。从历史上看，那达慕的组办者一直都是宫廷、各级政府或者达官贵人，民间少有资格和能力承办那达慕。而到了20世纪80年代中后期，随着人们生活水平的提高、民间文化的繁荣以及民间力量的提升，那达慕的民间性得到了空前的张扬，这一蒙古族特有的娱乐庆祝方式真正走向民间。这一时期，由民间自主、自愿组织那达慕已成为普遍现象。不论是敖包那达慕还是个人庆祝性那达慕，如老人寿辰宴那达慕、畜牧业丰收那达慕等，都由民间个人出资出力，全权负责，自行承办。就敖包那达慕而言，除了少量由政府资助的作为旗县"标志文化"的"旗敖包"之外，其余大部分敖包那达慕都由民间管理，轮流组织。

其次，那达慕的旅游功能大放异彩。旅游那达慕带来的经济收益可观，从而成为各地拉动经济增长的文化资源，每年名目繁多的"草原那达慕节"层出不穷。而那达慕的举办时间也由夏季延展到了冬季，出现了"银冬那达慕""冰雪那达慕"等。其间，除了"男儿三艺"的表演、文艺演出等传统内容之外，还将蒙古族手工艺、传统游牧生活等展览或展示，使那达慕的功能和内容发生了极大的扩展。

第三，那达慕作为传统民俗活动在回归的同时向大型化、专门化方向发展。各类敖包那达慕得到全面复兴，同时那达慕越来越综合化、大型化，很多民族和地区文化特色通过那达慕得以展现。如"挑战吉尼斯世界纪录西乌珠穆沁旗 2048 搏克大赛"那达慕、"800 骏蒙古马那达慕"等，不仅将三项竞技向大型化发展，而且以一项为突出点，辐射其他内容。不但有传统的三项竞技，而且有三项竞技以外的扩展内容，如套马比赛、马具展示等。另外，还将歌舞表演、服饰展示、贸易洽谈等都纳入其中。

第四，城市蒙古族那达慕、小聚居区蒙古族那达慕，甚至海外蒙古族那达慕的兴起，成为这一时期那达慕的一个重要特点，那达慕开始脱离草原而走向城市。城市那达慕是随着蒙古族走出草原进入城市以及城市化的加速而发生的，小聚居区蒙古族那达慕是随着民族、文化意识的回归和自我认同的需要而发生和发展起来的。

○那达慕上的套马

# Chapter One
## Origin and Inheritance of Naadam

In Mongolian, the word Naadam refers to a particular game or sport. For example, Eriingurvan Naadam refers to the Three Games of Men, namely, Mongolian wrestling (Bökh, [buh]), horse racing and archery. Normally, however, the word Naadam alone will not be used in life, whether in Mongolian documents or people's daily life. Instead, it is combined with the word Nair (meaning gathering and celebration) into the compound Nair Naadam which generally refers to Nair that involves Naadam.

In terms of contents, forms, time and space of the event, Naadam holds three connotations: ( i ) it only refers to competitive entertainment activities featuring wrestling, horse racing and archery; ( ii ) from the perspective of the form of organization it refers to the rally which involves competitive events of Naadam; (iii) from the perspective of social functions it refers to the prairie festival which emerged under the pastoralist economy.

As a prairie festival, Naadam is held during the event like State Great Khural, battle achievement celebrations, expedition rituals, royal banquets, throne ascending ceremonies, promotion celebrations for officials, the rally of Mengqi, the Living Buddha succession ceremonies, ovoo ceremonies, etc. Naadam not only serves as a platform for people to enjoy their time together, but also plays an important role in building shared values and enhancing cohesion. As it develops, it has also been termed differently in different periods and regions, for various functions and applications.

For several hundred years, Naadam has been developing and evolving and has perfected itself into a traditional festival for the Mongolian ethnic group.

## 1. Origin of Naadam

There are two mainstream views on the origin of Naadam: according to Ovoo theory, Naadam is a god-entertaining activity following ovoo rituals; according to Celebration Genghis Khan of Theory, Naadam came into being after Genghis Khan founded the Mongol Empire in 1206, if not earlier. Of course, some scholars do believe the origin of Naadam should date back to earlier times. Nagushanfu said, "The very beginning of Naadam culture of Mongolian ethnic group has already been recorded in historical documents after Mongolians stepped into civilized society. Instead, Mongolians, the master of North China nomlds, have a culture that ought to date back to more ancient times, which could be at least 3000 years ago if only the Huns were considered."

Ovoo, also called obo, is the outcome of Mongolians and other related ethnic groups' worship toward nature. The early

Mongolians believed in Shamanism, the history of which is as long as that of Naadam in folk memories. "Heaps piling in certain sites (namely obo) are often found in highlands, mountain passes, intersections, etc. Serving as shrines of local patron divinity and earth God, they are particularly worshiped. Thus ovoos are regarded as sites and junctions of local divinities according to the doctrines of Shamanism." writes Heissig Walther in his book The Religions of Mongolia.

"Following ovoo ceremonies, Bökh and horse racing are held to please Natural God and all the ovoo divinities who will then grant favorable weather, peace and health to both people and livestock." Actually, Naadam is an indispensable part of the ovoo ceremony which promotes the development of Naadam. The chapter Southern Xiongnu Modu Chanyu Biographies of Dong Guan Han Ji keeps the record that Chanyu, during the annual worship ceremony at Sanlong ancestral temple, enjoyed riding horses and camel fighting. The scene of royals' shooting willow twigs during rain praying of Khitan is also recorded in Volume 49 of History of Liao, "Huge tents with hundreds of stanchions were pitched in the preparation period. During the rain-praying ceremony, the emperor commemorated the former emperors in front of their portrayals and then shot willow twigs. The emperor shot twice, followed by princes and prime ministers, each of whom shot once. The emperor's sons and nephews shot after the emperor and empress worshiped the Sun God eastward." Descriptions of ovoo ceremonies and the following Naadam are more common in Qing Dynasty (1636-1911) in books like Military Arts and Courage of Qing Bai Lei Chao (Collections of Anecdotes in Qing Dynasty) and so on.

In fact, Naadam itself is a kind of ceremony intended to please the god following ovoo ceremonies. Both Naadam and ovoo ceremonies are inextricable and complementary to each other in constituting an integral process of ritual.

The website Intangible Cultural Heritage in China describes Naadam as follows: "Naadam originated in the early Mongol Empire, which was held grandly when Genghis Khan was elected the Mongol Great Khan (a ruler of all) in 1206." At that time, in order to inspect troops, preserve andt allocate pastures, Genghis Khan gathered leaders of tribes to hold Naadam together during Khuruldai (a magnificent gather or council each year) from July to August. However, only one game would be held, either archery, horse racing or Mongolian wrestling.

It is widely accepted that Naadam originated in 13th century and developed gradually during the following 800 years, the basis of which is the Yesüngge Inscription, also known as the Genghis stone (epitaph) in the Hermitage State Museum in St. Petersburg. In the first westward expedition from 1219 to 1225, Mongol army led by Genghis Khan marched into and conquered Khwarazmian Empire and returned to Mongol prairie in 1225. Then a grand celebration, namely Naadam, was held to celebrate the victory in Bukha-sujihai of western Mongol Emperor, during which Yesüngge (son of Genghis's younger brother Habtu Hasar the famous skillful archer) shot a target 335 alds away (Ald is an old Mongolian measure equal to the length between a man's outstretched arms. An ald is therefore approximately equal to 160 cm), and a stone inscription, namely Yesüngge Inscription at present, was awarded in honor of him, as commanded by Genghis. It's not hard to see that archery has been an event of competition and entertainment of celebrations at that time.

What is noteworthy is that it was not until Qing Dynasty

that the folk activity was directly called Naadam and was systematically held, though some contents of what we call Naadam today has existed long before. As far as ancient Mongols are concerned, Naadam is not a name universally used. In effect, it didn't become the proper noun carrying given connotations commonly known today until the Inner Mongolia Autonomous Region was established in 1947.

On January 1, 1948, the government of Hulunbuir League was established. Meantime, the proposal to rename Kanjur Miaohui (literally temple fair) as Hulunbuir Naadam was put forward at a symposium with over 100 attendants and it was approved by comrades in charge of Hulunbuir party and government affairs. Accordingly, the gathering on September 3 (August 1 according to the lunar calendar) of that year was called Kanjur Miaohui

The Genghis stone

Naadam, which was held 11 times afterward between 1948 and 1962 as an event of the whole League. Consequently, the name Naadam or Nair Naadam spread throughout the Hulunbuir.

Xilingol League Naadam had its name popularized in a similar way. In August, 1949, Sonid Right Banner held a Banner Nair (banner celebration). In order to differentiate it from the name called by previous kings, princes and aristocrats, the organizer decided to name the Nair as Naadam. Since then, the name Naadam spread in Xilingol region too.

The first Naadam of Inner Mongolia Autonomous Region in 1954 had its name spread throughout the Inner Mongolia Autonomous Region as well as other Mongolian ethnic enclaves.

## 2. Inheritance of Naadam

The history of Naadam' development and inheritance can be generally classified into six stages: gestation period before the 12th century, chrysalis period during Yuan Dynasty (1271-1368), maturation period between Ming Dynasty (1368-1644) and early Qing Dynasty, transformation period during middle Qing Dynasty and the Republic of China, inheritance and new-modeling period from the founding of new China in 1949 to 1980s, and diversification period since middle 1980s.

### 2.1 Gestation Period

From the 12th century to Yuan Dynasty, Naadam found its recreational development in the various individual activities and their contents, in which the prototypes of later developed Mongolian wrestling, horse racing and archery could be seen. They served the productions and daily activities of the nomads and the sacrifices and worships as a kind of occult and sacred show characteristic of witchcraft to please the God of Nature for harvest and well-being.

### 2.2 Chrysalis Period

During Yuan Dynasty, the chrysalis period, an integrated folk event bearing multiple functions and purposes like competing, entertaining, gathering and celebrating began to take form and further moved in the direction of finalizing and stylizing. At that time, the main activities of Naadam featuring Monglian wrestling, horse racing and archery were further developed with practical significance as a result of the establishment of Mongols' dominant role, growth of its military forces, expansion of its influence, and development of nomadic economy.

Naadam events became more like competitions with increasing performing and ornamental values, and participants like wrestlers became more professional. In June of the 6th year of Yanyou (1319 AD) during the reign of Emperor Renzong of Yuan, an official wrestling administration called Jiaoshu was established, and for the first time, emperors had their own professinal wrestlers to entertain themselves at court. It's said that Renzong granted 1000 guan (unit of currency) to each of the 120 wrestlers in June of the 7th year of Yanyou (1320 AD). It's therefore conceivable that not only was there a professional team of over 100 wrestlers but also a site built for watching wrestling games. What's more, it's known from historic texts of Yuan and later Qing Dynasty that Zhama feast had been prevailing for a certain period of time. Zhama feast, also known as Jusem feast, is hailed as "the best feast of Mongolian ethnic group". Zhama, according to a saying, is a Mongolian word which refers to the entire body of livestock plucked off the hair, and according to another saying, it's understood as a Chinese word. "Zha" means pretty and handsome, and, therefore, "zhama" refers to horses with beautiful ornaments, and "zhamayan" is a feast in which people usually gather by riding a gorgeous horse. Jusem is the transliteration of a Mongolian word for color, and attendees are supposed to wear a single color clothes to attend Jusem feast. These clothes are produced by professional tailors each year, bestowed by emperors, and daily changed with a uniform color for each suit. Jamah feast is a combination of songs, dances, clothing, banquets, competitions and recreations, and a kind of regular officially ritualized Naadam with strict procedures and formula in higher tiers of Nair in the court.

### 2.3 Maturation Period

Ming Dynasty and early Qing Dynasty, the continuous perfection period, saw remarkable advances Naadam. The professionalization of Naadam participants in became more obvious, Naadam's recreational function was strengthened, and the institutionalized and specialized trend for development took hold. The organization form of Naadam activities had basically been formularized and modelized.

During Ming Dynasty, the Mongolian ethnic group retreated to its homeland and held Zhama Feast as usual. The Caomuzi (notes about Yuan and Ming Dynasties) by Ye Ziqi of early Ming Dynasty stated that there was a biggest feast called Zhama in the north in which royals are ranked by finery and horses. It demonstrates that Zhama Feast was still prevailing on the prairie during Ming Dynasty though few documents of Naadam were preserved because of perennial civil wars and foreign aggretion. During the Manchu reign over Central Plains (comprising the middle and lower reaches of the Yellow River), great importance was attached to horse archery and wrestling. Hong Taiji (also referred to as Abahai, an emperor of the Qing Dynasty) once ordered the strong young generation to learn archery with hard bows and feather-plumed arrows, kids with wooden bows and willow arrows. Meanwhile he, to set an example, personally led courtiers to compete in archery and ordered Princes of the Second, Third and Fourth Ranks of the Eight Banners to lead their military chiefs to do so. At

Wrestling in the Qing Dynasty

that time, the Eight Banners troops played as the main force of the Qing army in conquering Ming. Naturally, they valued horse archery exercise. Shanpu Ying was set under national management and organization to help promote the Three Games of Men. Famous wrestlers could even get official title as reward, showing the popularity and prevalence of the activity and the relatively high social status of wrestlers. And wrestling was relatively mature in all respects. The Three Games of Men meanwhile served as a major competitive sport performance to entertain envoys of vassal states. As a way to display the power of vassal states, Naadam served some political purposes at that time.

### 2.4 Transformation Period

During the transformation period, from middle Qing Dynasty to the Republic of China, as an important part of social gathering, Naadam substantially extended itself. One manifestation is that it absorbed commercial trades. Another is the Three Games of Men highlighted their recreational functions as festival events, Major activities basically disengaged from practicability and wrestling in particular became completely recreational without any military function.

In each autumn during the reign of Qianlong, the Mongolian princes and dukes respectfully offered banquets to the emperor with Mongolian songs, wrestling and all kinds of programs, which were extremely similar to the visit of Yuan emperors at Zhama Feast. Just like what retinues of Yuan emperors did, retinues of Qing emperors visiting Mountain Resorts also wrote quite a few poems, like the circulated works of Ji Yun, Qiu Rixiu, Zhao Yi and so on. Among them, Zhao Yi once personally watched the show of Bökh and wrote a long poem Wrestling in Imperial Hunt which lively described the costumes at Bökh site, wrestlers' gestures when fixing eyes on and assessing each other, all kinds of wrestlers' moves when holding each other, and the winning scene with winner's unique and stunning skills.

The administration system of leagues and banners employed by Qing Dynasty made Naadam geographically vary from area to area to different degrees. League was the basic military and administrative unit of Mongolia as well as the inherit manor the emperor granted to the feudal lords at all levels within banners. Thus, banners held Naadam with various names and purposes. It became a significant gathering and celebration connecting intra-banners and extra-banners.

Bairin Right Banner Annals records that since the 8th year of Emperor Yongzheng in the Qing Dynasty(1730), over a thousand Lamas from 13 temples in the banner would gather for the yearly Miaohui in June at Daban Huifu temple, during which public ethnic cultural communications, sports and interflow of commodities went on in the solemn ceremonies of

Lamaism. Each banner appointed fine horses, wrestlers, archers and Mongolian chess players to take part in matches. A whole month would witness the extraordinary liveliness as well as active commercial activities with vendors from Beijing, Tianjin, Tongliao, Chifeng and other places. Alxa Custom Record writes that third king Luobusangduoerji of Alxa married a princess of Qing Dynasty, becoming a prince. To celebrate the great rejoicing, a remarkable Naadam was held in the thirtieth year during the reign of Qianlong (1766). Following the tradition of the Genghis Khan era, Qianlong gathered and amused with his descendants and named this Naadam as Urisen Nair. Thousands of nomads gathered here and about a hundred Mongolian yurts were set up. The task of training for the Three Games of Men was organized by all common people in eight sumus, and officials called Xieli, Guanqi, Zhangjing, etc. over the banner. Finally, 32 wrestlers were selected from several hundred of wrestlers, 120 from several hundred of archers, 80 from several hundred fine stallions. Large scale and configuration can be reflected from the Naadam fair.

During that time, not only did each banner hold Naadam with various purposes, but also banners and leagues together held Naadam to enhance exchanges and communications. Seven-Banners Naadam and Ten-Zhasag Naadam in Khalkha area were jointly hosted by adjacent 7 banners or 10 leagues regularly. In addition, the yearly-held traditional Ovoo Naadam continued to prevail.

As a crucial conponent and function of Naadam, commercial trades developed and continued to be enhanced during this transformation period. A Japanese Jyusanno Goto "Numerous worshipers gathered on Kanjur Miaohui and Cham Festival. Han merchants crowded here to trade. It seemed that bustling cities popped up around the temples overnight." Apart from Hulunbuir, Dolon Nor region of Xilingol League also hosted inter-league assemblies from Emperor Kangxi of Qing Dynasty and therefore became Lama temple-centered ties of fair trade connecting present Inner Mongolia and Mongolia. The Miaohui in June, Kanjur Miaohui and Dolon Nor Fair, as essential channels for commodities interflow and business trades, became a gold mine for merchants traveling to Mongolia, and Naadam the "great fair of north-south China commodity exchange".

### 2.5 New-Model Period

From the founding of Inner Mongolia Autonomous Region to the early 1980s, Naadam developed into a large comprehensive government organized gathering with an exclusive name.

All of the Naadam during that time were directly named Nair Naadam which became the most accessible and suitable stage for ethnic culture display. Since the middle and late

The Mongolian festival in 1952

1950s, the Ovoo Naadam which kept most traditions gradually died away. And the government-organized Nair Naadam serving political and economic objectives became the dominant type.

From the Nair Naadam of Kanjur Hulunbuir League in1948, Ulanqab Banner, Ike Joo Banner and Bayannur Banner and other banners held the Nair Naadam successively. And the first Inner Mongolia Autonomous Region Nair Naadam was held in 1954. At that time, apart from the traditional Three Games of Men, ritual agendas like hoisting national flag, singing national anthem, briefing on the work by leaders, publicizing policies of CPC, awarding model workers, competing in production etc. went on as well as modern sports like tug-of-war, basketball match and so on. In some area like banners in eastern Inner Mongolia, the name Naadam was simply referred to general sports meeting, all being track and field events and ball games instead of the traditional Three Games of Men. During this period, Naadam commercial trade still had a certain role to play and the exchange of commodities was still a key part in Naadam.

### 2.6 Diversification Period

Since the middle 1980s, Naadam has entered diversification period with expansion in its contents, sizes and types, the pattens more complete, the characteristic more prominent, and the festive trend more evident.

Firstly, the dominant role of folks in Naadam is increasingly highlighted. In the past, the organizers had always been royals, governments of different levels, high-level officials but seldom did civil society have the qualification and ability to host it. Since the middle and late 1980s, however, with better living standard, richer folk culture and power, ordinary people became capable of holding Naadam, and the way of celebrating and entertaining peculiar to Mongolia ethnic groups with folk characteristics was unprecedentedly highlighted. It has become a general phenomenon for the folk to autonomously and voluntarily hold Naadam. Both Ovoo Naadam and Naadam for individual celebration like birthday party for the elder and thrived livestock etc. were funded and taken in charge by folks themselves. As for Ovoo Naadam, except for a few of that were funded by the government as culture symbols of banners and counties, most were managed and organized by civil society in turns.

Secondly, Naadam greatly promoted tourism. Naadam tourism brought reasonable economic benefits, and became cultural resources which drove economic growth. Each year Naadam with various names emerged in an endless stream. As for the holding time, normally Naadam was held in summer but now there are winter Naadams like Silver Winter Naadam, Snow Naadam, etc. Besides the traditional Three Games of Men and artistic performances, there are also Mongolia handicraft art and traditional nomadic life display.

Thirdly, in the process of turning into a folk-custom activity, Naadam developed into a large-scale and specialized festival. All kinds of Ovoo Naadam thrived. Meanwhile Naadam became larger, more and more comprehensive, facilitating the display of ethnic and local cultures. Naadam of Bökh Contest to Break Guinness World Records in West Ujimqin Banner of Xilingol League and alike had greatly enlarged the scales of the three games and promoted the developments of other games like horse lassoing match, saddlery display, songs and dances, costume display, trading negotiations, etc.

Fourthly, the emergence of urban Mongolian ethnic Naadam, small enclaves Naadam and even overseas Naadam constituted an important feature of that time. Naadam started leaving prairie for cities. Urban Naadam was driven and facilitated by urbanization of Mongolian Ethnic group; small enclaves Naadam occurred and developed together with the returning of national and cultural awareness and the need of self-identification.

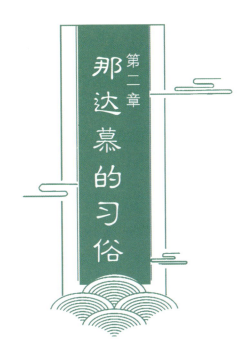

第二章 那达慕的习俗

那达慕的习俗是与那达慕有关的娱乐、饮食、节日服饰、仪式仪礼、家庭活动、亲友往来等民俗事项的总称。在长期的历史积淀中，那达慕已经形成了丰富多彩的活动和习俗。

# 一、
## 那达慕的活动

### （一）"男儿三艺"及其他

　　那达慕中的"男儿三艺"以搏克、赛马、射箭三项为代表，在不同的地域，在那达慕的实际发生中，有所不同。有的地方三项同时举行，有的地方以其中两项为主，外加地区特色项目，如蒙古象棋、嘎拉哈、赛驼、掷布鲁等。

　　在传统意义上，"三艺"是男儿必备的技艺和本领。他们从小被教育和训练成了"手执弓箭，头枕箭筒，把自己的尸骨抛弃荒野，才是真正好男儿的贵重的尸体"的荣誉感；歌颂"以露为饮，以涎为食，以风为骑，以剑为友"的刻苦精神，赞誉"像狮虎似的勇敢"、"像海青似的凶猛"，"在乘马的尾上飘扬起云和雾，在战马的鬃上扬起太阳红光"的英雄气概。在这样的训导和性别角色形塑下，成就了蒙古族男儿刚毅、坚韧、豁达、乐观、威武、神勇的个性特征。而那达慕中的技艺正是考验男子这些特质的最佳手段，又是他们展现自己男子气概的最佳方式。当然，在那达慕的发展中，"男儿三艺"并非完全是男儿专属，各项比赛中都有女子的参与。

多彩中国节

那达慕

### 1. 搏克

搏克，就是蒙古式摔跤，在蒙古语里具有"坚韧""结实""牢固""耐久"之意。一个真正的"搏克"，必须具备该词所指的特质，不仅坚韧于身，还须坚强于心。对于蒙古族而言，搏克是"智"和"勇"的完美化身，是不同于常人的英雄人物。他们具有坚强、结实、灵巧、智谋的英雄气概。如果说"男儿三艺"是那达慕的核心内容，那么搏克应该是"男儿三艺"中的核心。在那达慕的历史发展中，搏克的传承相对而言，最悠久，最稳定，也最完整，而搏克的文化符号形式也更鲜明。

摔跤从汉文古籍记载看，秦汉时期已出现，当时称之为角力。观角力戏是汉代风行的一种娱乐活动，而且作为娱乐观赏进入了中原王朝的宫苑。20世纪50年代陕西客省庄第104号墓出土的角力铜牌，后被考证为匈奴人之物。铜牌上镌刻了匈奴角力比赛的情景：两个匈奴人各把自己的马拴在树上，两人开始了角抵比赛。他们长裤短靴，上身赤裸，似乎两人都是抢抱对方的腿，或搂对方的腰，

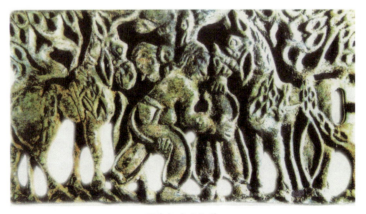

○匈奴角力铜牌

以图将对方摔倒。金启孮先生研究认为，铜饰牌上的匈奴人角抵不像正式比赛，似乎是偶然在一起的游戏，由此可以推测在匈奴人中角抵必然很盛行。1931年在辽的东京遗址（今辽宁省辽阳市）出土了一个八角形的辽代白色陶罐，罐腹绘有八幅小儿角抵图。日本的鸟居龙藏认为，罐上所画是契丹小孩摔跤的形象，且属连环画性质。依据金启孮先生的研究，契丹、女真的"跋里速"（摔跤）戏，是上承自匈奴、柔然，而蒙古则沿自契丹。可以说蒙古摔跤源于匈奴，具有漫长的历史。仅就蒙古族传统搏克服饰来看，与当初匈奴人的摔跤着装大体相似，搏克服饰已有较长的历史传统。

清代著名文人赵翼，在观看木兰围场的摔跤比赛后，写下了《行围即景·相扑》一诗："黄幄高张传布库，数十白衣白于鹭，衣纔（才）及尻露裲裆，千条线缝十层布。不持寸铁以手搏，手如铁锻足铁铸。班分左右以耦进，桓桓劲敌猝相遇，未敢轻身便陷坚，各自回旋健踏步……"这首诗为我们全面、生动地描绘了当时搏克比赛的诸多符号特征，如服饰、技巧、仪礼等。可见至清代摔跤已是那达慕中核心的内容，当时搏克的竞技技术也已经达到了相当高的地步。

在内蒙古各地，尤其搏克较为盛行的地区，至今仍然流传着很多搏克故事。这些故事是基于每个人物的真实生活背景和当时搏克比赛记录（有些是虚构出来的），叙述着搏克在蒙古族生活中的地位，英雄化地再现和传递着搏克精神。康熙五年（1666年）清政府举行的全国性的那达慕盛会上，乌珠穆沁搏克手安召在1024名搏克选手中独占鳌头，留下了盛名。19世纪初，巴特尔朝克图参加清廷京师盛会，又以头名载誉而归。19世纪中叶的搏克手都仁扎那，更是传说和民歌中的人物。长调民歌《都仁扎那》就是为他战胜了当时著名的常胜搏克手而创作，并被后人传唱至今，"都仁扎那"也成为蒙古族著名搏克手的代名词。后来的僧格、劳来、其木德、额尔敦巴雅尔、关其格扎布、查干扎纳、哈达、巴图苏和、巴雅尔巴特尔等都是乌珠穆沁草原养育的"都仁扎那"似的搏克健儿。一名搏克手的良好竞技技能不仅为他带来竞技场上的荣耀，同时还会带来极高的社会声誉，同时更是一个地区民众崇高的集体荣誉，甚至是关乎社稷民生的大事。搏克身体表达着力量，对于社区，对于一个地域而言，具有神力，是力量和丰饶的象征。比如在乌珠穆沁旗白音敖包祭祀那达慕上，每年吸引远近著名搏克手的参与。搏克们认为在敖包那达慕上的获胜将提升一年的"黑目力"（气运），可以所向无敌。牧人则认为，属于自己苏木嘎查的搏克胜出能为自己的苏木嘎查带来福运。

　　搏克是不分等级、没有时间限制、一跤定胜负的具有很强竞争性的项目。由于搏克没有体重等级的划分，所以摔跤手要充分考察自身和对手的身体重量情况、力气的大小、摔跤技巧等之后才能进行摔跤活动。例如：50公斤重的人要与100公斤重的人进行搏克比赛时，显然体重上处于劣势，看上去有些不公平，可实际上各有各的优势。体重相对重的一方显然在摔上占优势，但是对手如果体重轻、个子小，动作敏捷、搏克技术娴熟的话，体重也可能成为失败的原因之一。因此，双方都各有利弊，搏克手要充分了解这一情况，尽量避开自己的劣势，充分发挥出自己的优势，才能一跤定输赢。传统的搏克比赛，时间上没有要求，因此还有僵持几日决不出胜负的。没有胜负，就继续。这种搏克蒙古语称作"握压搏克"（桩子搏克，耐力搏克），"握压"拼的是勇气和耐力。无法被对方摔倒，就继续坚持。如果上午没有结果，中午吃饭，下午继续比赛……什么时候被对方或将对方摔倒为止。现代大型那达慕中，对此做了些许的调整。

　　一般在那达慕会场主席台的正前方设立专门的搏克帐幔，这是那达慕比赛场地的象征。帐幔多为白色，上面绘有蓝色的佛教祥瑞

041

图案，如鹿、经轮等，搏克手们在那里等候上场。搏克赛正式开始前，搏克手排列两队等待入场。排在右侧，即西边的为优秀的、佩戴"将嘎"的搏克，新手或无"将嘎"的搏克则排在左手。在每队之前有一位长者，形成如两扇门的入口通道。两组对阵跤手的领头者将两臂搭在前方长者的肩上，俯身待发。每次出场，小型那达慕两边各有8位，大型那达慕则各有16位搏克手。一般而言，第一轮第一个安排上场的是重量级的搏克手，如跤王等，与他交手的是年轻的新手。在反复三唱"搏克因斡力亚"，即邀跤曲之后，两边跤手从两位长者中间跃入场地，作鹰舞飞跃状，跳入场内，并向主席台行礼。邀跤曲唱词简单，曲调悠长，大意为"请带搏克入场啊——"，一般唱三遍后搏克手们跳跃入场。过去都由长调歌手现场演唱，如今都使用录音，用广播播放。

○搏克手入场

邀跤曲是搏克比赛中贯穿始终的音乐，邀跤曲一唱，如同吹响战斗的"号角"，象征着搏克比赛的开始。

入场后搏克手自然分成左右两队，以顺时针方向绕场漫步，等待主持人介绍著名搏克手的佳绩，并安排对手。念到谁的名字时，搏克手举"右手"表示在场，并与对手点头、双手相握开始比赛。搏克手们非常注重比赛的礼节，交手前要互相握手，比赛决出胜负后仍握手示敬。败者向主席台和观众敬礼并快速离开场地，胜者则跳跃三次，并向主席台致敬后跑步离场。搏克入场"舞"，蒙古语称

"德波乎"或"玛格西拉特",模仿的是飞禽走兽之姿,如雄鹰、麋鹿、雄狮等,这是搏克古老的仪式,具有神性和特殊的寓意。入场舞蹈说明了与游牧文化的关系,模仿的这些动物被视为是传说中的祖先,或具有保护山水的神力,被认为具有社会和文化方面的意义。通过模仿它们的动作,展示搏克手的威武雄壮、生龙活虎、饱满的斗志和生命力。

搏克最基本动作可概括成昭格斯策(站式或跤架)和别日查[把(握)式]两种,掌握这两种基本动作是搏克的基本功,因为好的站式和上佳的把(握)式是比赛获胜的关键。在站式和把式中又有多种技法。搏克技法种类繁多,而且各地也略有不同。1988年由东乌珠穆沁旗文化历史学会出版的《乌珠穆沁搏克》(1)丛书中,将乌珠穆沁搏克技巧总结为基本技能10部,技巧345种,包括缠、挑、挂、压拽、踩拽、扭拽、躲拽、虚拽、挚拽、横打、反握腕、斜握腕、抓后腰、抓小袖等。

○搏克入场舞(席银柱 摄)

搏克有着浓郁的民族特色和地方特色,从形式上来讲分为乌珠穆沁式、呼伦贝尔式、鄂尔多斯式和沙力博尔式。在内蒙古阿拉善等地区,具有地方特色的搏克,即"沙力博尔"搏克,不论从服饰还是从比赛规则上有别于其

○"沙力博尔"搏克比赛

他三种。"沙力博尔"在西部蒙古语中意为"短裤",搏克手着短裤竞技,因此将此命名为"沙力博尔"搏克。阿拉善那达慕中的"男儿三艺",指的是"沙力博尔"搏克、乘马射箭和赛驼。"沙力博尔"搏克的服饰有短裤、盖头。跤服的颜色分为蓝色和绿色,蓝色代表天空,绿色代表草原,盖头是红、黄、蓝色的绸缎做的。比赛前,跤手遮着盖头出场,当裁判员掀开盖头时,跤手们才知道自己的对手是谁。阿拉善素有"驼乡"之美称,阿拉善"沙力博尔"搏克的起式和技艺很大程度上都模仿了公驼相互争斗的架式,动作技巧的名称也与公驼攻击方法的名称相同,有前攻、猛背、偷袭、后推、左拉右拧、内外夺脚、旋转猛压、上压、空旋、单打、松肩、硬抗、上翻下扣等。

在多数那达慕上,以成人搏克赛最为普遍,偶有儿童搏克赛。在官方举办的大型庆典那达慕上,也会增加如团体赛、女子搏克赛、老年搏克赛等。对于很多民间的敖包那达慕,或小型的那达慕,搏克手无赛前特殊训练和准备。举行那达慕时,有兴趣者都可报名,名额满限,即开始比赛。因为平日牧业生活的繁重和艰苦锻炼了蒙古人的肌体,为搏克摔跤奠定了身体基础,练就了搏克手强壮的体魄和坚毅的性格。作为劳动的间歇,三五成群地进行摔跤是他们娱乐消遣的一种方式。可见,搏克与蒙古族日常生活的紧密程度。

## 2. 赛马

马,对于蒙古人而言是工具、是财富,更是朋友和伴当。我们甚至可以说,作为马背民族,马就是蒙古族的符号。在牧业地区各类型的那达慕中,赛马均处于核心位置,并在某些类型的那达慕中有被突出和丰富的趋向。赛马中隐含的丰富的文化因子仍被继承和表达着,只是在不同类型的那达慕中被呈现的程度有所不同。如马赞辞,一般在政府举办的大型那达慕或专项的以马文化为主题的那达慕中才会仪式化地表达。而"绕桑"仪式则是所有那达慕赛马前进行的一项内容，只是繁简不一。

　　蒙古族先民早在青铜时代和早期铁器时代就有养马的文化遗迹。公元前 2 世纪至公元 3 世纪初，匈奴东胡时期，马已成为游牧社会不可缺少的家畜。尤其是公元 9 世纪后，蒙古人从额尔古纳河西迁斡难、克鲁伦、土喇三河之源时，马已经普及于蒙古草原。约翰·普兰诺·加宾尼于 13 世纪中叶出使蒙古时感叹道：蒙古人"拥有如此之多的公马和母马，以致我不相信在世界的其余地方能有这样多的

○蒙古马

马"。

　　蒙古人在与马朝夕相处过程中，形成了自己独特的驯马、养马，以及与马相关的竞技、娱乐活动。彭大雅在《黑鞑事略》中详述了蒙古人的养马之法："自春初罢兵后，凡出战归，并恣其水草，不令骑动。直至西风将生，则取而鞯之，执于帐房左右，啖以些少水草，经月臕落，而日骑之数百里，自然无汗，故可以耐远而出战。寻常正行路时，并不许其吃水草，盖辛苦中吃水草，成臕而生病，此养

马之良法。"1279 年元灭南宋，统一中国，制定了一套国家制度，把牧民按十户、百户、千户、万户编制起来。"上马则备战斗"，"下马则屯聚牧养"。在这种制度下，蒙古族的适龄男子，都受到了有计划、有组织的骑射训练，从而使蒙古族的骑马运动得到普及和发展，练出了一支强大的骑兵部队。道森在其《出使蒙古记》中写到："小孩刚刚两三岁的时候，就开始骑马和驾驭马，并骑在马上飞跑，同时大人就把适合于他们身材的弓给他们，教他们射箭。"马不仅在蒙古人日常生活中具有较高的地位，而且在战争中更占有极高的军事地位。成吉思汗的 13 个"古列延"（军事组织）中，能骑善射者达 3 万之众。13 世纪赛马也成为那达慕中三大竞技之一。元代诗人萨都刺在《上京即事五首》诗中描写了当时精湛的骑射技艺："紫塞风高弓力强，王孙走马猎沙场。呼鹰腰箭归来晚，马上倒悬双白狼。"蒙古大汗国始，蒙古有了专门的宫廷宴飨——"诈马宴"，到了清代"诈马宴"仍盛行，而且赛马在各类那达慕中广为开展。《清稗类钞·宴塞蒙古》刊载了清乾隆皇帝在秋八月巡幸木兰观看蒙古人表演马术

○调吊中的赛马

的情景，赵翼《檐曝杂记·蒙古诈马戏》中则记述了激动人心的套马场面。

从最早的记录看，赛马的距离往往都在几十公里以上，"近则三四十里，远或百余里，待命斗胜负"。速度，是赛马的必然追求，但耐力更是一个重要方面。赛马要取得好成绩，驯马、控马之术必不可少，赛马不仅要有好的马匹、优秀的骑手，更为重要的是精到的吊马技术，这三者有机结合才能取得比赛的胜利。不论在历史文献中，还是在民间实践中，赛马的调吊是参加那达慕前的重要准备环节。牧人根据各自马匹情况、参加比赛项目类型进行调吊，一般从那达慕举行前一个月左右开始。因为吊马技术属于家庭，具有一定的隐秘性，也有诸多的禁忌。

吊马首先要选好适合调吊的马匹，俗话说："好马骑乘才知道，好友长交才明白"，牧人认为马的脾性、耐力好坏必须经过骑乘才可知道。民间也有专门的相马人士，根据马的毛色、体态、步伐等判定其"潜质"。就毛色来说，认为净白、肝棕、雪白、亮黑、赤红、铁青、竹黄等颜色的马匹为吉祥之骏。从马的形态来说，马头要细瘦，如飞鹿；眼睛大而有神，睫毛且长。脖子如麋鹿长而扁，胸宽体瘦，背长而细、胯宽而长等。牧人根据这些特性加上平日的观察以及骑乘，从马群中挑选出有"潜质"的马匹进行吊控。吊马通常根据吊马手的时间、精力以及马匹的状况确定吊控数量。虽然每个家庭有所不同，但有其通用的原则。首先拔汗、调控饮食，控制饮水次数和时间，以便调节其脾胃。其次，吊控中的马需要绑在阴凉通风处，防止过热过凉，并隔天训跑一次。在训期内一天只让喝一次水。根据赛程，训跑距离也有所不同。远程马一般不超过 10 公里，鞍马 5 公里。但由于现在草原处处是围栏，训跑的距离也相应缩短了许多。还值得注意的是赛后需要遛马至少半个小时，让马匹休息 4-5 个小时后才能让它饮水、吃草、打滚，使全身放松，保证马匹的健康。马的特性各异，需要采取不同的调吊技法。有的马需要掉膘，须用冷水梳洗；有的则需要上膘，则用温水梳洗。对不同比赛类型的赛马，采取的方法也不同。鞍马一般不予梳洗，远程马则需要每日梳洗，让它减肥膘变得轻巧有力。除了以上一些调训方法外，吊马期间还有很多的禁忌：主人不得喝酒，不得与人发生争执；所吊马匹不可绑在拉货物

○赛马专用工具

的车上，忌讳不洁之物；所吊之马要有专用的马鞭、毛刷、马鞍等用具，并将它们放置在高处，保证其"清洁"等等。吊马是极其精细的活儿，如同伺弄婴儿一样，需要精心、细腻。因而，民间有"即便不洗自己的头，也得给马匹梳洗"的说法。由此我们可以说，在那达慕上所见的赛马，已然不是马匹的比赛，而是马主人对马的理解、对马的调教以及对马的情感的表达了。

赛马比赛一般分为远程马赛、二岁马赛、走马赛、鞍马赛等。此外，在大型那达慕中还有高难度的马术表演和竞技比赛，如锡林郭勒的马上拾嘎拉哈比赛，阿拉善的骑射以及内蒙古自治区专业马术队的表演等。赛马比赛的起点，根据赛程的不同，设在远离会场的不同地方，但终点都在那达慕的主会场。以远程马赛和二岁马赛最为普遍，通常在早上6—7点，天气凉爽的时段进行。一般为直线赛跑，赛程为10、20、30公里不等，先达终点为胜。远程马比的是耐力和速度，一般不分组，参加的人数少则几十人，多则上百人甚至几百人。骑手年龄最小的只有7、8岁，最大的不超过12、13岁。走马赛，主

要是比赛马步伐的稳健与轻快。走马与跑马不同，跑马是狂奔，马的前后蹄同时前进，走马是走，马的前后蹄交错前进，决不能奔跑。走马赛的骑手都是成年人，赛程一般为 10~20 公里。马上拾嘎拉哈赛是马上竞技的一种，比的是技巧和勇力。比赛以 4 人为一组，在 300 米的直线上隔段放置 5 枚用哈达包裹的嘎拉哈，选手从远处策马而来，从马背上倾斜拾起嘎拉哈。比赛以选手在一次赛程中用时最短、拾得嘎拉哈数最多为标准确定胜负。

那达慕上的赛马也要做一些特别的装扮。在蒙古人看来，马鬃、马尾具有神力，被视为是马的"黑目力"（气运）所在，古时人们常用来进行占卜。为在比赛中防止马鬃挡住马的眼睛，将马的顶鬃高高梳起，并用彩色绸缎或绸线缠系，如同小辫儿一样让它翘立，同时，

用红绳或各色绸缎束裹马尾（九节下方三指左右的位置）。这是非常古老的传统装饰，在早期的岩画中仍有遗留，可追溯到较为久远的年代。牧人认为赛前装扮赛马，可以提升赛马的运气，获得神的福佑，

○赛马装饰

同时也能"提醒"赛马抖擞精神，挑战比赛。除此之外，不同的地区不同的家庭也会给赛马其他的一些装饰，如马脖子上，佩带铜铃或五色"将嘎"，或在马额头戴上铜镜等等，人们将自己对马的怜爱和祝福都融进了其中，祈愿赛马避免坎坷，平安、顺利地到达终点。

赛马开始前还要进行"祈福"性的"绕桑"仪式，蒙古语称作"桑额日古勒乎"或"玛日赛拉乎"。"桑"是指煨祭仪式，同时指煨祭时在香炉里燃烧的松叶、柏枝及其火焰等。"额尔古勒呼"，蒙古语

动词，有"转、绕"等意。"玛日赛拉乎"由绕"桑"时演唱的歌曲"玛日赛"而来，"拉乎"则是它的动词词缀。在吊马手的牵引下，一般由骑手骑着装饰的赛马，唱着"玛日赛"歌，环绕点燃艾草、檀香、柏枝等香料的香炉顺时针方向转三圈，以祈福赛马征服险阻，载誉而归。"玛日赛"是藏传佛教格鲁派（黄教）祭拜的佛，可保佑众生，远离水、火、风、狮、兵器、偷盗、口舌（争吵）等灾祸。"绕桑"仪式就是向"玛日赛"佛祈愿，通常都由儿童连续哼唱"唵嘛玛日赛，玛日沁宝姆布莱，唵嘛所亥"，大意就是"唵嘛玛日赛，佛在你左右"等几句唱词，直到绕"桑"仪式结束。多数那达慕上，没有现场演唱，而是播放提前录制的"玛日赛"曲。"绕桑"仪式中的"玛日赛"曲各地称谓有所不同，有的地方则称作"ginggao"歌。"绕桑"仪式本身也略有不同。有的地方，要唱"万马之首"，要在赛马头上洒"酸奶汁"。而有的敖包那达慕上，如锡林郭勒东苏尼特查干敖包"绕桑"仪式更为隆重。领头者要骑乘白马，手持系有"宝恩道好日勒"佛像的旗杆，随后是乘马吹海螺的队伍以及比赛的马匹。在海螺声和玛日赛曲的伴随下顺时针方向绕敖包三圈，向敖包神灵和山水、天地之神祈福。从现代那达慕赛马绕"桑"仪式的唱词以及仪式本身来看，都与佛教有着紧密联系，它是佛教文化渗透到那达慕"男儿三艺"中的一种表现。

### 3. 射箭

弓箭，蒙古人称"诺木·苏木"，"诺木"是弓，"苏木"是箭。蒙古人自古崇尚弓箭，喜好骑射，把它视为男子汉的象征和标志，当作他们随身携带的武器和吉祥物。射箭自然也成为那达慕的重要活动项目。

骑射是北方的自然和社会环境赋予游牧民族的生存本领，是狩猎和作战之必需。《汉书·匈奴传》上记载，匈奴"儿能骑羊，引弓则射鸟鼠，少长则射狐兔"。南宋人彭大雅在他的《黑鞑事略》里对13世纪蒙古人自孩提时便乘马骑射的情形进行了记述："孩时绳束以板，络之马上，随母出入；三岁索维之鞍，俾手有所执射，从众驰骋；四五岁挟小弓、短矢。"13世纪的波斯史学家费志尼，在他的《世界征服者史》中写到成吉思汗极其重视狩猎，目的不单是为了猎取野兽，更是为了习惯狩猎训练，熟悉弓马和吃苦耐劳。意大利人约翰·普兰诺·加宾尼于13世纪中叶出使蒙古数次，他在《蒙古游记》中记载：

"男子除了从事造箭或照料畜群外不管别事。他们从事狩猎和练习骑射，他们不分老少都是射箭能手。"成吉思汗规定：兵士们必须携带两张或三张弓，或至少一张好弓以及三个装满箭的箭袋。当时涌现了众多的射箭能手，成吉思汗的名将木华黎、其弟

○13世纪的蒙古骑兵

哈萨尔之子也孙格等等都是优秀的射手。而哈萨尔的后裔所形成的蒙古部落也以"科尔泌"命名，科尔泌，即"弓箭手"之意。可见，弓箭以及射箭之术对蒙古族历史以及生产生活的重要性，而这种重要性也促使它成为"男儿三艺"和那达慕的核心内容。

蒙古族射箭，分骑射、立射及远射，远射目前基本已不见。比赛中对弓箭的式样、重量、长度、拉力都不限。骑射，是催马起跑后在奔跑的马背上取弓、抽箭、搭箭、射击。参加骑射的人数不限，对马和箭都无统一要求。射场一般有宽4米，长85米至100米的跑道，设3个靶位，每靶相距约25米，从第一靶开始依次在2米高的

木架上挂一个彩色布袋。射手的一马三箭要在规定的跑道上射完，共射三轮为九箭，最后以中箭多寡决定胜负。在鄂尔多斯、阿拉善、赤峰等地较为盛行。立射，就是站立射靶，那达慕中较为普遍的一种类型。各地比赛中男女分组比赛，有时也分专业和业余组。射程一般为男30米、女25米。每人一轮5支箭，分3轮，最终以中靶箭数环数多少而评出优胜者。蒙古族射箭活动用的靶，在早期有草靶、牛羊皮靶，近代出现了毡靶或棉布袋靶。比赛用的弓有传统的榆木弓和柳木弓，高档次的为牛角弓和钢弓、塑弓。现代射箭，在距射手15至20米处设一靶牌，靶心向外依次为黄、红、兰、黑、白5种颜色的圆环，射中最里面的得100分，依次为80、60、40、20分。此外，还有一种靶的靶心是活动的，箭中靶心会自动掉下来。蒙古族射箭一般采取大拉锯的方法，弓开得十分满，拉弓弦的手用大拇指扣弦，箭尾卡在拇指和食指的指窝处。

○弓、弓套、箭、箭囊、月靶

那达慕传统的三项内容都是从蒙古族生活中发展而来，与民众的生活密不可分。射箭是在游猎社会产生的，并在蒙古族历史发展中发挥了重要的作用。但随着蒙古族生活方式的改变，射箭比赛发展不均衡，有些地区出现了整体式微的趋向。比如在乌珠穆沁地区，那达慕中射箭处于式微地步，传统的射箭比赛，从上世纪50年代便已消失，在大小那达慕上基本都以搏克、赛马为主，辅以蒙古象棋、嘎拉哈比赛，而无射箭比赛。现代那达慕中的射箭比赛是2005年"有识之士"开办射箭团体，招收学员，在那达慕中慢慢推广后才恢复起来的。但在科尔沁地区，射箭比赛始终是那达慕中的重要内容，保持着传统的弓箭和传统的比赛规则。

那达慕的"男儿三艺"充分展现了蒙古人与自然、与人和谐相处之道，搏克更多表达的是人与人之间的关系在密切之中又充满了对抗，在对抗之中又展现着人与人之间的融合。在赛马比赛中，更多展示的是人自身及其生产工具之间的和谐；而射箭则是张扬的、扩张的、开放的，表达的是人与自然之间的张力与紧张。蒙古人对力的崇拜，对坐骑的赞美，对弓矢的称颂，在民间文学作品中随处可见。在漫长的历史推进中不断完善的"男儿三艺"是一种力、勇、技、智的较量和征服，那达慕通过搏克力的较量、赛马速度的拼搏、射箭精准的考验得以淋漓尽致的展现。

### 4. 蒙古象棋

蒙古语称象棋为"沙塔拉"，亦作"喜塔尔"，是那达慕中仅次于搏克、赛马、射箭的活动，在内蒙古各地区有较好的群众基础。传说成吉思汗纵横欧亚时期，蒙古象棋已在蒙古族当中盛行。值得一提的是，蒙古象棋与国际象棋有许多相近之处，因此蒙古象棋的佼佼者常常也是国际象棋的高手。

○蒙古象棋

业界研究认为，在古印度，有种棋叫"却图郎卡"，由大象、战车、骑兵和步兵等4种棋子组成。公元7世纪传到波斯，被称作"沙特拉兹"。13世纪初，随着蒙古草原丝绸之路的不断延伸，波斯的"沙特拉兹"也随之传入蒙古高原。15世纪末，"沙特拉兹"从波斯传入欧洲，并逐渐演变定型为现代国际象棋。"沙特拉兹"被带入蒙古草原后，结合蒙古族传统生活习俗及文化特色，在棋子名称、走法、规则上加以改进和完善，最终形成了具有鲜明草原文化特色的蒙古象棋。

关于蒙古象棋的起源，学者认为，最早记载蒙古象棋的汉文文献是明朝永乐年间的《艺仙集》，该书介绍了蒙古象棋的基本弈法和规则。原书已佚，但有关蒙古象棋的内容转载留存于清乾隆二十三年（1758年）成书的《口北三厅志》。此外，清康熙年间徐兰所撰《塞上杂记》、清道光年间的叶名沣所著《桥西杂记》等都记有蒙古象棋棋法，其所记内容与《口北三厅志》所辑基本相同。《口北三厅志》中蒙古象棋的棋制和走法如下："蒙古棋局纵横九线，六十四罫。棋各十六枚：八卒、二车、二马、二象、一炮、一将，别以朱墨。将居中之右，炮居中之左，上于将一罫，车、马、象左右列，卒横于前。其棋形而不字，将刻塔，崇象教也。象刻驼或熊，迤北无象也。多卒人众为强也，无士不尚儒生也。棋不列于线，而列于罫，置器于安也。马横行六罫，驼横行九罫，以驼疾于马也。满局可行，无河为界，所谓随水草以为畜牧也。卒直行一罫至底，斜角食敌之在前者，去而复返，用同于车，嘉有功也。众棋还击一塔，无路可出，始为败。"可见蒙古象棋有许多独特之处，如象刻成骆驼或者熊，是因为北方没有大象，马和驼是草原上重要的交通、运输和作战工具；与中国象棋相比，蒙古象棋没有"士"这个棋子，这反映了游牧马背民族的社会结构与中原宫廷结构的不同，也反映了在古代的蒙古族军事组织当中以及军事战斗中，最高将领必然是与自己的士兵并肩作战，甚至是身先士卒。其没有中间的河界，则反映了蒙古族游牧生活，即逐水草而居的特性，同时也直接反映了蒙古族在广袤草原驰骋，甚至一度扬威于整个欧亚大陆的映射。

蒙古象棋比赛一般分成人组和儿童组，参赛人数为 2 的倍数，即 16、32、64 位选手等，并以此类推。在锡林郭勒、鄂尔多斯等地区，蒙古象棋较为普及，人们喜欢在茶余饭后，闲暇时对弈一局，不论老少长幼都可以参战，以展示自己的棋艺。

一直以来在官方举办的大型那达慕、家庭那达慕上都有蒙古象棋比赛。近年来，各种比赛较为频繁，一年可达上百场。蒙古象棋的棋盘为正方形，由颜色深浅交替排列的 8 行 8 列共 64 个小方格组成。棋盘每边有 8 个小方格，浅色的称白格，深色的称黑格。棋子也分为两种颜色，浅色的称白子，深色的称黑子，一共 32 枚，双方各执 16 枚棋子，即每方都有诺颜（王），哈昙（后）各 1 个，哈萨嘎（车）、骆驼、马各 2 枚，厚乌（子）8 个。棋子的名称各地有时不同，有的地方将“子”称为“犬”，“后”称为“狮”。蒙古象棋的棋子可谓是艺术品，人物、兽类、车都是立体造型，形态逼真、栩栩如生。如雕刻的马，就有各种不同的姿态，有奔马、跑马、走马、立马，还有母子马。骆驼有公驼，也有母子驼。这些木雕或骨雕或石雕或玉雕的棋子是牧人长期观察的结果和牧民生活体验的生动展现，富有草原生活气息。

○那达慕蒙古象棋比赛

○东乌珠穆沁旗旗庆那达慕象征财富和吉祥的金色嘎拉哈

### 5. 嘎拉哈比赛

在羊后蹄和小腿的连接处有一块游离的骨头，俗称"嘎拉哈"，蒙古语称作"沙嘎"，汉语称为"躁骨"或"羊拐"。这种骨头有呈现不同形状的六个面，有宽有窄、有凸有凹、有正有侧。呼伦贝尔地区有民谚赞曰："高高山上绵羊走，深深谷地山羊过，向阳滩上骏马跑，背风弯里黄牛卧。倒立起来叫不顺，正立抓个大骆驼。"蒙古人用五畜的名称给嘎拉哈的各面命名。牧人认为沙嘎具有某种"魔力"，代表着"财富"，"拐多之家牛羊多"，说的就是这个意思。沙嘎预示着五畜兴旺，因此，牧民享用了美味的羊肉后，沙嘎都不能随意扔掉，而是将其收集起来，进行修整、装饰，单独或相互搭配，一到冬闲季节，不论男女老少，都提着羊拐袋子玩耍起来，把赢得对方羊拐看作一大乐事，由此也创造出了畜牧特色的各种娱乐游戏。牧人根据五畜以及畜牧生活中不可缺少之狗、勒勒车等来命名嘎拉哈，并摆造出各种形状和可能的"场景"来进行"叙事"，再现日常生活的"场景"。

在蒙古人的生活中，沙嘎又是一种信物，是友谊和信誉的象征。因此，牧人非常珍视沙嘎，不论是羊、牛、驼还是狼、羚羊等的沙嘎，都是每家每户珍藏的"宝贝"。过去，人们也有收集起沙嘎，达到一千之后装在袋子里将其封存，再从一开始重新收集的习俗。

沙嘎有上百种玩法，有的专属于儿童，作为启智游戏，有的老少皆宜。在锡林郭勒地区沙嘎比赛多在秋冬季老人祝寿宴那达慕时举

○嘎拉哈扔四样比赛

行，较为忌讳在春天接羔时节玩沙嘎，认为对牲畜生长不利。沙嘎比赛，是那达慕较为普及型的项目，因为简单易学，人人都可参与其中。一般而言，有弹、射、欻、扔四样等几种比赛。

### 6. 赛骆驼

素有"沙漠之舟"的骆驼，在古代蒙古民族的经济生活和军事行动中有着特殊的地位。蒙古人视骆驼为吉祥之畜、"万牲之王"，作为上乘牲礼用于九九八十一大礼之首。赛骆驼主要是内蒙古阿拉善盟，新疆博州、巴州和青海海西州等那达慕的传统项目，也是锡林郭勒、呼伦贝尔等地区冬季那达慕的重要内容。

赛驼也如赛马一样，需要调吊。一般在赛前半个月开始"吊"驼，少给水，喂些含蛋白质的精料，以至备战。骆驼的奔跑速度每小时最快可达 70~80 公里，赛驼多选在冬季举行，比赛类型主要有长距离赛、环形跑道赛、接力赛以及射箭赛。赛程一般为 10~30 公里。

比赛前，要在高处点燃一堆火，由参赛的主人牵着骆驼向火堆焚香，并绕香以顺时针方向转三圈，祈求吉祥如意。比赛时，赛手不分男女，身着艳丽的参赛服骑在驼背上，在起跑线排成一行。裁判员发令后，众骑手挥鞭驱驰，以先到达终点者为胜。也有的在赛途中置靶进行射箭比赛，以中靶的多少定胜负。赛后按到达终点的顺序绕着象征时运的火堆缓步跑三圈，并献酒祭火，酬谢火神的护佑。

## 7. 掷布鲁

"布鲁"，蒙古语意为"棒"，形状像一把镰刀，是流行于内蒙古东部地区那达慕的项目。

布鲁是最古老的狩猎工具，后演化成放牧工具和防身武器。早期的布鲁大都是用榆木制作，长度80厘米左右，后出现了头部带有金属的布鲁。按用途和形状的不同，布鲁可分为"心形布鲁""铅布鲁"

○清代镔铁布鲁、链锤布鲁

和"海雅木拉布鲁"三种。"心形布鲁"用铜、锌、铁、铅铸成鹊卵大小的椭圆形小球，然后用铁线串起拴在布鲁头上，多用于野外行走或夜晚出行时当作防身武器。"铅布鲁"在布鲁头部用刀刻制细而深的花纹并灌入铅而成，用于掷远和打猎。"海雅木拉布鲁"头为扁形，握柄为圆形，是日常生活中最普遍使用的布鲁。

布鲁比赛分为掷远布鲁和掷准布鲁两种。掷远布鲁叫"海雅木勒"，掷准布鲁叫"图拉嘎"。也有二者兼备既能掷远又能掷准的，头顶处包有铅头或铜箍环。掷远时按一定的距离，用规定布鲁掷远，掷出最远者为胜。投准比赛以 3 根圆形木柱为目标，柱高 50 厘米。每人投 3 次，直接投准所有目标得 10 分，间接投中所有目标得 8 分，直接投中两根木柱得 6 分等，最终以得分多者为胜。

以上所介绍的是那达慕的主要竞技类活动内容。那达慕的类型繁多，在蒙古族散居地区那达慕中也有一些独具特色的竞技活动，如云南通海兴蒙乡的舞龙、划旱船等。这些活动具有鲜明的地方色彩，是当地自然生态环境、地方历史传统的节日化表达。

## （二）歌舞及仪式展演

歌舞表演及仪式性展示，也是多种类型那达慕的主要内容或重要内容，一般作为开幕式的活动拉开那达慕的序幕。历史上，元代的"诈马宴"那达慕中便有歌舞、宴飨、竞技等内容。

蒙古族是歌唱的民族，人人都能哼唱几首民歌。蒙古人认为，歌唱不是用嗓子，而是在用心。所以，没有不会歌唱的人，也没有唱不好的歌。歌唱渗透在蒙古人的日常生产生活之中，如同每日的柴米油盐是最普通却也是最不可或缺的内容。那么，那达慕这样的节日，自然也就离不开歌舞。各地那达慕的歌舞表演，以地方特色歌舞为主要内容，凸显地方特色。如新疆蒙古族那达慕中，有萨瓦尔登舞、江格尔弹唱；在内蒙古锡林郭勒那达慕中，有长调表演；科尔沁地区那达慕中有科尔沁短调民歌、安代舞等等。那达慕的歌舞，渲染了节日的气氛，烘托了那达慕的欢乐和祥和。除了开幕式上的表演性歌舞之外，那达慕期间歌舞不断。对于草原牧人而言，人们的居住相对较远，平日的相聚不多，因此各种各样的那达慕成为亲朋好友相见相聚欢庆的日子。人们在享受闲暇，欣赏传统比赛项目之外，借此机会，饮酒欢宴，歌之舞之。

入场仪式是现代那达慕中地区资源集中体现和展演的舞台，是现代那达慕仪式化表达的重要一环。入场仪式展演一般包括国家仪式符号、蒙古族传统礼仪符号及地方民俗符号等。通过入场仪式，将本地区、本旗县政治、经济、文化各领域象征资源以一种内在的叙事顺序组合起来，符号化地展示地区所拥有的共同和特色资源。在官方举办的庆典类那达慕入场仪式中，各种符号的展演尤为突出。比如东乌珠穆沁旗建旗50周年那达慕入场仪式包括国旗护卫队、会旗队、会徽队、标语牌队、儿童方队、武警战士、搏克代表队、牧民马队、苏木、镇代表队、彩车队、迎宾献礼队等；包头市下辖的达茂旗那达慕大会入场仪式包括国旗队，黑、白苏勒德队，八省区服装展示队，骆驼方队，特技骑马表演等。从入场仪式，我们可以快速领略到这一地区那达慕的特色。

○那达慕开幕式搏克代表队

## 二、那达慕的仪俗

节日集中展示着文化传统，集中表达着民族情感，可以说是活态的"文化博物馆"。那达慕作为蒙古族的传统节日，其本身就是综合性文化载体，蕴含着丰富多彩的民族符号象征和情感诉求。

### （一）数字"玄机"

每个民族对数字都有各自不同的喜恶和象征，蒙古族也不例外。蒙古族民俗文化中的数字喜忌在那达慕中得以一一展现，暗含着蒙古族对数字的审美想象。

那达慕很多项目以"二"为基数，并以其倍数安排参加人数，如8、16、32、64到1024、2048等。不论是搏克、蒙古象棋、嘎拉哈比赛都是如此。人数的多少标志着那达慕的规模、规格以及组织者的身份地位。一般而言，那达慕的规模以参加比赛的人数多寡来判定。在锡林郭勒地区，有16~32搏克的称为小型的那达慕，64~128搏克的称作中型那达慕，256~512搏克的称为较大型的那达慕或叫有81奖赏的那达慕，而参加1024搏克的则称为大型那达慕。旧时，对于不同层级的那达慕，都有较为严格的搏克赛的人数规定。民间的敖包那达慕一般不会超过 128 个搏克，而旗县政府组织的那达慕才可有 512 名搏克手。而且大部分敖包那达慕的搏克数量是固定的，如东乌珠穆沁旗道特淖尔镇寺庙敖包洪格尔敖包那达慕有 128 名搏克，西乌珠穆沁旗王盖敖包那达慕则是 64 名搏克。除了那达慕参赛人员数量之外，那达慕的奖励也以"二"的倍数，以参加人数的四分之一为准。参加 128 名，奖励前 32 名；参加 64 名，奖励前 16 名，以此类推。不论是搏克、赛马、射箭，还是那达慕其他项目的奖励都是如此。

"三"这个数字对于蒙古族具有特殊的意义。"三"表示上、中、下三界，过去、现在、将来三时，是表示多的最小奇数。日常生活中蒙古人敬酒要敬三杯，饮酒之前须以右手无名指蘸杯中酒三敬：敬天（朝天）敬地（朝地）敬祖先（沾一下自己的前额），唱歌要唱三首完整的歌，等等。因此，那达慕"男儿三艺"中的"三"是一个象征性的数字，是一个相对的概念，在"三"中集合了蒙古族男儿必须掌握的基本本领，又概括了蒙古族考验和衡量英雄和好汉的价值标准。在那达慕具体的实践中，可以少于三或多于三。

再如数字"九"。蒙古族以"九"为尊，认为"九"不仅含有多数、无限多的意思，而且是吉祥如意的象征。《蒙古秘史》（267 节）载成吉思汗时谒见者"皆以九九为数来献"。据《蒙古风俗鉴》记载："自古规定：最高奖赏为九九，以下为五九，二九，一九等数，并参照奖品的重量定数。不论送给谁的礼物，直到给汗（皇帝）的礼物，最高的就是九九，也就是每种九件，共九种。""九九礼"作为蒙古各部朝贡的一种形式，源于成吉思汗时代，之后作为吉祥、完满的象征，在庆典、祭祀、节日及娱乐活动中使用。那达慕一直遵循着这一传统的奖励礼俗，"九九八十一大礼"只有在重要的大型那达慕上才会使用，而且不能超过这个数字。一般情况下，小型的那达慕会以三件、单个九件等礼物来奖励。"九九八十一礼"包括驼、牛、马、砖茶、毡子、银碗、哈达、靴子等等，都是日常生活所需却又具有吉祥之意的物件。而获得"九九八十一大礼"是参加那达慕最为荣耀和受人尊重的事情。

○ 那达慕比赛冠军的奖励——白驼

## （二）授予仪式

那达慕中隐含着许多仪式性的表达，其中最具特色的是青年搏克授予"将嘎"和老搏克退役授予"达尔汗"称号的仪式。

"将嘎"是搏克的一种装饰，是搏克荣誉的象征，也是凝结搏克气运的神圣之物。主"将嘎"用缎制哈达制作成项圈，并垂以蓝、红、黄、绿、白等五色彩条。这五色代表了金黄的世界，碧绿的草原，红色的晚霞，白色的云彩，蓝色的天空。只有在相当级别的那达慕上获得冠军的搏克，才有资格佩带"将嘎"。此后每得一次冠军，再增添一束五彩绸带，"将嘎"也就越来越饱满和充实。搏克往往还将戒指、金银和宝物放进"将嘎"里，一些老搏克手"将嘎"上显得破旧的彩绸，是他们资历和荣誉的表征。"将嘎"的授予也是神圣的仪式，旧时"将嘎"只有寺庙活佛或官方政府才有资格授予。而且"将嘎"的大小、多少都有严格的规制，不可任意添加。现在，由政府授予，但不同地区授予条件不尽相同。如东乌珠穆沁旗规定："在128名搏克手的赛事上，夺冠三次者可被授予'将嘎'。"而2004年西乌珠穆沁旗制定了《授予蒙古搏克将嘎条例》，进一步规范和细化了授予条件。即：在64名选手参加的个人赛中，前后获得过12次冠军；在128名选手参加的个人赛中，前后获得过4次冠军；在256名选手参加的个人赛中，获得冠军等可授予"将嘎"。

"将嘎"凝聚和寄托着蒙古人对力量、对英雄崇拜的精神追求和向往。"将嘎"作为神圣之物，也被应用在放生仪式和赛马装饰上。敖包祭祀仪式上，进行放生仪式的时候将五色"将嘎"套在放生的家畜羊、马脖子上或将五色彩条编系在鬃毛上，献牲给神灵，使它神圣化，从此不再骑乘或宰杀。赛马比赛上，给屡次获胜的马匹也佩戴"将嘎"，作为一种荣誉的象征，表示赛马的非同寻常。搏克的"将嘎"也发挥着同样的功效，授予搏克"将嘎"亦被认为赋予了搏克以"神性"，具有了神力。搏克比赛时，要模仿雄鹰、猛虎、凶狮的动作舞动双臂，跳跃入场。而"将嘎"如同雄狮鬃毛，让搏克威力无穷，不同于凡人。

除了授予"将嘎"外，蒙古族还有授予搏克称号的习俗，关于这点清朝时已经有明确记录。据金梁《满文秘档·太宗赏三力士》载："（天聪六年正月）令们都、杜尔麻、特木德黑三力跪于上前，听候命名，赐们都'阿尔萨兰土射图布库'名号，并赏豹皮长袄一；赐杜尔麻'扎布库'名号，并赏虎皮长袄一；赐特木德黑'巴尔巴图鲁布库'名号，并赏虎皮袄一。刀一、缎一、毛青八，并谕以后如有不呼所赐之名而仍呼原名者，罪。"这里所赐荣誉称号，分别为：第一名获得"阿尔萨兰"（狮）的称号，第二名获得"扎"（象）的称号，第三名获得"巴尔"（虎）的称号。在内蒙古地区，尤其在锡林郭勒盟，也有专门"授予称号"的搏克"锦标赛"。获胜者被授予"阿布日古"（跤王）、"阿尔萨兰"（狮）、"扎纳"（象）、"纳沁"（隼）、"哈日查该"（雕）等荣誉称号。青海、甘肃蒙古族中有在搏克比赛结束时，给获胜的搏克系上红色绸缎，将他高高举起欢呼的习俗。卫拉特蒙古人中，夺冠的搏克手被称为"嘎拉芒奈"（意为额头，比喻争到首位），获第二的称之为"阿尔班芒奈"（喻为第一名的十分之一），获第三的

○东乌珠穆沁旗旗庆那达慕搏克"退役"仪式

为"呼和布哈"（灰公牛，喻力气大）。而在蒙古国，优秀搏克手只授予称号而不佩戴"将嘎"。

"搏克退役"仪式，蒙古语称为"搏克达尔汗拉"，即授予搏克手"达尔汗"称号。"达尔汗"，在这里是"终身的""荣誉的"意思。成为"达

尔汗"搏克，是功成名就的象征，一般年龄50岁以上的著名搏克手，因为年老而不能继续争雄于跤坛，才能获此殊荣。授予仪式通常在那达慕大会开幕仪式后，搏克比赛正式开始之前举行。搏克手被授予"达尔汗"称号后，宣告退役，不得再参加任何形式的比赛。

授予仪式并不繁复，象征意义较为浓郁。两位搏克手，如同比赛一样穿戴整齐，在三唱"邀跤曲"后跳跃入场，在主持人历数他们跤坛佳绩的赞辞中，绕场漫步，接受众人的注目礼。随后，两位搏克手完全遵照正式比赛程序，仪式性地表演。经过一段搏克技巧的展示后，摔成平局，作为退出跤坛的最后一战。"达尔汗"称号授予仪式，同时也是年轻搏克"将嘎"授予仪式。被授予"将嘎"的搏克手并排而立，跳跃入场后，走到主席台前，向主席台和周围的观众行礼，由政府领导将"将嘎"授予他们。与此同时，代表"达尔汗"搏克荣誉的"将嘎"也要传给有潜质的年轻搏克手，寓意传承搏克技艺与运气。在蒙古人心目中，成为"达尔汗"搏克意味着荣誉和终身成就，也象征着搏克的代代相传和英雄辈出。

### （三）奖励及祝赞

蒙古族是一个极其注重"礼"和"赞"的民族，鼓励和赞美是其日常生活之态度，因此，"礼物"的流动以及祝赞仪礼更是节日、祭祀等特殊场合重要内容和必不可少的环节。那达慕上，不仅奖励和赞颂胜者，还要鼓励和"调侃"败者。搏克末尾者称为"少仁搏克"，意即"沾土搏克"，意即"一上场就被摔倒在地的搏克"。赛马的最后一名，称作"金座子""肥胃""脂球"等等，并以调侃的方式为其成为末名，找出各种客观理由进行"辩解"，如忙于牧活儿匆忙参赛，骑手是谨慎稳重的老头等等，并鼓励他们总结经验，吸取教训，养精蓄锐，在下次那达慕中取得成绩。蒙古人认为，很多时候输赢成败都是一时的，不是最后定论，这次的冠军在下次的比赛中就不一定是赢家。因此，这种处事态度和心理促成了那达慕比赛的最后一名都要嘉奖以资鼓励的传统。

祝赞是蒙古族民间传统文学形式，以吟唱者的即兴吟诵为主，运用比喻手法较多，且语言凝练流畅，讲究节奏的抑扬顿挫。各地区、各时期、不同类型的那达慕祝赞辞体例、颂赞内容略有不同，一般在遵循本地区赞辞韵律和体例的前提下，祝赞人根据现场实际情况自由发挥。那达慕的祝赞主要有"搏克祝赞""马赞"及"弓箭赞""射手祝词"等。

"搏克祝赞"是从体、力、技、智、德等不同角度对搏克手进行全面的赞美。有一首祝赞词唱道："能把高山挟在腋下的，胸膛宽阔的搏克。能把黄河搬空的，有顽强毅力的搏克。能把悬崖举起的，力大无比的搏克。"对冠军搏克赞美道："他有着庞大强健的身躯，举世闻名个个颔首赞许；他有着炉火纯青的技艺，也有着无坚不摧的意志力；他精神抖擞斗志昂，披荆斩棘从不停歇。犀利的达赖阿布日古，全国闻名的达尔罕阿布日古。"

"马赞"和赛马比赛的名次称号联系在一起，从冠军到第九名都有各自独特的赞诵。其中，"首马赞"一般介绍马的出身和成长，交代马的长相，强调马的气势，刻画马的神态，描绘马的装扮，以及对小骑手的赞美祝福，并授予"喜庆之首""吉祥之骏""宝驹""万马之首""飞隽"等不同的称号。从赛马称号来说，无统一规格，各地也有一些差别，如"升空太阳"，有的地方是第二、三名的称号，有的作为最后一匹马的称号。从赛马类型来看，因为以远程马比赛最为普遍，所以赞辞多为快马，即远程马赞。此外，也有走马赞辞。祝赞仪式开始，小骑士们穿戴赛马服，骑上获奖马匹由各自主人牵引绕那达慕会场三圈至主席台前听候授予称号。有一首乌珠穆沁赞辞如下："吉祥如意、众生安康如此美好的一日，超度之地邀请尊贵的喇嘛，祭拜山水之神的神圣的敖包。在这盛会上，要问跑到第一的这匹神骏属谁，它是浩硕斯琴亲王旗的××府的××苏木的臣民××的马群中之万马之首……它奔跑如疾风，蹄声如雹点，嘶鸣如蛟龙……它有月帚形的鬃毛，有鱼儿般的眼睛，有莲花般的耳朵……"等极尽溢美之词来高声唱颂获得冠军的赛马。祝诵后，还要用酸奶涂抹赛马的额头，赏吃奶豆腐，祝福比赛获得更好的成绩。

对那达慕夺冠射箭手，授予"莫尔根"（神箭手）称号，对连续三年夺冠者授予"达尔汗莫日根"（神圣/尊贵的射箭手）荣誉称号，并与搏克、赛马祝赞一样，在那达慕的闭幕式上由祝赞人对获得名次的射箭手吟唱弓箭赞和射手祝词。有一首《射手诵辞》祝赞道："左手握神弓，右手搭灵箭，双臂似托起山峦，胸膛如草原阔宽，把紧韧的弓弦拉圆。当飞行的箭翎发出呼啸，骏马为之嘶鸣，骟驼为之噪叫，山峰为之摇晃，大海翻起狂澜，蓝天彩虹呈现，而我们只能惊愕和赞叹。能射穿山峰的神箭手，利箭搭弓疾如电闪，无论在人海中，还是在颠簸的马背上，左右开弓箭箭中的。"那达慕上除了祝赞神箭手之外，也有赞美弓箭的赞词。

那达慕是全体蒙古人的节日，不论贫富，不分男女老幼均参与其中。千百年来，那达慕把蒙古人的诗情充分调动了起来，创造了富于诗意的祝赞和奖励礼俗，寄托着希望，表达着祝福。

多彩中国节

那达慕

三、
饮食文化

蒙古族的饮食文化在那达慕中也有充分地展现，不论是白食（奶类食品）还是红食（肉类食品），不论是日常的餐食还是隆重的饮食之最，都可一见。那达慕的特色饮食主要可分为祭祀供品和日常饮食两大类。供品主要包括敖包祭祀以及庆典那达慕上的全羊、羊背子、别灵（用红糖、熟面、黄油，由喇嘛制作）、肉粥、马奶等；日常饮食包括奶茶、奶豆腐、黄油、手把肉等。

奶食，俗称"白食"，蒙古语称"查干·伊德"。蒙古族崇尚白色，视白色为吉祥、纯洁。奶食品种类繁多，是蒙古族食品中的上品。除了最常食用的牛奶外，还用羊奶、马奶、骆驼奶制作的各种奶食品。最常见的奶制品有黄油、奶皮子、奶酪、奶豆腐、奶油，黄油渣等。白食的制作工艺可分为三类，包括自然凝固、搅拌发酵、温火烧制。用自然凝固的方法制作奶食品有：奶油、白油、黄油、黄油渣、奶豆腐、奶酪等。搅拌发酵的奶食品主要有"策格"（马奶）"艾日格"（酸奶子）、奶酒等。温火烧制的方法制作的奶食品主要有奶皮子。

肉类食品的统称，蒙古语称为"乌兰·伊德"，其意为鲜红的肉食品。品种也很多，主要包括：全羊、整羊背子、手扒羊肉、羊肉串、

涮羊肉等等。全羊，是蒙古人在重大节日、婚礼寿筵上款待尊贵客人的传统食品。全羊必须是绵羊，以二三岁的羯羊为上品。全羊只

○蒙古包外晾奶干

○分食羊背子

用不带蹄子的四肢（两条前腿各带四条肋骨）、腰背部和尾巴、胸腔骨和去掉下颌的头。用温火烧煮，不放佐料，出锅前只放少量盐。所以煮"全羊"，也叫"清水煮全羊"。也可以用烤制的方法，烹制全羊，称为"烤全羊"。煮全羊时要掌握好火候。出锅时，把四肢按原来的部位放在大托盘里，背部放上，胸腔骨放左，最上面放羊头，头朝前尾向后，羊头上放奶酪，以示隆重。整羊背子，蒙古语称"乌查"，是蒙古族宴请尊贵客人时摆放的传统佳肴。在老人寿辰那达慕上常用到。"乌查之宴"的礼节很隆重。

饮食礼仪在那达慕中也得到了充分体现，主要包括德吉礼、萨察乎礼（敬献礼）、米拉乎礼（涂抹礼）。"德吉"，意指"上、初"。德吉礼是蒙古族饮食习俗中强调进餐顺序的一项礼节，并将"食物之上"要敬献天地诸神。在平时，熬好早茶后将第一杯茶，即早茶之德吉敬献于天地、诸神及祖先。在家中进餐时把饮食的德吉献给长辈、老人和父母，以此表达自己的恭敬之意。在敖包祭祀那达慕、庆典那达慕中，都要重新制作新鲜的奶食、肉食用于祭祀，祭祀后作为"贺

○那达慕"酸奶五神骏"祝赞仪式

希格"（祭祀后对祭品的"分割"和享用）分享。"萨察乎礼"，意指"向诸神祭洒的奶子或其他食物"。而萨察礼则指进食前或进行祭祀仪式时，向天地诸神祭洒饮食，感谢神的赐予，并祈求神赐予其幸福安康的一项祭祀礼仪。蒙古人认为，所有饮食都由天地、祖先所赐，因此在食用饮食前进行萨察礼，以表感恩之情。如在饮酒时用右手无名指沾杯中酒弹3次；食肉时切3小块抛向天空等。敖包祭祀中，祭祀者绕敖包3圈，并敬献奶食。祭祀仪式的最后，还要祭洒五色风马。"米拉乎"，意指"将少许奶油或其他食物涂抹于某种东西上"。如那达慕赛马祝赞时，用酸奶涂抹赛马，并喂食奶豆腐就是一种米拉乎礼，以此祝愿赛马吉祥如意。那达慕中，还有一种饮食礼仪可以称为"分享礼"或"分食礼"。祭祀仪式后，将祭祀供品，如奶食、肉食作为"贺希格"分食或带回家与家人分享，以此表示获得了神的护佑。

# 四、
# 服饰文化

　　那达慕，可谓蒙古人的服饰"秀场"，从大漠深处到西南边陲，从草原牧人到城市白领，在那达慕这一天，男女老幼身着盛装，神采奕奕。从参加者的袍装到参赛者的服饰，无一不展示着多彩的蒙古族服饰文化。

　　蒙古族服饰，主要包括长袍、腰带、靴子、帽子、佩饰等。蒙古族分布地域辽阔，自然环境、经济状况、生活习惯各不相同，也形成了各具特色、丰富多彩的服饰。"蒙古族服饰"2008 年被列入国家级非物质文化遗产名录，对 28 个蒙古族部落的服饰进行了全面确认整理和严格审定后，《蒙古族服饰内蒙古自治区地方标准》于 2012年 6 月 1 日发布，2012 年 8 月 1 日实施。根据该标准，蒙古族服饰可分为巴尔虎服饰、布里亚特服饰、呼伦贝尔厄鲁特服饰、扎赉特服饰、扎鲁特服饰、科尔沁服饰、奈曼服饰、敖汉服饰、阿鲁科尔沁服饰、巴林服饰、翁牛特服饰、喀喇沁服饰、克什克腾服饰、乌珠穆沁服饰、浩齐特服饰、阿巴嘎服饰、苏尼特服饰、察哈尔服饰、四子部服饰、达尔罕服饰、茂明安服饰、土默特服饰、鄂尔多斯服饰、乌拉特服饰、阿拉善和硕特服饰、土尔扈特服饰、阿拉善信仰伊斯兰教蒙古人服饰、喀尔喀服饰等。如果加上甘肃苏北蒙古族、青海蒙古族、云南蒙古族等跨区域性服饰种类的话，可达数十种。在各地那达慕上，这些服饰鲜艳夺目，异彩纷呈，成为那达慕最靓丽的风景线。

那达慕"男儿三艺"的服饰也各具特色。

"数十白衣白于鹭，衣纔（才）及尻露裲裆，千条线缝十层布。"这是清代诗人赵翼对当时搏克服饰的描写。现代搏克的服饰，与历史上无二样，一直保持并传承了下来。搏克上身穿"昭德格"，下身穿"班扎拉"，即白布制成的宽大多褶长裤。外套吊膝，即"陶秀"，用鲜艳的缎子做料，用各色锦线、金银线绣边，再用刺绣和粘贴工艺描出龙、凤、狮、虎四雄以及蝙蝠、万字符等各种图案。双膝部位绣有圣火、祥云等吉祥纹样。这些吉祥图案昭示着搏克手拥有像火一样旺盛的精力，像四雄一样力大无比。搏克服饰上的装饰纹样都是由女人一针一线缝制出来的，正如蒙古族有句俗语称："男人会摔跤，女人不会缝制很遗憾；女人会缝制，男人不会摔跤不完美。"因此，在搏克赛场上不仅可领略蒙古族男人的威武雄壮，也可领略蒙古族女性的娴淑灵巧。

"昭德格"是最具蒙古族特色的摔跤服饰。"昭德格"一般由香牛皮制作，偶见用粗面革、毡子和布料制作的。不论用什么材料制作，领口、袖子、四周一带一定要用香牛皮或粗革层层镶边，用皮筋、丝线、麻筋等密缝起来，并在这些部位和后腰两侧，镶嵌银泡钉或铜泡钉，便于搏克手比赛时抓牢。泡钉的数量根据其形状大小有512、256不等，这个数字与搏克比赛人数——2的倍数有着内在的关系。在"昭德格"的心口处，有个五寸见方或圆月型的银镜或铜镜。镜上雕刻着龙、凤、狮、虎四雄及象、鹿等图案，象征搏克手如同猛兽一般英勇、威武。也有饰以各种吉祥纹样和蒙古文篆字，如"乌珠穆沁""苏尼特"等，标识着所属地域。一般著名搏克手都亲自缝制自己专用的"昭德格"，平日，无比赛时将它折叠包裹好放置在高处，远离"不洁"之物。

○搏克服"昭德格"

参加赛马的骑手也有专门的服饰，主要包括裙袍和骑士帽。裙袍颜色以粉红、天蓝、白色等亮色为主，用柔软的绸料制作，前后开襟，以保证轻便、吸汗。在衣襟、袖口、裙边处绣有动物或吉祥图案。骑手的头饰有尖顶圆帽、船形帽等，也有用彩绸来包头做装饰。帽顶有流苏，帽前缝有小镜子或绣有吉祥图案，帽后有穗儿。远程马赛时，为了尽可能降低赛马的负重，骑手一般不穿鞋子，只穿布袜；即便穿鞋，也选轻便的布鞋。

多彩中国节

那达慕

五、
居住文化

　　那达慕少则一日，多则七日，多在宽阔的草原上举行。草原上的人们几乎倾城而出，一家老小带着"家"来参加那达慕。因而，蒙古包成为移动的家，成为整个那达慕的节日生活空间。节日期间，除了观看比赛、参加比赛之外，亲戚朋友的聚会是其最重要的活动。人们在蒙古包里招待亲朋好友，饮酒高歌，享受节日的闲暇。草原上的牧人，平时的生活主要以小家庭为主，除了附近"艾里"（户）

○在蒙古包迎候亲朋好友

之间的走动之外，很少有大型的聚会。那达慕则提供了一个亲戚朋友见面、聊天，联络感情、凝聚社会关系网络的机会。那达慕是公共的开放性的节日，除了本旗县、本地区人员外，吸引着外部旗县甚至外来旅游者、商贩等各种身份者的加入，成为本地区与外界联络互动的媒介。而蒙古包也自然地成为接待外来者的场所，成为那达慕节日活动的一部分。

蒙古包是蒙古族传统的建筑，便于拆装，是"逐水草而居"的牧民们随身的家园。一顶普通的蒙古包只需要两峰骆驼或者一辆勒勒车就可以搬运，两三个小时就可搭盖起来。传统的蒙古包由架木、苫毡、鬃绳三个部分组成。架木结构有哈纳（支架）、陶脑（天顶）、奥尼（撑杆）、乌德（门）。普通的蒙古包，高约十尺至十五尺之间。蒙古包的大小，要以哈纳的多少区分，通常分为4个、6个、8个、10个和12个哈纳的蒙古包。苫毡由顶毡、围毡、外罩、毡门头等组成。还有覆盖陶脑（顶）的方形盖毡，称作"乌日和"，拉开可通风采光，盖严可挡风避雨。鬃绳，是用马鬃马尾搓成，包括扎带、围绳、压绳、坠绳。蒙古包的门一律朝南或东南方向，蒙古包的中央放置炉灶，周围摆设木质的碗柜、板柜、板箱、方桌等。蒙古包的正北一般悬挂成吉思汗像，西北侧供奉佛龛，两边柜子上摆放供品。西南主要摆放男人们的放牧用具，如：马鞍、马鞭等。蒙古包中间长条桌上摆满点心、糖果、奶食品，不论是谁进入蒙古包，热情的主人都会端上一碗热腾腾的奶茶。

现在因牧民基本都已定居，即便在牧业地区也很难看到形形色色、各种规制的蒙古包群落。唯有在那达慕这样的节日场合，蒙古族的传统民居及居住习俗得以集中展现。如2006年东乌珠穆沁旗建旗50周年那达慕期间，主会场左右两侧按照各苏木在本旗所在地理方位安置了500座蒙古包，建造了一座"移动的城镇"。这是那达慕期间各个苏木、嘎查牧民临时的家，也是为游客提供那达慕期间蒙古族特色食宿的地方。可以说，那达慕将分散于草原深处的苏木嘎查的人们聚集到一起，形成了那达慕节日期间的联合体，再现了"游牧王国"的盛况，建构起族群历史记忆中的"库列延"的想象。

　　传统的敖包祭祀那达慕中，蒙古包更是神圣的空间。祭祀前一日或几日前，敖包祭祀的组织者举家搬家到敖包祭祀地，经喇嘛念经净化之后搭建蒙古包。此后，敖包祭祀相关的准备、敖包祭祀后的那达慕的安排、分享敖包"贺希格"、敖包祭祀组织任务的交接仪式等事项都在蒙古包里举行。如东乌珠穆沁旗白音敖包祭祀那达慕，每年祭祀前七日组织者便到达祭祀地准备敖包祭祀那达慕相关事宜。因该敖包祭祀的组织者为 17 个家庭，按照蒙古族传统，蒙古包以右为上，右边第一家为敖包总长，第二家为次长，依次以年龄长幼排开，年龄最小的位居左，形成小型的蒙古包群落，形成敖包祭祀的空间。

六、
商贸交流

　　从农历四月至八月，草原上的各种类型的那达慕交替举行，而商业贯穿于期间，成为草原上牧人交易和买卖的"流动"平台和渠道。在今天的草原那达慕中，仍可见大江南北的小商贩，他们整个夏季都在草原上，一个那达慕接着一个那达慕"流动游走"。

　　历史上，那达慕的商业功能在游牧生产方式下发挥着重大的作用，是"中国南北物资交流的大商会"。甘珠尔庙会每年阴历八月初至中旬举行，一般进行九天，是巴尔虎草原上八旗喇嘛隆重的庙会。起初，甘珠尔庙会的商贩只来自呼伦贝尔各个游牧旗，后来内蒙古的昭乌达、哲里木、锡林郭勒等盟以及外蒙古喀尔喀、车臣汗部各旗的蒙古人也来参加。光绪三十一年，中日、中俄签订协约开放海拉尔、满洲里商埠，允许外国人来经商之后，俄、日及欧美等国商人也来甘珠尔庙会进行商业活动。当时甘珠尔庙会各地商贩都有自己固定的位置：门东向北是卜奎（齐齐哈尔）、多伦商铺，门西向北是北京、奉天商人，北门外还有俄国商摊。由此，巴尔虎草原上出现了独一无二的，也是世界闻名的甘珠尔庙会集市。除呼伦贝尔之外，在现锡林郭勒盟多伦诺尔地区，自清康熙始举行蒙古各盟盟会，成为以喇嘛寺庙为中心的沟通漠南与漠北地区蒙古族集市贸易的枢纽。届时，锡林郭勒、察哈尔、昭乌达盟各旗和漠北车臣汗、吐谢图汗部等蒙古部落周围数百里的蒙古牧民，扶老携幼，骑马乘车，赶着畜群，驮载毛皮、野兽裘毛前来参加庙会和贸易交换；来自东北和内地的汉、回、达斡尔族商民，亦从四面八方云集于斯，进行互市交易。

今天，随着定居和城镇化步伐的加快，牧人的商业和物资交易形式发生了根本性的变化，因此，那达慕的商业功能也发生了巨大的变迁，那达慕的商业被植入了新的内容。那达慕从过去较为直接的物资交流功能转变为当下以旅游和消费为主的较为间接的第三产业功能，并借助招商引资等手段吸引广告和企业赞助，从而发挥着更为重要的经济功能。在现代大型那达慕当中，通过企业赞助或广告获取收益，渐次成为其重要的运作方式。这对于缓解举办那达慕的资金压力，提高那达慕的经济收益起到一定的作用。

旅游小贴士

### 额尔古纳

在《史记》以及 14 世纪用波斯文写成的《史集》中都记载了一个关于蒙古族起源的传说：蒙古人因战败遭到其他部落残杀，仅剩下两男两女得以逃出劫难，他们来到一个地方，周围都是山林，中间有良好的草原，这个地方叫做"额尔古涅昆"（额尔古纳河畔山岭），他们在这里生息繁衍，世代相传，直至今日。流经呼伦贝尔草原的额尔古纳河，也就成为蒙古民族的发祥地。额尔古纳河作为蒙古民族的母亲河，不仅哺育了蒙古民族，也滋润了两岸的土地，见证了蒙古族的发祥历史。

额尔古纳河是黑龙江的源头之一，蒙古帝国及北元时期是中国内陆河。1689 年《中俄尼布楚条约》签订，额尔古纳河成为中国与俄罗斯的界河。

来到额尔古纳旅游，被誉为亚洲第一湿地的额尔古纳湿地（又名根河湿地）不可错过。这是中国目前原生态保持最完好、面积最大的湿地。景区有一望无际的灌木丛和草甸，野生动植物资源极为丰富，每年在这里迁徙停留、繁殖栖息的鸟类达到 2000 万只以上，是世界上最重要的丹顶鹤繁殖地之一，也是世界濒危物种鸿雁的重要栖息地之一。

最佳季节：

额尔古纳主要是草原和林区，最佳旅行季节为每年 7 月至 9 月中下旬，盛夏季节气候宜人，水草最为肥美。喜爱冰雪的游客不妨在 11 月至次年 2 月中旬的冬季到此一游，一定会满意而归。

交通路线：

1. 飞机或火车到达满洲里；可随旅游巴士或跟团游额尔古纳。

2. 自驾游路线：起点自满洲里，全程约 245.6 公里；沿满洲里市中央街行驶 38.7 公里，左前方转弯进入 X904，沿 X904 行驶 142.6 公里，右转进入额尔古纳市。

# Chapter Two
## Naadam Customs

Naadam, as a custom, is an umbrella term for entertainments, foods, costumes, rites, family gatherings and other folk events related to Naadam festival. Various and interesting activities and customs have accumulated over the history.

# 1. Activities of Naadam

## 1.1 The Three Games of Men and Other Activities

In Naadam, the Three Games of Men mainly refer to Bökh (Mongolian wrestling), horse racing and archery. Details of the events may be different in different regions. In some places, these three games are held in one Naadam, while in some other places only two of them are included with the third game coming from Mongolian chess, shagai, camel racing and "bulu" throwing which bear distinctive regional features.

Traditionally Mongolian men are supposed to master the skills and techniques needed in the Three Games. They are brought up to be "honorable tough guys holding a bow and arrows, resting their heads on a quiver and daring to leave their bodies in wildness after death". They admire the hardworking spirit of "drinking dew, feeding on saliva, riding on wind and befriending swords". They also praise people who are "as brave as lions and tigers, as intrepid as the fiercest eagles" and manly guys on horseback who embrace cloud, mist and sunlight. With such education and expectation, there is no single Mongolian man who is not resolute, tenacious, open-minded, optimistic, masculine and brave. These characteristics and skills are perfectly shown and tested by Naadam which, in turn, serves as the best platform for people to display their manliness. But over the long history of Naadam, we can see that the Three Games of Men are not limited to men; women also participate in them.

### 1.1.1 Bökh

Bökh, also known as Mongolian wrestling, means "tough", "strong" and "enduring" in Mongolian. A qualified wrestler must possess all the characteristics dictated by the word "Bökh", which means he or she should be both physically and mentally strong. Mongols see wrestlers as the perfect embodyment of wisdom and bravery and as outstanding heroes for their toughness, flexibility and wisdom. Just as the Three Games of Men are the core of Naadam, wrestling is also the kernel of the three games. Over years of development, the long-standing Bökh has always been the most stable and well-reserved activity and it also carries the more distinctive symbolic meaning.

According to ancient Chinese documents, Mongolian wrestling appeared in as early as the Qin and Han dynasties (221BC-AD220), when it was called Jueli (the competition of strength). Watching Jueli competition was so popular in Han Dynasty (202BC-AD220) that it was even brought to Chinese imperial palaces. In 1950s, a bronze medal for Jueli competition was excavated from the 104th tomb in Keshengzhuang, Shanxi Province and it was later found out to be the belongings of Xiongnu tribe's. The scene of Jueli was engraved on the medal: after tying the horses to trees, the two bare-chested wrestlers tried to topple their opponents by grabbing each other's legs or waists. Jin Qicong's studies reveal that the wrestling game described on the bronze medal is more like a game that happened occasionally instead of an official competition, which further implies that Jueli was quite popular then among the Xiongnu. In 1931, an octagonal white clay pot was unearthed from the site of what was Dongjing city in Liao Dynasty (907-1125), known as Liaoyang city in Liaoning Province today, and the pot was painted with eight scenes of Jueli of kids. Japanese Torii Ryuzo believed those were Khitan kids and the scenes constituted a comic. According to Jin's studies, Jueli competition of Khitan and Jurchen peoples were handed down from the Xiongnu and Rouran tribes and then Mongols' Jueli was from

Khitan. It means that Mongolian wrestling originates from the Xiongnu, thus having a long history. Traditional costumes for Mongolian wrestlers are almost the same as those of Xiongnu, which shows that Bökh costumes also have a long history.

Zhao Yi, a famous man of letters in Qing Dynasty, wrote a poem, Wrestling in Imperial Hunt, to describe the scene of a wrestling competition held on Mulan hunting ground: "With the yellow tents set up, wrestlers finally showed up; their costumes, made from several layers of clothes with a particular stitch, were as white as the feather of egrets, long enough to cover their hips. Though not armed, the wrestlers had strong arms and legs as if they were made from iron. Knowing the opponents were tough, they were all circling around, waiting for the right moment to attack." The poem vividly describes many elements of Mongolian wrestling, such as the costumes, skills and courtesy. It also proves that wrestling was an essential sport in Naadam festival in Qing Dynasty during which time the skills of wrestling had already become quite advanced.

Stories about Bökh are widespread in Inner Mongolia, especially in areas where the competition prevails. Based on people's life experiences and records of wrestling competitions, though some may be imaginary, these stories are the epitome of Bökh's important role in Mongols' life and of the spirit of Bökh. In 1666, the fifth year of the reign of Emperor Kangxi, the Qing government held a national Naadam, in which the wrestler Anzhao from Ujimqin established his extraordinary fame by outdoing the other 1,023 wrestlers. In the early 19th century, Bartee Kaoketu participated in the event and took the first place and all the honors with him. In the mid-19th century, there appeared a wrestler called Durengzaan, who later became the hero of many legends and folk music stories. For example, the long tune song Durengzaan is one of the pieces of folk music to praise his triumph over an ever victorious wrestler. The song is handed down to present time and Durengzaan has become a synonym for famous Mongolian wrestler. Wrestlers like Sengge, Laotai, Qimed, Erdenbayar, Gonchayzhab, Tsagaanzaan, Khada, Batusukh and Bayarbatu were all as great as Durengzaan, nurtured by the vast steppe of Ujimqin. Good skills can help a wrestler not only win in competitions but also earn great reputation in the community. What's more, the Bökh championship is the collective honor of a community and can even be significant to the whole society, as Bökh stands for a mysterious power, strength and abundance to a community and a region. The Naadam held in Bayan Ovoo rituals in Ujimqin, for example, attracts many wrestlers every year. They believe that to win in Ovoo Naadam can bring them a whole year's luck to win in all competitions. And herdsmen believe that the success of the wrestler from his sumu or gachaa (villages) can bring fortune to all people in the sumu or gachaa.

There are no weight classes or time limit in a match and Mongolian wrestling is a highly competitive sport in that winning or loss is determined within one bout. Without weight classes, wrestlers have to consider both themselves and opponents' weights, strength, wrestling skills and so on before a match. For example, it may seem unfair for a man weighing 50 kilograms to compete with a man weighing 100 kilograms, but actually the two both have their own advantages. The man with 100 kilogram's weight obviously has the advantage in weight and thus in throws, but it also stands to reason that his weight may contribute to his loss if his opponent is small, agile and skillful in wrestling. So every wrestler should weigh up advantages and disadvantages and fully draw on strengths to win a competition. Since traditional Bökh has no time limit, there have been occasions where a competition lasted for several days. If no winner emerges, the competition will go on. In this occasion, the competition is called "Woya" or Patience Bökh. As we can tell from the name, it's all about patience and courage. If the competition isn't over in the morning, then it will go on after lunch and will not end until one of them get toppled by the other. Modern large-scale Mongolian wrestling, however, has modified this rule.

Exciting Bökh (by Xi Yinzhu)

In front of the main platform in the Naadam venue, there is usually a special tent, indicating the competition field of Bökh. Usually it is a white tent embroiled with blue Buddhist auspicious patterns, such as deer and prayer wheels. Wrestlers wait in the tent and then enter the Bökh contest field in two queues when the competition starts. Excellent wrestlers wearing "jiangga" (a silk necklace representing honor) queue at the right side or the west while those green-hands or without "jiangga" queue up at the left side. Led by an elder, each team forms a passage leading to a door. Each wrestler in the queue rests his arms on the shoulders of the person before him and keeps a bending gesture while waiting. In smaller Naadam, there are eight wrestlers in each queue while sixteen for larger Naadam. Normally, the first competitor is an excellent wrestler, such as a Wrestling Giant, and the opponent is a green hand. After repeating three times of Bökhiin uriya, a song as an invitation to wrestling, two competitors from each queue dance like flying eagles into the contest field and salute towards the main platform. With simple lyrics and beautiful tunes, the Bökhiin uriya expresses a basic meaning of "welcoming competitors to the contest field". The song is usually played three times and then the wrestlers can dance and jump into the contest field. The invitation song used to be sung by long-tuned singers live but now it is recorded and broadcast by radios. Running through the whole competition, Bökhiin uriya indicates the beginning of a Bökh like a bugle call in a war.

After the march-in, wrestlers queuing in two lines go round the contest field clockwise, and at the same time the host introduces each wrestler and announces detailed arrangements of the competition. When called, the wrestler lifts his right hand to show he is ready, nods to his opponent and shakes hands with him before their competition begins. Wrestlers observe match courtesy strictly by shaking hands both prior to and after a bout. When a contest is over, the defeated competitor will salute the main platform and audience and then leave the contest field quickly, while the winner will jump three times and salute the main platform and then turn to leave. The dance performed prior to a Bökh competition is called "Deveeh" or "magshikh" in Mongolian and it requires wrestlers to imitate the gestures and poses of animals, like eagles, deer and lions. This is a traditional ritual that has divinity and special meanings. This dance indicates the close relationship between these animals and nomadic culture: they are seen as Mongolians' ancestors possessing the magic power to protect the nature and thus are important in social and cultural aspects. By imitating the movements of the animals, wrestlers fully demonstrate their strength, high spirit, fighting will and vigor.

March-in dance of Bökh (by Xi Yinzhu)

The basic movements in Bökh fall into the following two general categories: Zogsich (standing gestures) and Bёrcha (grappling gestures), which are also seen as the basic skills to win a competition. The standing and grappling gestures involve many Bökh techniques varying from region to region. The first volume in the Bökh in Ujimqin, a series of books published in 1988 by the Culture and History Association of East Ujimqin

Banner, summarizes 10 different basic skills and 345 techniques in Ujimqin Bökh including clinching, fighting, dragging, throwing, and grabbing wrist or waist and so on.

Featured by distinctive ethnic and regional characteristics, Bökh can be divided into four forms: the Ujimqin-style, Hulun Buir-style, Ordos-style and Salibor-style. The Salibor-style Bökh in areas like Alxa in Inner Mongolia differs from the other three types in costumes and rules. "Salibor" is the Mongolian word for shorts and the Salibor-style Bökh is so called because competitors all wear shorts. In Alxa, the Three Games of Man are Salibor-style wrestling, archery on horseback and camel racing. Costumes of Salibor-style Bökh include shorts and veils. The clothes for wrestling are blue or green, blue for the sky and green for the grassland, and veils are made of red, yellow or blue silks. At the beginning of each competition, competitors enter the contest field veiled, and only when unveiled by the judge can they know who their opponents are. Alxa is known as the home of camels and thus there in the Salibor-style Bökh,

March-in of Salibor-style wrestlers (by Cainiao Blog)

the starting gestures and techniques are, to a large extent, the imitation of camels fighting each other. The techniques are also named after the attacking methods by camels, which are lunge, sneak attack, backward push, pounce and so on.

Although adults are the main force of Bökh, there are also children competitors occasionally. Group contests and Bökh for females and elders are also held in some official large-scale Naadams. For Ovoo Naadam or small-scale Naadam, wrestlers don't undergo special training or make preparation before competition. Anyone interested in Mongolian wrestling can sign up and the match begins when there are enough competitors. Heavy everyday tasks in nomadic lifestyle have already prepared wrestlers with physical strength and strong will. At the intervals of hard work, Mongols tend to wrestle with each other as an entertainment. We can tell that Bökh is closely related to Mongols' daily life.

### 1.1.2 Horse Racing

Horse is tool, wealth, friend and accompany to Mongols. It stands to reason that horse is a symbol of Mongols, an ethnic group growing on horseback. Horse racing is one of the core sports items in all kinds of Naadam in pastoral areas and is getting more and more important and colorful in certain types of Naadam. These Naadams still carry on the cultural meanings of horse race though different kinds of Naadam show different degrees of these meanings. For example, chants of horses are only sung as a ceremony in large-scale Naadam held by governments or Naadam featuring horse culture. The ceremony of Sang Erguleg is performed prior to all horse races in Naadam though its procedures may differ in complexity

Cultural relics reveal that Mongols started horse husbandry as early as the Bronze Age and the early Iron Age. During the second century BC to the early third century AD, horses had gained an indispensable place in Mongolian nomadic society as a domestic animal. Especially after the time of late ninth century AD when Mongols moved from Argun River to the origin of Onon, Kuulu and Turla Rivers, horses were everywhere in Mongolian steppe. John of Plano Carpini was accredited to Mongol Empire in the mid-13th century and he once said with admiration, "here people raise so many horses, I don't think there's a place in the world that can rival Mongolia in the number of horses."

Over years of raising horses, Mongols have adopted their unique ways of raising and training horses and developed special competitions and entertainments relevant to horses. Peng Daya described vividly in his book Hei Da Shi Lue (Introduction to Mongolia) their ways of raising horse: early in spring when the war is over, war horses can all feed themselves on water and grass freely and no one is allowed to ride on them. But when west wind is coming, they have to be tied around tents under control and fed with only a little water and grass. Several months later horses become slim and strong so that they never sweat even after several hundred kilometers of ride. By then these horses have become more durable and suitable for wars. In normal marching, horses can't feed on water or grass unless they're extremely exhausted for people fear that tired horses can fall ill if they feed and get too much weight. This is how to raise a strong horse." In 1279, the Jurchen-ruled Yuan Dynasty ended the reign of the Southern Song, unified the whole country and built a set of national systems. For example, Mongolian herdsmen were grouped into units of ten, a hundred, a thousand and ten thousand for better control. When there comes a war, they ride their horses to battle; otherwise, they setlle together to raise the horses. Required by this system, Mongolian men had to go through well-organized training on archery and horse riding, which contributed to the development of horse racing in Mongolia and cultivated an excellent cavalry. In his Envoy to Mongol Empire, Dawson, a British man, wrote that "(Mongolian) children of two or three years old have already started to learn riding and controlling horses and archery on horseback with bows proportionate to their build". Horses not only have an important role in Mongols' daily life, but also possess high military status in wars. Genghis Khan established thirteen military organizations in which soldiers good at horse riding and archery reached nearly 30,000. In a group of five poems named Views in Shangjing, by the Yuan poet Sadula, he described the riding and shooting skills of Mongols: With bows as strong as the wind in the northern-frontier area, the nobility are riding in the hunting ground; Calling their hunting eagles and carrying their arrows, they do not come back until very late, but they get two white wolves hanging besides their horses. Since the Mongol Empire, Mongolians began to hold a roy-

Archery on horseback

al banquet called Zhama banquet, which still remained popular in Qing Dynasty. Along with that, horse racing was also held in all kinds of Naadam. The chapter of "Banquet of Mongols" in Qing Bai Lei Chao records the scenes of Emperor Qianlong watching a horse-riding performance in his tour to Mulan hunting ground in August. Zhao Yi also described the exciting horse racing competition in an article called Zhama Banquet of Mongols in his miscellany.

According to the earliest records, the distance of a race is usually dozens of kilometers, "usually thirty or forty li (one li equals 500 meters) and sometimes over a hundred li". Try as every competitor may to win in speed, stamina of horses is also an important element. Therefore, to win in a horse race, skills of training and controlling horses are essential. Good breeds of horse, superior jockeys and excellent skills of horse training constitute the three key elements to win a race. No matter in historical records or actual races, horse training has always been an important preparation prior to a horse race in Naadam. This preparation has many diversions depending on conditions of horses and types of competitions, usually starting a month before the event. As skills of training horses are so privative and handed down within a family, there are lots of techniques that cannot be revealed and also many taboos.

Horse training begins with choosing the right horses. As the old saying goes, "it takes rides to know whether a horse is good just as it takes communication to know whether a person is friend". For a herdsman to know about a horse's temperament and stamina, he has to ride on it, and there are also horse experts who can judge a horse's quality by observing its fur, figure, motion and so on. Judging by fur, horses that are pure white, liver-like brown, snowy white, shiny black, red, irony green or bamboo-like yellow are considered to be good ones with fortune. Judging by figure, a good horse should have a slim head like deer, bright eyes and long eyelashes. The neck should be long and flat like deer, the chest broad, the back long and slim, and the hip wide. These traits plus everyday observation and riding experience are criteria for a herdsman to choose the right horses for strict training and the number of horses depends on the time and energy of horse trainers and conditions of the horses. Although varying from family to family, horse training still has its universal principles. First is to sweat horses and control the frequency and timing of feeding them, so as to regulate their spleens and stomachs. Second, horses should be tied in cool places with good ventilation so that they will not get too cold or hot and they need to run a certain distance every two days. During the preparation, horses can only drink water once a day. Running distances are also different according to the distances of the races they are going to compete in. Horses for endurance races are required to run no more than 10 KM and horses for jump races run no more than 5 KM. But as grassland is actually enclosed by fences nowadays, the training distance is much shortened. After a race, it is necessary to walk the horses for at least half an hour and, for the sake of their health, they should have four to five hours to fully relax themselves before drinking, eating or rolling on the ground. Horses are different from each other and hence need various kinds of training methods. Some horses may need to lose weight so they should be washed with cold water, while some may need to gain weight so they should be cleaned with warm water. Horses competing in different types of races also need to be treated differently. Horses for jump races don't need washing, but those for endurance races need to be washed every day to lose weight and become light. There are also taboos during the preparation. For example, the owner should not drink alcohol and argue or fight with anyone. Horses should be kept far away from cargoes and other ominous things. Tools used for training such as horsewhips, brushes and saddles should be kept in high places to keep "clean". The training of horses asks for as great care as requested for treating a baby. So folks say that "even if you don't wash your own hair, you have to wash your horse". By this saying we can say that horse racing in Naadam is far more than the competition of horses; it's also the understanding, training and love of owners to horses.

There are endurance race, race for two-year-old horses, horse-walking race, jump race and other types of horse races. Apart from those races, large-scale Naadams also hold equestrianism performances and competitions, such as competitions of picking up shagai from horseback in Xilingol, horseback archery contests in Alxa and performances of the professional equestrian unit of Inner Mongolia. Races different in distances start from different places in the venue but all end in the main venue of Naadam. Endurance races and races for two-year-old horses are the commonest types which usually take place at six or seven o'clock in the morning when it is cool and comfortable. Usually the track is straight and the distance is 10, 20 or 30 km. The person first to arrive at the end is the winner. In endurance races, stamina and speed are the most important factors. There is no grouping among competitors, and there can be dozens or even several hundreds of people, usually between 7 and 13 years old. For horse-walking races, whether the horses' gaits are steady and light is the key to win. Different from running horses who

Endurance race in Naadam

gallop with both front and back legs moving forward together, walking horses have to move with cross steps and definitely cannot run. Jockeys in horse-walking races are all adults and they race for 10 to 20 km. The competition of picking up shagai from horseback is a real test of skills and courage. Four competitors are in one group. On the 300meter course, there are five shagai wrapped with Khata placed on the ground at certain intervals. Mounted competitors have to reach down

Competitors picking up shagai from horseback

from one side of their horses' backs and pick up shagai one by one at full gallop. The winner will be the competitor who picks up the most shagai in the shortest time.

In Naadam, race horses are usually specially dressed up. A horse's mane and tail are considered to have magic power and luck. So in ancient times, Mongols used them for fortune telling. People use colorful silk clothes or strings to wind up race horses' manes like braids so that the hair won't cover their eyes. Their tails are also wrapped up with red strings or silks. This old traditional decoration is recorded by rock paintings, which dates back to a distant epoch. Herdsmen believe that dressing up race horses can bring luck and bless to the horses and can cheer them up for competitions. Apart from decorations on mane and tail, families in different regions have their special ways of decorating a horse. Some may hang a bronze bell or colorful "jiangga" on the horse's neck; some may put on a bronze mirror on the forehead. These decorations are more about people's love and bless for their race horses. They wish that the horses can reach destinations safely and smoothly.

There's a ceremony of sangerguleg prior to a race to pray for blessings. Mongols also call it Marsaileg. Sang refers to the whole ceremony and also the burning pine leaves, cedar leaves and fires in burners. Sangerguleg is a verb in Mongolian which means to circle around and rotate, and the word marsaileg originates from the song Marissa, which is sung in the Raosang ceremony, and-leg is a suffix to change the word into a verb. Jockeys riding on decorated race horses also have to sing the song Marsai. Led by the trainers of the horses, the jockeys circle around the burner clockwise for three rounds to bless the race horses a successful return. Marsai is the Buddha in Gelug (a school of Buddhism) who can protect people from many misfortunes including flood, fire, wind, lions, wars, burglary and quarrels. In Sangerguleg ceremony, children pray to the Buddha by humming lyrics like "Om Marsai, the Buddha is with you" until the ceremony is over. But in most Naadams, there's no live show of Marsai but a radio broadcast of it. The song's name varies in different areas and in some places people call it "ginggao". The procedures of the ceremony also have certain divergences. In some places, people sing a song called "The Lead of Ten Thousand Horses" and sprinkle sour milk on race horses' heads. In some Ovoo Naadams, like those in Tsagaan Ovoo, East Sonid of Xilingol, the ceremony is of a more grand scale: the leader ride on white horses and hold a flagpole wrapped with a cloth painted with Buddha, followed by a procession of race horses and people blowing conches. Accompanied by the sound of conches and the song Marsai, all people and horses circle around the ovoo three times, praying to the Gods of ovoo, of mountains and river, and of sky and earth. The lyrics of songs in Sangerguleg ceremony and the event itself show the close relationship with Buddhism and they're all the epitome of Buddhist culture in the Three Games of Men.

### 1.1.3 Archery

In Mongolian, bow is called "nom" and arrow "sum". Regarding them as symbol of masculinity, Mongolians have been loving bow and arrow and enjoying horseback archery since ancient times and in the past they always carried them both for attack and for luck. Naturally archery has evolved into an important sports event of Naadam.

The natural and social environment in high-latitude areas have endowed nomadic people with the technique of horseback archery, a must for their survival, hunt and fight. According to "Traditions of the Xiongnu" in Book of Han, a history of China's Former Han Dynasty, Xiongnu people "can ride sheep or goats and shoot birds and mice by bows and arrows from a young age; when they grow older, the targets become foxes and rabbits." In Hei Da Shi Lue, the author Peng Daya describes some scenes about Mongolian children riding horses in the 13th century. The book says, "at an early age, a (Mongolian) child ties a board on the back of a horse, sits on it and follows his mom to go around. At three, he ties himself on the saddle so that he can hold a bow and an arrow and gallop a horse with a crowd. By four or five, he has already learnt how to use small bows and short arrows." According to History of the World Conqueror written by Persian historian Juvayni in the 13th century, Genghis Khan, the founder of Mongol Empire, attached great importance to hunting. His purpose was not only to hunt animals but to get his people to adapt to hard training, master archery and horse-riding skills, and obtain the ability to endure hardships. In the mid-13th century, an Italian named John of Plano Carpini visited Mongolia several times and he wrote in his book The Story of the Mongols that "(Mongolian) men do nothing but make arrows and raise herds. They often go hunting and practice horseback archery. Almost all Mongolian men, no matter young or old, are expert at shooting arrows." Genghis Khan ordered that Mongolian soldiers must carry two or three bows with them, or at least one quality bow with three bags full of arrows. Encouraged by their king, numerous excellent archers appeared at that time, including the famous military officer Moholai and Genghis Khan's nephew Yesüngge, whose father is the Khan's brother Hasar. Later, descendants of Hasar established a Mongolian tribe named "Khorchin", which refers to "archer". It can be concluded from the aforementioned information that archery plays a critical role in Mongolia's history and its people's life and production, so much so that it has developed into the core of Naadam as one of the Three Games of Men.

Mongolian archery includes three types, namely mounted archery, target archery and long-distance archery, though the last one is rarely seen now. Naadam puts no limitation on the type, weight, length or draw weight of bows and arrows. Mounted archery requires an archer armed with bow and arrow to shoot while riding on a running horse. The number of participants in Naadam's mounted archery contests is not limited, nor is there requirement of uniformity for about an archer's horse or arrows. The field for shooting usually includes a horse-racing track, which is 4 meters in width and 85 to 100 meters in length. Three targets are placed on each field at intervals of about 25 meters, and each target is a 2-meter-high wooden frame with a colorful cloth bag hanging on it. Archers are required to shoot three arrows while riding on the requested track, and they need to finish three rounds with nine shots. The winner will be the one who hits the most targets. Mounted archery is still popular in areas such as Ordos, Alxa and Chifeng. Target archery, in which archers shoot in a standing position, is a relatively common form of archery competitions in Naadam. Participants are grouped by genders or sometimes by degrees of professionalism. Normally the distance to the target is 30 meters for males and 25 meters for females. There are three rounds for each competitor and five shots in each round. The number of arrows that hit targets and the points of rings that they hit will be counted to decide who is the champion. Targets used by Mongol archers were at first made by grass or skin of cattle, sheep and goats and later in the early modern times by felt or cotton bags. As for bows used in competitions, traditionally they are made out of elm and willow, or cattle's horns, steel and plastic for high-class ones. In modern archery competitions, an archer stands about 15 to 25 meters away from a target that consists of five rings with different colors,

Archery competition in Naadam

which, from the central one to the outermost one, are yellow, red, blue, black and white. An archer will get 100 points if shooting the innermost ring, and get 80, 60, 40 and 20 points respectively for the outer rings. In addition, there is a kind of target with a movable center which will fall off if being shot. A Mongol archer usually holds the string at full draw, using thumb to grasp the string and placing an arrow's fletching on the joint between thumb and forefinger.

The three games of Naadam have been deeply intertwined with Mongols' daily life, which is exactly the source of the games. Created in Mongolian nomadic society of hunters, archery has played a vital role in Mongolian history. But nowadays, archery games are developing in an uneven manner due to the changes of Mongols' life style and even tend to decline in some areas. For example, in Ujimqin, an administrative subdivision of Inner Mongolia, traditional archery competitions have disappeared since the 1950s. For a long time, virtually all contests in Naadam festival of Ujimqin have been occupied by "Bökh" (wrestling) and horse racing and some minor competitions such as Mongolian chess and "shagai" (ankle bone) games, while archery has always been absent. The renaissance of archery in modern Naadam is attributed to the efforts of some insightful people who began to found archery organizations and recruit students in 2005, and since then archery games have gradually spread in Ujimqin. But different from Ujimqin, the Khorchin region always regards archery as an essential part of Naadam and has maintained traditional bows, arrows and rules of competitions up to now.

The Three Games of Men amply demonstrate the harmony between Mongolians and nature and the friendship among the people themselves. Wrestling stresses the contradictory relation between two persons who, being both rivals and friends, keep fighting while enjoy harmony. Horse racing highlights the harmony between human and production tools. As for archery, a sport involving actions of opening and stretching, it represents a tie of both ease and tension between mankind and the environment. Mongolians worship human's force, admire horses and praise bows and arrows, and in Mongolian folk literature you can easily find evidences for those characters. Gradually improving along with the advancement of times, the Three Games of Men are about competing and conquering with force, guts, skills and intelligence. The Naadam festival is thoroughly displayed through the competition of force in wrestling, speed in horse racing and accuracy in archery.

### 1.1.4 Mongolian Chess

Mongolian chess

Called "shatar" or "hiashatar" in Mongolian, the Mongolian chess is a sport with significance only next to the mentioned Three Games of Men, enjoying wide popularity all over Inner Mongolia. It is said that shatar was already well received among Mongols as early as in the 13th century when Genghis Khan was waging invasive wars over a large part of Eurasia. In addition, shatar shares a lot of characteristics with the international form of chess and therefore many excellent shatar players are also chess masters.

According to the chess academia, in ancient India there was a form of chess called "chaturanga", which consisted of four kinds of chess pieces,including elefantry, chariotry, infantry and cavalry. In the seventh century, this chess was introduced to Persia where its name changed to "shatranj". Then, the stretching of Silk Road over Mongolian-Manchurian grassland in the early 13th century brought "shatranj" into Mongolian plateau. On the one hand, at the end of the 15th century, shatranj spread to Europe and later evolved into the modern form of chess. On the other hand, in Mongolian plateau, shatranj's rules and its pieces' names were adapted according to Mongolian tradition and culture, finally giving birth to the Mongolian chess with typical nomadic features.

Actually, the origin of shatar, namely Mongolian chess, is not mentioned in some important historical materials about Mongols such as The Secret History of the Mongols and Genghis Khan. But according to some scholars, the earliest Chinese literature with records about shatar is Yi Xian Ji (A Collection of Arts), written during the reign of Emperor Yongle (1402-1424) of Ming Dynasty, and it introduced the basic rules of shatar. Although Yi Xian Ji has been lost, its content about shatar is quoted in Kou Bei San Ting Zhi (A Record of Three Northern Cities), a book finished in 1758, the 23th year of the reign of Emperor Qianlong of Qing Dynasty. In addition, similar information about the chess can also be found in other books of Qing Dynasty, including Sai Shang Za Ji (Notes of Life in Border Area) written by Xu Lan during the reign of Emperor Kangxi (1661-1722) and Qiao Xi Za Ji (Notes of Life in Qiaoxi) by Ye Mingfeng in the reign of Daoguang Emperor(1820-1850). Kou Bei San Ting Zhi describes the rules of Mongolian chess as follows: "The Mongolian chessboard consists of eight rows and eight columns, i.e. 64 squares. It has two sets of chess pieces colored red and black, each containing 16 pieces, including eight soldiers, two chariots, two horses, two elephants, one cannon and one general. A general starts at the right square beside the midpoint of the last line and a cannon starts at the left square, but the cannon is one row above the general. Chariots, horses and elephants stand beside them and soldiers in front of them. Different from Chinese chess, the pieces of Mongolian chess are shaped like animals but have no characters carved on them. The general takes the form of pagoda, signifying Mongols' belief in Buddhism. The 'elephant' in the chess is actually camel or bear instead of elephant because elephants do not exist in northern areas. The chess has a large number of soldiers as Mongols view a large number of people as a symbol of power. It has no advisor(a type of piece in Chinese chess) for Mongolian Empire has no civilian staff. Pieces are placed in squares instead of on lines, indicating that Mongols care about protecting their tools. A horse can move diagonally in a large rectangle of six squares, but a camel, namely 'elephant', can do the same in a rectangle of nine squares, as camel runs faster than horse. Pieces can move over the whole board without the obstruction of a river (another feature of Chinese chess), representing Mongols' nomadic life to move with the change of seasons. When a soldier moves to the last rank of the board, it can advance diagonally to capture the enemy's pieces and transform into a chariot for its reward. If one side's general is blocked by pieces of the other side and cannot get out, then the side loses the game." From this paragraph, we can see that Mongolian chess has many unique features. For example, an "elephant" is carved into a camel or a bear because there is no elephant in the north while horses and camels are important tools for transportation and fighting. Compared with Chinese chess, shatar has no "advisor" for two reasons. One is that the nomadic people had a different system of court officials compared with that of Han ethnic group living on the plain. Another is that in ancient battles, a Mongolian general must stand side by side with his soldiers and even sacrifices himself to protect them. As for the absence of river on the chessboard, it not only shows that Mongols live a migratory life but also reveals that in ancient times they defeated all enemies on the grand grassland and put the Eurasia continent under their boots.

Shatar players in competitions are usually divided into two groups, the adults and the children. The number of players is even, such as 16, 32 and 64. Shatar is quite popular in Inner

Shatar in leisure time

Mongolia like Xilingol and Ordos where people love playing chess in their leisure time and both the young and the old are free to join in and show their skills and knowledge about the chess.

Shatar has been a regular game for a long time in not only grand Naadam festivals held by the government but small ones by families. In recent years, chess competitions have been held more frequently, up to over 100 times in a year. Shatar is played on a square-shaped chessboard of eight rows and eight columns, which constitute 64 small squares with two alternate colors, one being deep and the other light. On each side of the board there are eight small squares. The light-colored ones are called "white square", the dark-colored ones "black square". Similarly, the pieces of light color are "white piece" and the ones of deep color "black piece". Out of the total 32 chess pieces, each of the two sides has 16 pieces, among which are one "noyin" (king), one "bers" (queen), two "tereg" (chariot), two camels, two horses and eight "huu" (child). As the names of these pieces vary in different regions, sometimes "child" is called "dog" and "queen" becomes "tiger". The pieces of Mongolian chess are virtually pieces of art. Three-dimensional figures of human, animals and vehicles are all carved vividly. Just under the category of horses, for example, so many different images have been created to represent various behaviors of horses, such as galloping, running, walking and standing. There is even a scene that a pony accompanies its mother. As for camels, there are images of male camels and also female ones with their children. Made of wood, bone, stone or jade, these pieces of vivid figures come from herdsmen's long-time observation in their life with livestock, and thus the pieces of shatar are full of nomadic characteristics.

### 1.1.5 Shagai Games

Usually, Shagai refers to a bone on the joint between the hind foot and the shank of a goat or sheep. In Chinese it is called "zaogu" or "yangguai". This kind of bone has six uneven faces with various widths and lengths and with inward or outward curves. Some faces are referred to as the obverse sides and some the lateral sides. In Hulunbuir, Inner Mongolia, a folk song goes like this: "Sheep walk on high hills, while goats pass through deep valleys. Horses run on the sunny side of riverbanks, and cattle lie in corners against wind. If a shagai stands upside down, it means bad luck; but if it stands in the right way, then you get a big camel." This ballad shows that Mongolians use five kinds of animals to name different faces of shagai. As a sheep or goat has only two pieces of this special bone, shagai is relatively rare and herdsmen regard it as some sort of "magical" object that represents wealth, just as expressed by a Mongolian saying that "the family who have lots of shagai must own lots of Livestock." As a symbol of health and reproduction of livestock, shagai cannot be thrown away after sheep or goats are eaten. Instead, people will collect those bones and polish and decorate them. Shagai can just stay as individual bones or be paired with others. During the spare time in winter, every Mongolian, despite age and gender, will take their own bags of shagai and play with friends. Winning other people's shagai is a great pleasure to them. Then a range of shagai games with nomadic features come into being. For example, Mongolians name shagai after the fore mentioned five types of livestock and other animals and tools inseparable from their life such as dogs and Lele carts. In games, people like putting bones into special shapes to resemble different scenes in real life and make up their own stories. In addition, shagai also stands for friendship

Competition of shooting shagai

and trust in Mongolia. Thus Mongols cherish shagai very much, viewing it as a "treasure", no matter it is from a goat, sheep, camel, wolf or antelope. In the past there was a custom to collect 1,000 pieces of shagai, put them in a bag and start collecting again from just one piece of bone.

Of the hundreds of forms of shagai games, some are specially designed to help children develop intellectually, and some suit people of all ages. In Xinlingol, shagai games are usually held on the Naadam that celebrates the elderly's birthdays, but it is inappropriate to play shagai in spring when lambs are born as people think it will hinder the growth of young animals. Shagai is so simple and easy that it can be played by everyone, and thus it has become a common sport in Naadam. Generally there are four major methods for playing shagai, including flipping, throwing, shooting and "chua" (grabbing shagai while throwing a sand bag).

### 1.1.6 Camel Racing

Praised as "Boat in Desert", in ancient times the camel was crucial for the economy and military force of Mongols. In Mongolia, the camel is thought auspicious as "King of All Animals", and in "nine-nine gifts" of a ceremony, the camel is the first one. Camel racing is a traditional sport of Naadam in areas including Alxa League of Inner Mongolia, Bortala and Bayingolin Mongol Autonomous Prefectures of Xinjiang, and

Camel racing in winter (by Sarensuhe)

Haixi Mongol and Tibetan Autonomous Prefecture of Qinghai. It also occupies an important position in the winter Naadam in Xinlingol and Hulunbuir.

Like horses, camels need to be well prepared before races. They will be fed with less water but more fodder rich in protein for half a month before competitions. Camels can run at up to 70 to 80 kilometers per hour. Usually held in winter, camel races include four major types, namely long-distance race, round-track race, relay race and archery race. Generally the total distance of a race is 10 to 30 kilometers. Before a race starts, a fire is lit on a high place, owners of camels go up to it and light incense by the fire, and then competitors take their camels to walk three rounds clockwise around the incense for good luck. When the race begin, both male and female competitors wearing brightly-colored clothes ride on the back of camels and line up in a row before the starting line. Once the judge gives orders to start, riders immediately begin whipping and galloping the camels, trying to win the championship by

109

being the first one to reach the destination. In some races, some targets are set along the track and the winner is the one who shoot the most targets. After the competition, riders slowly run three rounds around the fire that represents luck, starting from the first rider to reach the destination to the last one. Then competitors sprinkle some alcohol over the fire as sacrifice for the God of fire to thank him for protecting and blessing them.

### 1.1.7 Bulu Throwing

"Bulu", a Mongolian word for "stick", with a shape like sickle, is a popular sport in the Naadam of eastern Inner Mongolia.

As the oldest hunting tool in the world, bulu later evolved into an instrument for herding animals and defending oneself. The early bulu was usually made of elm, with about 80 centimeters in length, and later bulu with head covered in metal came into being. Based on usages and shapes, bulu can be divided into three groups, which are "heart-shaped bulu", "lead bulu", and "hayamul bulu". A "heart-shaped bulu" is a stick whose head is tied with a string of metal balls as big as magpie's eggs made by bronze, zinc, iron or lead; it is often used for defense

when people are walking in the wild or at night. A "lead bulu" has patterns of thin lines carved deeply at the head and is filled with lead; it is designed for throwing games and hunting. A

Fagoted iron bulu and hammer bulu in Qing Dynasty

"haramul bulu", with a flat head and a round handgrip, is the most commonly used bulu in Mongolian daily life.

There are two types of bulu games, "distance throwing" and "target throwing". The bulu used for one type is called "haimul" and the other type "tulag". There is another kind of bulu fit for both two games, and its head is wrapped with lead or a bronze hoop. For distance throwing, players stand at a certain distance to throw out a designated bulu, and the one who throw it farthest wins the game. In target throwing, three wooden columns with a height of 50 centimetres are set as targets. Every player is given three opportunities to hit targets by bulu. The rules for scores: in a throw, hitting all three targets directly means the player can get 10 points, shooting them indirectly means 8 points, reaching two columns directly represents 6 points, and so on. The winner is the one who gets the best score.

The above information only covers the major sports of Naadam, as the festival has evolved into so many kinds of different sports and cannot be all included. Besides, the Naadam held in scattered Mongolian communities also incorporates some unique activities, such as the dragon dancing and the on-land boat dancing in Xingmeng Township in Tonghai, Yunnan Province in southwest China. With distinctive local identities, these sports are the festive expression of the local natural and ecological environment, history and traditions.

### Song, Dance and Ritual Parade

As an important part of many forms of Naadam, song, dance and parade usually appear at the opening ceremony as a prelude to the grand festival. As early as Yuan Dynasty, there was a kind of Naadam called "Zhama Banquet" ("Zhama" in Mongolian means whole cattle or sheep) which already incorporated song, dance, gourmet food and competitive sports.

111

With a love for singing carved on the nation's soul, every Mongolian can hum several ballads at least. Mongolians think that it is the heart, instead of the throat, that sings a song. Therefore in their view, everyone can sing well and every song can be sung beautifully. Just like the daily meals, song has permeated Mongolians' everyday activities as the most ordinary and also the most inseparable element in their life. Then, naturally, such a great event like Naadam is sure to have song and dance. Naadam celebrations in different areas feature different songs and dances with local identities. For example, in Xinjiang, the Naadam includes dancing "Sawardeng" and singing the Epic of Jangar, while within Inner Mongolia, the Naadam in Xilingol involves long songs and the festival in Khorchin incorporates short folk songs and "Andai" dance. Song and dance help create a kind of festive atmosphere, adding the happiness and harmony to Naadam. Apart from appearing at the opening

Group dance at the opening ceremony of Naadam

ceremony, singing and dancing can also often be seen throughout the Naadam. As herdsmen living on grasslands rarely visit each other in ordinary days, various Naadam celebrations provide them a good opportunity to gather together with relatives and friends. In such precious leisure time, people not only watch traditional sports events but also feast, drink, sing and dance, enjoying the festival to their heart's content.

Enjoying great importance in modern Naadam, the opening ceremony fully exhibits a wide range of resources that an area boasts. The displayed resources are in the form of symbols, usually covering national rites, Mongolian traditional etiquette and local folklore. In this way, the political, economic and cultural features of different areas are transformed into symbols and can be told just like stories so that audience can understand the common or unique resources of these places. Performance of these symbols is prominent at opening ceremonies of Naadam festivals held by governments. For example, to celebrate the 50th anniversary of the foundation of East Ujimqin Banner, Xilingol, the local government arranged a grand parade for the opening ceremony of this year's Naadam, and the performers comprised guardians of the national flag, teams to exhibit the flag, emblem and signs of the Naadam, children, armed police and soldiers, wrestlers, herdsmen and horses, government representatives from sumus and towns, floats, and other teams to welcome guests and present gifts. As for the Naadam celebration of Darhan Muminggan United Banner in Baotou, Inner Mongolia, performers of the opening ceremony consisted of national flag guardians, teams carrying black and white Sülde banners (a pole with circularly arranged horse or yak tail hairs of varying colors arranged at the top), clothes exhibiting teams from eight towns of the banner, camel riders and horse riding performers. From an opening ceremony, audience can get a quick glimpse of the features of Naadam of this place.

## 2. Naadam Traditions

Festivals, as a living "cultural museum", display a nation's cultural traditions and express its people's emotions. As a traditional Mongolian festival, Naadam is a comprehensive carrier of profound Mongolian culture, symbols and emotional appeals.

### 2.1 Secrets Behind Numbers

Every nation has its own likes and dislikes toward numbers, and the Mongolian is no exception. The lucky and taboo numbers in Mongolian folklore are fully revealed by Naadam, implying how the nation appreciates different numbers and imagines their meanings. "Two" is the base for the number of participants of many games in Naadam, including 8, 16, 32, 64, 1024, 2048 and other multiples of two. This rule applies to sports such as wrestling, Mongolian chess and shagai. Naadam's scale and the organizer' status are shown as to how many competitors participate in these competitions. In Xilingol, a "small" Naadam has 16 to 32 wrestlers, a "medium" one 64 to 128, a "relatively large" one 256 to 512 (also known as Naadam with 81 rewards), and a "large" one 1,024. In the past, there were strict limitations on the number of wrestlers in Naadam of different levels. For example, the Ovoo Naadam held by individuals had to contain no more than 128 Bökh players, while the number of players for the Naadam organized by a town government could reach 512. Most Ovoo Naadam festivals have a fixed number of Bökh combatants, such as 128 for the Temple Ovoo Naadam and Hongor Ovoo Naadam in Duutnuur, East Ujimqin Banner, and 64 for Wanggai Ovoo Naadam in West

Ujimqin Banner. Besides, the number of awards needs to be even as well, usually the quarter of the number of contestants. If there are 128 players, those ranking in the top 32 will be rewarded, and if 64 people participate, the first 16 will get awards, and so on. It is the same for wrestling, horse race archery and other games.

"Three" also carries special meanings for Mongols. In Mongolian beliefs, this number indicates the upper, middle and lower realms, implies the past, present and future, and also serves as the smallest odd number traditionally used to describe something of a huge quantity. Usually when Mongolians propose a toast, they need to drink three cups of alcohol and before drinking, they use the ring finger of the right hand to dip the alcohol to offer three times of ritual respect. The finger will first point to the sky and then the ground and finally touch the forehead to show respect to heaven, earth and ancestors respectively. When it comes to singing, Mongolians also need to sing three complete songs. And there are many other similar rules. In such connection, "three" in the title the Three Games of Men of Naadam is more of a symbolic number rather than just a specific one. It compasses the basic skills that a Mongolian man should master and also sums up Mongolians' criteria to judge a true hero. In real life, the games of Naadam can be more or less than three types.

"Nine" is special as well. For Mongolians, nine is the number of honor, which not only implies a large or infinite quantity but also represents good luck. It is written in The Secret History of the Mongols (section 267) that visitors to Genghis Khan always "bring with them eighty-one (nine timing nine) pieces of gifts" to show their respect for the king. Also, according to Mongolian Customs, "since ancient times a rule has been set that the reward of the highest level is nine types of gifts with each type containing nine pieces, that is nine multiplied by nine, and the next level is five types with nine pieces for each one, namely five multiplied by nine, and then lower levels are two multiplied by nine and finally one multiplied by nine. From ordinary people to Khan (emperor), no matter who is the receiver of gifts, the highest standard is always 'nine-nine', namely nine kinds of gifts with nine articles for each type." The "nine-nine gifts" originated from the reign of Genghis Khan as a form that all Mongolian tribes adapted to pay tribute to the imperial court, and later it developed into a symbol for auspice and completeness that frequently appears in all kinds of celebrations, rituals, festivals and recreational occasions. This tradition of rewarding is still kept alive in Naadam. The great "nine-nine gifts", namely eighty-one articles, only appears in important, large-scale Naadam festivals and the quantity of awards cannot exceed eighty-one. In most cases, the rewards for small Naadam festivals only consist of three types with nine pieces for each type. The nine-nine gifts usually include daily objects that carry auspicious meanings, such as camels, cattle, tea bricks, felt blankets, silver bowls, khadags, boots, etc. For recipients, the "nine-nine rewards" is the greatest honor they get in Naadam, with which also comes great respect.

### 2.2 Rewarding Ceremonies

There are a lot of ceremonies in Naadam that imply profound meanings, and the most distinctive ones among them are the ceremonies to award the silk necklace "jiangga" to young wrestlers and the title "Darkhan" (meaning "invincible") to retired wrestlers.

More than just a decoration, "jiangga" is also a symbol of honor in Bökh competitions and a sacred object that embodies the Bökh spirit. "Jiangga" is a necklace made of silky khata, adorned with blue, red, yellow, green and white cloth strips. The five colors stand for the golden earth, green grassland, red sunset glow, white cloud and blue sky. Only the wrestlers winning in important Naadam festivals have the privilege to wear "jiangga", and every further championship later will grant them one more strip of ribbon which will add to the "jiangga" greater weight and significance. Sometimes wrestlers will put rings, gold, silver and other treasures in "jiangga". For some aged Bökh players, the worn-out "jiangga" is yet a symbol of their seniority and honor.

The awarding ceremony of "jiangga" is very sacred. In the past, only living Buddhas or government officials had the right to award the necklace. The size and number of "jiangga" are also strictly stipulated and cannot be changed casually. Now in modern times, "jiangga" is awarded by local governments with rules varying in different areas. For example, the East Ujimqin Banner states that "in a Bökh game with 128 players, the wrestler winning three times is eligible to be awarded jiangga". In 2004, the West Ujimqin Banner established the Regulations of Awarding Jiangga in Bökh Competitions, which further standardizes and details the awarding rules of jiangga. According to the regulations, the wrestlers entitled to receive "jiangga" are:

"Jiangga" for Mongolian wrestlers

the one winning 12 times in an individual competition with 64 players, the one taking championship for 4 times in an individual game of 128 players, and the winner of an individual contest featuring 256 players.

As an epitome of Mongolians' respect and pursuit for strength and heroic spirit and also a holy object, "jiangga" is often used for animal release ceremonies and racehorses' decorations. Before animals are freed in ovoo sacrifice rituals, people will tie colorful "jiangga" to the necks of the released sheep, goats or horses, or braid cloth strips of five colors with their hair, so that these creatures will become sacred gifts to god and cannot be ridden or killed any more. In horse race horses winning multiple times will also wear "jiangga" as a sign of honor and excellence. "jiangga" has the same meanings for wrestlers. The holy necklace is regarded to be able to give Bökh contestants a kind of "sacred nature" and formidable power. When entering the Bökh arena, wrestlers need to jump up and wave arms to imitate movements of eagles, tigers and lions. In this process, "jiangga", just like lion's mane, endows athletes with great strength that the ordinary cannot possess.

Apart from "jiangga", different Bökh titles are also rewarded to excellent wrestlers, which have already been recorded in The Secret Record of Manchu written by Jin Liang during Qing Dynasty. According to the chapter "Emperor Taizong Awards Three Men with Great Strength", in the first lunar month of the 6th year of Tiancong (the era name of Emperor Taizong), namely the year of 1632, "the three men with unusual strength, Mendu, Durma and Temudekhi, were ordered to kneel down to receive the emperor's rewards. Mendu got the title of 'arslan' and a long coat made of leopard skin; Durma received the rank of 'zaan' and a long coat made of tiger skin; Temudekhi was rewarded with the title of 'bar' and a same coat with Durma. Besides, each of them got one knife, a large piece of silk and eight pieces of wool-yarn cloth. The emperor stipulated that anyone would become guilty if they called the three men their original names instead of their titles." The fore mentioned three titles have different meanings. "Arslan", meaning lion, is given to the champion of a Bökh game; the runner-up gets "zaan", elephant; the person at the third place receives "bar", tiger. In Inner Mongolia, especially in Xilingol League, there are Bökh tournaments designed for wrestlers to win ranks. Winners will be awarded different titles including "aburag" (titan), "arslan" (lion), "zaan" (elephant), "nachin" (falcon), and "Khartsgai" (hawk). Mongolians in Qinghai and Gansu Provinces will tie red silk on the winner of a Bökh game and raise him high with happy cheers. Among Oirat Mongolians, a Bökh champion will be called "galmangnai" (meaning forehead, which indicates winning the first place), the runner-up "arbanmangnanai" (meaning one tenth of the champion) and the third-place winner "huhbuh" (meaning gray bull, which indicates great strength). In the state of Mongolia, excellent wrestlers will only be awarded with ranks without "jiangga".

The retiring ceremony of Bökh players is called "Bökh darkhanla" in Mongolian, namely awarding wrestlers the rank of "darkhan", which means "lifelong" and "honorable". Receiving this title is the highest achievement of a wrestler. In most cases, only famous wrestlers who are over 50 years old and cannot continue the wrestling career have the privilege to obtain the rank. Usually the ceremony begins after the opening ceremony of Naadam and before Bökh competitions. Once receiving the rank of "darkhan", a wrestler will retire and cannot attend wrestling games of any forms any more.

The procedures of awarding "darkhan" are not complex but embedded with profound implications. At first, two wrestlers in formal and neat dresses will sing the song of "Wrestling Invitation" three times and then enter the arena with jumps. Under audience's gaze they will walk around the field, with the emcee's complimenting on their glorious achievements. Then the two wrestlers will follow the standard procedures of a formal competition to perform a Bökh game so as to show audience a series of Bökh skills. The final battle for them will end up with a tie. The awarding of "jiangga" to young wrestlers will also be held along with the "darkhan" awarding ceremony. Young athletes will stand side by side, jump into the field, and then walk to the rostrum to salute people on the platform and the surrounding audience before government officials award them "jiangga". At the same time, the "jiangga" of "darkhan" wrestlers will also be passed on to their young counterparts with great potential, implying the inheriting of Bökh skills and good luck. In Mongolians' mind, the rank of "darkhan" is a lifetime achievement of remarkable honor and also represents that the game of Bökh can be passed on from generation to generation with excellent wrestlers emerging endlessly.

### 2.3 Awards, Wishes and Compliments

Putting great stress on "courtesy" and "compliment", Mongolians lives everyday life with much encouragement and praise to each other. Therefore, gifts, wishes and compliments are a necessary part of grand occasions such as festivals and rituals. In Naadam, people not only award and praise winners but also encourage and "joke about" losers. The wrestlers ranking in the last are called "shoren Bökh", meaning "the wrestler with earth", that is "the one who is thrown on the ground at the very beginning of a game". The last one in a horse race is named "golden saddle", "fat stomach", "ball of fat", etc. But people will also find various objective excuses for the horse racer's failure: maybe he has been too busy with caring for livestock to prepare for the game, or his rival is a cautious old man with lots of experience, etc. Moreover, people will encourage him to learn from the failure and strive for a better result in next Naadam. In Mongolians' mind, a success or failure just is temporary since the present winner may turn into a loser next time, so it cannot be used to make a final judgment on a player. This attitude contributes to a tradition that every contestant in Naadam, even the last one, shall receive awards.

As a form of traditional Mongolian culture, wishing and praising mainly consist of impromptu chanting which often adopts metaphors, rhymes, and concise and fluent language. The wishing and praising chants have different types, and their styles and contents also vary in different times and regions. Usually, in accordance with the local chanting tradition on rhymes and styles, a chanter will perform freely according to the situation at that time. The major subjects of Naadam chanting are Bökh, horse, archery, archers, etc.

"Bökh chanting" is to praise a wrestler from comprehensive aspects including body shape, strength, skills, intelligence and morality. A song goes like this: "The wrestler has such a broad breast that he can tuck high mountains under his arm. The wrestler has such great perseverance that he can pour out all the water in the Yellow River. The wrestler also has such remarkable strength that he can even lift up steep cliffs." Another chant praises a Bökh champion like this: "He has a big strong body upon which everybody around the world will nod in approval. He masters unrivaled skills with an indestructible will. His morale is so high and energy so abundant that he has defeated countless rivals. What a sharp wrestler, a nation-renowned darkhan wrestler!"

As for "horse chanting", each horse, ranking from the first one to the last in a race, has a chant especially for itself. The praise for the champion horse, for example, introduces its family background and experience of growth, portrays its appearance, manner and dress, offers wishes to its little rider, and awards the horse with all sorts of beautiful titles, such as "the luckiest horse", "auspicious beauty", "treasure horse", "the leader of all horses", "flying falcon", etc. Without a set standard, titles in different regions can diversify a little bit. For instance, in some areas the title "rising sun in the sky" is given to horses at the second or third place, and even in some it is awarded to the last one. According to horse types, horse chanting is mainly for race horses, namely horses running long distance, as they are the major type to compete in games, although the chants for walking horses are also not uncommon. At the beginning of the chanting ceremony, young riders in racing dresses will ride on the prize-wining horses and the owners of the horses will lead them to walk three rounds around the Naadam arena before stopping at the front of rostrum for the horses to receive their titles. A chant in Ujimqin goes like this: "How beautiful it is today! Everything goes well and every living creature is happy and healthy. We gather at this holy place to invite distinguished Lama and pay respects to the sacred ovoo owned by the Gods of mountain and river. Please answer me, in this grand ceremony, who is the handsome horse leading the race? It is the head of thousands horses all over XX sumu at XX county in Khoshuusiqin Prince Banner... It runs like a fierce wind, clop like hail hitting the earth, neigh like a dragon swimming in water... Its mane looks like a moon-shaped broom, its eyes long and

Horse chanting for horses running endurance race

thin just as two fishes, its ears shaped like lotus flowers..." The song goes on with numerous beautiful phrases to compliment the champion horse. After singing, people will rub some yogurt on the forehead of the horse and award it a treat of milk tofu to wish it greater achievements in future.

When it comes to archery, the title for the winner is "mergen" (sharpshooter) and for the champion of three consecutive years, it is "darkhan mergen" (holy/distinguished shooter). Like Bökh and horse chanting, people will sing to prize-winning archers the chants of bow and arrow and songs of good wishes at the closing ceremony of Naadam. The Song of Archers goes like this: "A sacred bow held in the left hand and a magical arrow in the right hand, the archer with a breast as broad as a prairie puts up his arms, stretching the bowstring to the furthest point as if he is raising a mountain. When the arrow dashes out with a sharp whistle, horses neigh, castrated camels

123

howl, mountains shake, sea waves surge, the sky clears and a rainbow appears, all for the power of this shot. We, the audience, can only be shocked and marvel at the scene. The sharpshooter, who is able to shoot through a mountain, can fit an arrow on the bowstring so quickly that his targets can be shot from all directions, whether he is among crowds or on a jolting horseback." Apart from archers, bow and arrow are also the subjects of chants in Naadam.

Naadam is a festival for all Mongolians. Without regard to age, gender and wealth, everyone can enjoy the happy event. Over the past centuries, Naadam has been inspiring Mongolians' poetic heart, and so many beautiful traditions of chanting and rewarding embedded with people's sincere hopes and blessing have been created.

## 3. Food Culture

Naadam fully displays the Mongolian culture of food. From the white food (dairy products) to the red food (meat), from ordinary meals to the grandest feast, all of these can be seen in the festival. Foods in Naadam consist of two major types: sacrifices and everyday foods and drinks. Sacrifices are especially prepared for ovoo religious practice and Nair Naadam ceremonies, mainly including whole sheep, uchi dishes (cooked sheep's backs), "byelang" (a dessert consisting of brown sugar, cooked flour and butter, made by Lama), meat porridge, horse milk, etc. As for daily meals, there are milk tea, milk tofu, butter, hand-held mutton and so on.

Dairy products are usually called "white food" or "Tsagaan idee" in Mongolian. White is worshiped in Mongolia as a color of luck and purity. The numerous kinds of dairy products enjoy high status among Mongolian foods. Apart from cows'

Dairy products for the festival

milk, the most familiar milk to us, the milk of sheep, goats, horses and camels are also processed into other forms, among which the commonest ones are butter, clotted cream, cheese, milk tofu, cream and butter crumbs. There are three types of processing techniques of white food: natural curdling, stirring for fermentation, and mild boiling. Foods made by natural curdling include cream, white fermented butter, butter, butter crumbs, milk tofu, cheese, etc. Those going through stirring and fermenting are "tsegee" (fermented mare's milk), "airag" (similar with yogurt), milk wine and so on. Food made by boiling with slow fire is mainly milk skin.

Meat products are called "ulaan idee" in Mongolian, namely "red food". Mongolians have lots of meat dishes, including whole sheep, sheep's backs, hand-held mutton pieces, mutton kebabs and instant-boiled mutton. Whole sheep is a traditional dish prepared for distinguished guests in important festivals and feasts like wedding or birthday parties. The cooking material must be sheep, and two- or three-year-old castrated ones are the best. Only the sheep's four legs without hooves, the waist part of the back, tail, chest and head without jaw are used for cooking. The mutton is stewed by slow fire without any spice except for a pinch of salt before the meat is ready. Therefore the stewed whole sheep is also named as "stewed whole sheep in plain water". Sheep can be roasted as well, thus becoming the dish of "roasted whole sheep". The key for roasting is to control temperature. Before being served, the four legs of a sheep should be placed on a big tray according to their original positions on the sheep's body, then the back is put in the middle of the tray, the chest on the left, the head on the front. The head should point forward and tail backward. Some cheese will be put on the head to show the significance of the occasion. Cooked sheep's back is called "uchi", a delicacy for important

Whole sheep for ovoo ceremonies

guests. This dish often appears in the Naadam festivals held for the elderly's birthdays, namely "the feast of uchi" which involves complex and solemn rules of behavior.

Naadam is also a platform to show a whole picture of Mongolian dining customs, including "deej", "sachih" and "miliah". "Deej", namely "best" or "first", is a custom of dining order in Mongolian meals, emphasizing that "the best food" should be given to the Gods of

heaven and earth. Usually, in the morning, Mongolians will offer the first cup of tea to heaven and earth, Gods and their ancestors. When eating at home, Mongolians will give the priority
of dining to the elderly, relatives of higher kinship status and
their parents as a sign of respect. In Nair Naadam and sacrificing rituals of Ovoo Naadam, people will make fresh dairy
products and meat dishes as sacrifices which will be shared as
"kheshig" (originally meaning to cut and share sacrifices) after
rituals. "Sachih" means "milk products and other foods offered
and scattered to gods", and the custom of "Sachih" requires
people to throw foods and drinks to sky and earth before meals
or during sacrificing practice. This is to thank gods for their
giving and pray for happiness, safety and health. For Mongolians, all food comes from heaven, earth and ancestors, so they
practice the "Sachih" custom before every meal to express their
gratitude. For example, when drinking alcohol, Mongolians
will dip the ring finger of
the right hand into the
cup and flick the finger
three times; when having
meat, they will cut three
small pieces of meat and
throw them toward sky. In
ovoo sacrificing rituals,
people will walk three
rounds around the ovoo,
offer dairy foods to gods,
and scatter five-color
"wind horse" (pieces of pa-
per for prayer). As for
"miliah", it means "rub-

Offering of dairy foods to Gods of ovoo

127

bing a little cream or other food onto something". One example is that during horse chanting in Naadam, people will smear some yogurt on the forehead of a racing horse and treat it with milk tofu to wish it good luck and well-being. There is another tradition related with food in Naadam, the "sharing" custom. After a sacrificing rite, people will bring back to home sacrifices called "kheshig", such as dairy products and meat, to share with family members, which indicates that they are now protected and blessed by gods.

## 4. Costume Culture

Naadam, to some extent, can be seen as a show of Mongolian costumes. From the most remote place deep into the desert to the border of south-west China, all the people of different ages in all walks, such as herds in grassland and white collars downtown, dressed up in great joy to celebrate this great day. From ropes of attendees to costumes of contestants, they all exhibit the colorful Mongolian costume culture.

Mongolian costumes mainly consist of ropes, belts, boots, hats, ornaments. A vast distribution in area of the Mongols comes together with different natural environments, economic situations and living habits, forming a distinctive costume culture rich in colors and styles. In 2008, Mongolia costume was listed as national intangible cultural heritage. Following a full recognition and strict examination, Mongolia Costumes, the local standard over Inner Mongolia Autonomous Region, was announced in June 1, 2016, and put into force in August 1 of the same year. According to the standard, Mongolian costumes can be classified as Barga costume, Buryats costume, Hulun Buir-Olot costume, Jalaid costume, Jarud costume, Khorchin costume, Naiman costume, Aohan costume, Arkhorchin cos-

Mongolian costume in Ujimqin Banner (by Sarensuhe)

tume, Bairin costume, Ongniud costume, Kharchin costume, Kheshingten costume, Ujimqin costume, Khaochid costume, Abag costume, Sonid costume, Chahar costume, Dorbod costume, Darhan costume, Muminggan costume, Tumed costume, Ordos costume, Urat costume, AlxaKhoshut costume, Torghut costume, Alxacostume of Mongolia who believe in Islam and Khalka costume. If the trans-regional costumes of Mongolians in other regions such as northern Gansu Province, Qinghai Province and Yunnan Province, are also counted in, there will be over dozens of Mongolian costumes. During the Naadam festival in different regions, these dazzlingly bright-colored costumes are so eye-catching that they always become the most beautiful scenery.

In addition, costume of the Three Games of Men in Naadam festival also boast for its distinctive characteristics.

"Standing in the field are dozens of wrestlers in white elaborate suits sewed by layers of fabrics, hanging to their buttocks", described Zhao Yi, a poet in Qing Dynasty, in one of his poems picturing Bökh costume. The modern Bökh costume inherits and keeps the traditional style. Wrestlers wear Zodog in upper body and Banzal, a kind of fat and pleated pants. The hanging-to-knees coat, known as "Taoxiu", is made of colorful satin and embroiled by various golden and silver threads. There are images of four creatures—dragon, phoenix, lion and tiger, as well as bat and the symbol 卐 , on the costume through embroiling and sticking. On the knees part of the costume, patterns of holy flame and auspicious clouds are embroiled to indicate that wrestlers own fire-like vigor and are strong as those four creatures. All those patterns on Bökh costume are sewed stitch by stitch from women's hands. As the Mongolian saying goes: a wrestler husband without a wife good at stitching is not a perfect couple, and vice versa. Thus, Bökh competitions are not only a platform to show men's power and strength, but also a great opportunity for women to display their virtues and dexterousness.

Zadgo is the wrestling costume which has the most distinc-

Bökh costume

130

tive Mongolian characteristics. Most of Zodog are made of sweet cattle hide, few made of high leather, felt and cloth. No matter what kind of material, the neckline, sleeve and hem of costumes shall be edged by layers of sweet cattle hide or high leather and sewed by rubber band, silk thread and or fibers. Silver or copper blister nails are embedded in above parts of Zodog and the two sides of lower back. There are 512 or 256 blisters in different sizes embedded in Zodog, indicating an inner connection with 2, the number of Bökh competitors. At the middle back of Zodog is a silver mirror or bronze mirror which is five inches square or in the shape of full moon. Patterns of the four creatures—dragon, phoenix, lion and tiger, as well as elephant and deer are engraved in the mirror, symbolizing the power and gallantry of wrestlers. Some are decorated with auspicious patterns and Mongolia seal characters such as Ujimqin and Sonid which mark the belonging area. Those famous wrestlers usually sew their own special Zodog and carefully put it in the high place after carefully folding and packing it, in case of

Costume for riders

131

the contamination of "filthiness".

Riders in horse racing also have their own costumes, mainly including gowns and knight hats. Most in bright colors such as pink, sky blue and white, the gowns are made of soft silk fabric with openings both in the front and back to ensure its handiness and function of absorbing sweat. Auspicious patterns or animal embroidery can also be seen in the parts of lapel, sleeve and edge of skirt. Headwear of riders differs in its style from pointed round hat to boat-shaped hat. Some riders just bundle around their head with colorful silk as a decoration. On top of the hat there is a tassel, back side of a fringe, front side of a sewed tiny mirror and embroiled auspicious pattern. During the long distance horse race riders usually wear cloth socks instead of shoes to lighten the loads of racing horse. If they have to wear shoes, the portable cloth shoes will be their favorite choice.

## 5. Residential Culture

Naadam festivals are usually held on wide grasslands, lasting from one day to a week. At that time, almost all Mongolians will carry all their belongings to attend the grand event, and then Mongolian yurts will become movable homes where people live during the entire period of the festival. Apart from watching and participating in competitions, the gathering of relatives and friends in yurts is the most important activity for Mongolians. People will drink and sing to fully enjoy the festive leisure. The life of herdsmen on grasslands is usually limited within their own small families with some visits among neighbors called "ail" (household) while large-scale gatherings are very rare. Therefore, Naadam is a precious opportunity for Mongolians to meet and chat with each other, thus deepening

The exterior of Mongolian yurt

people's relationships and strengthening their social networks. Naadam is an inclusive public holiday, attracting not only local residents but also people of all walks of life outside the region, such as tourists and traders. In this way, Naadam serves as a bridge linking the local area with the outside world. Then Mongolian yurts, as a place to entertain strange friends, also become an inseparable part of the festival.

Yurt is the traditional dwelling of Mongolians. Easy to dismantle and reassemble, it is a portable home for nomads who need to move with seasons. An ordinary yurt can be carried by just two camels or one Lele cart and only takes two or three hours to build. Traditional Mongolian yurt consists of three parts: frame, felt cover and mane ropes. The frame includes "khana" (wall), "toono" (roof), "uni" (rafter) and "uud" (door). Usually a yurt is about ten to fifteen chi high (one chi is about 1/3 meter). The size of a yurt is judged by the number of "khana", which is usually 4, 6, 8, 10 or 12. The felt cover is comprised of roof felt that surrounds walls, outside cover, door curtain and a square piece of felt called "oerkh" to cover "toono" (roof). This piece of felt can ventilate the house and let the sunlight pour in when lifted and guard the inner home from wind and rain when put down. Mane ropes, made of horses' mane and tails, are used to wrap and strengthen walls and rafters, and at the center of the roof hangs a rope that can steady the whole structure when tightened. Generally the door of a yurt points south or southeast. Kitchen range is set in the middle of the room, surrounded by wooden cupboards, cabinets, chests and rectangle tables. A portrayal of Genghis Khan is hung at the due north of a yurt, while a Buddha niche is placed at the northwest with cabinets on both sides to place offerings to Buddha. The southwest part is mainly reserved for men's herding tools, including saddles and whips. On the long table in the middle of the yurt are all kinds of snacks, candies and dairy foods. Enthusiastic Mongolian hosts will always offer a bowl of hot milk tea to whoever comes into the yurt.

People setting up an Mongolian yurt

As most herdsmen have settled down, it is rare in normal days to see groups of Mongolian yurts of various types and forms even in pastures. Only in grand festivals like Naadam can traditional Mongolian dwellings and relevant customs be fully displayed. In 2006, for example, during the Naadam for the 50th anniversary of the establishment of East Ujimqin Banner, 500 yurts were set up on both sides of the main arena according to the locations of every sumu in the banner, resulting in a "mobile town". During the Naadam period, this "town" was the temporary home of herdsmen from different sumus and gazams and also the place to offer tourists with unique Mongolian food and accommodation. It is safe to say that through Naadam, all people scattered in different sumus and gachaas in the depths of grasslands gather together, thus recreating the spectacular scene back in the "nomadic empire". In this way, the memory about "kuriyen" (meaning circle, an arrangement of a yurt in medieval Mongolia) of Mongolian ancestors is kept alive in the imagination of people today.

Groups of Mongolian yurts during the Naadam festival

135

Mongolian yurt is a sacred place in traditional Ovoo Naadam. One day or a couple of days before the sacrificing ceremony, organizers of a Naadam festival will move with their whole family to the ritual site where the lama will chant scriptures to purify this area before organizers begins to establish yurts. Then, the yurts will be the place for preparing the ovoo ritual, sharing "Khesig" and handing over tasks during the organization of the ceremony. In East Ujimqin Banner, for example, where the Bayan Ovoo Naadam is held every year, the organizers will arrive at the ritual site seven days before the sacrificing ceremony for sufficient preparation. The organizers for this Naadam are 17 families. According to Mongolian traditions, being on the right side shows a higher status of a person. Therefore, in this small group of organizers' Mongolian yurts, the family of the general director settles on the rightmost side, that of the deputy director next to them, the rest going on according to the ages of the organizers, and in this way the youngest organizer settles on the end of the left side. All of these yurts will serve as the space to practice the ovoo sacrificing ritual.

## 6. Commercial Culture

From the fourth month to the eighth month in the Chinese lunar calendar, as a wide range of Naadam festivals are held, commercial activities also prosper, enabling Naadam to be a platform for nomads to buy and sell goods. Peddlers from all corners of the country are still commonly seen in today's Naadam festivals. Throughout the whole summer, they keep traveling on wide grasslands from one site of Naadam to another.

In the past, the commercial function of Naadam was vital for nomadic people, so much so that the festival was regarded as "a large trading center for northern and southern China".

The Kanjur Miaohui (Kanjur Temple Fair) in Hulunbuir, Inner Mongolia, for example, was a grand meeting for the lamas of the eight banners of the Barag Grasslands (called Hulunbuir Grasslands today) in Qing Dynasty. It was held from the beginning to the middle of the eighth lunar month, usually lasting for nine days. At first, only people from the nomadic banners of Hulunbuir came to the miaohui to sell goods, but later Mongolians from Inner Mongolia's leagues like Juu Uda, Jirem and Xilingol and Outer Mongolia's banners including Khalkha and Setsen Khan also came to the event. In the 31th year of the reign of Emperor Guangxu of Qing Dynasty, namely 1905, China signed treaties with Japan and Russia to open the two ports of Hailar and Manzhouli for trade. After that, businessmen from Russia, Japan, Europe and America also came to join in Kanjur Miaohui. At that time vendors from different regions had their fixed trading areas. The northeastern part belonged to people from Bukui (today's Qiqihar, a city in Heilongjiang Province) and Duolun; the northwestern part was preserved for people from Beijing and Fengtian (today's Shenyang, the capital city of Liaoning Province); beyond the north gate of the fair there were Russian stalls. All of these peddlers and stalls of various regions and countries made Kanjur Miaohui of Barag Grasslands unique and world-renowned. Apart from Hulunbuir, the area of today's Duolun County in Xilingol League also had meetings of different Mongolian leagues since the reign of Emperor Kangxi (1661-1722) of Qing Dynasty. With lama temples being their center, these gatherings evolved into a trading hub for Mongolians from areas north and south of Gobi Desert. At that time, herdsmen living in a several-hundred-mile radius from Xilingol, Chahar, Juu Uda and other Mongolian tribes at the north of Gobi Desert, such as Setsen Khan and

Tüsheet Khan, would all come to these gatherings. Riding on horses or taking carts, they would travel with all family members, no matter the young and the old, followed by their herds and animals that carried fur and skin of livestock and wild beasts, to participate in the temple fairs and exchange products. Those who also came from far away were ethnic Han Chinese, Muslims and Daur people.

Today, as more and more herdsmen have settled down and urbanization on grasslands is accelerating, the nomadic way of trading and exchanging has changed fundamentally, which brought a huge impact on the commercial function of Naadam. The festival has been infused with new elements, transferring from a channel for direct products exchange to an indirect platform of service industry centering on tourism and consumption. What's more, Naadam plays an important economic role for it invites businesses to invest in the grand event and then

Nomadic peddlers during Naadam festivals

harvests profits from advertisements and corporate sponsorship. Nowadays, sponsorship and advertisements have become important methods to fuel large-scale Naadam festivals, helping to ease the financial pressure of organizers and to raise the revenue of Naadam.

## Tips for Tourism

## Argun

In Records of the Historian and Jami' al−Tarikh written in Persian, there is a same tale about the origin of Mongolia. It is said that only two men and two women survived after Mongolians went through the slaughter of other tribes because they lost the war. The survived men and women escaped to a place surrounded by forests and fertile grassland amid. Named as Ergüne khun (mountains beside the Argun River), this place has turned into the home to Mongolian people since then. The Argun River, which runs across the Hulunbuir grassland, becomes the birthplace of the Mongolian ethic. As the mother river, the Argun River not only long fed the Mongo−lian people, but also moistened the fields along the banks and witnessed the origin of Mongolian.

The Argun River is one of the sources of Heilongjiang River. Back to the period of Mongolia Empire and Northern Yuan Dynasty, the Argun River was an inland river of China. Later, it was defined as the boundary river between China and Russia when the Treaty of Nerchinsk was signed.

The Argun wetland (also called Genhe wetland), which enjoys the reputa−tion as "the most beautiful wetland in Asia", is a destination that should never be missed if any tourist travels to Argun. It is China's biggest wet−land with the most well−preserved original environment. There are end−less bushes and meadow in the wetland, as well as extremely abundant wild fauna and flora. Every year, over 20 million birds stay here during their migration or live and breed here. The Argun wetland is one of the most important breeding grounds for red-crowned cranes around the world and one of the important breeding grounds for the world's endangered swan goose.

The Best Visiting Seasons:

Argun mainly consists of grassland and forest, thus the best visiting season is from July to the middle and end of September every year. During mid-summer, the weather is pleasant with abundant rainfall, and grass flourishes to present the most beautiful scenery. For those who love the view of ice and snow, they can also be pleased to visit here at winter from November to the middle February next year.

Tour Routes:

1. Tourists can reach ManzhouLi by air or by train, then take a tour bus or join the tour group to visit Argun.

2. Self-driving route: starting from ManzhouLi, the whole journey is 245.6 kilometers. Tourists can drive along the Central Street of ManzhouLi for 38.7km, then turn left to road X904 for 142.6km, and turn right to Argun.

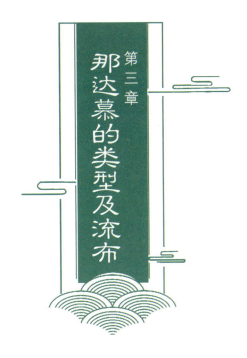

第三章 那达慕的类型及流布

　　中国境内的蒙古族主要聚集在内蒙古自治区、辽宁省、吉林省、黑龙江省、新疆维吾尔自治区、青海省、河北省，还有部分则聚居或散居在甘肃、宁夏、四川、云南、贵州、北京等地。蒙古族的聚居地规模差别大，大到一个自治区，小到一个村庄；聚居地的范围广，从东北到西北，从内蒙古到大西南，遍布大江南北。境外而言，蒙古族是蒙古国的主体民族，俄罗斯、日本、韩国、欧洲、美国等欧亚国家也有少量的分布。那达慕作为蒙古人重要的节日，以它的开放性、适应性、综合性满足不同的需要，呈现出多样化的特点。每年不同地域的蒙古人采取不同的形式举办那达慕，不仅有传统的敖包祭祀那达慕，还有政府举办的服务于政治、经济和文化目的的大型庆典那达慕，以及作为旅游资源开发的旅游那达慕。当下，更有家庭那达慕、都市那达慕、散居区那达慕等。不同地域、不同类型的那达慕中既有传统的核心符号，即"男儿三艺"的保持和发展，还有地域特色的衍生符号的扩展，更有新的具有时代特色符号的展演。

# 一、
# 敖包那达慕

那达慕作为蒙古族集会娱乐的重要方式，从一开始就与蒙古族的信仰文化密切相连。在与敖包祭祀结合的过程中，那达慕中的核心符号完全脱离了生产的必需，而成为文化的构成；从基本的生存技能，发展成为宗教信仰中的精神追求和表达；从实用性转变为表演性和娱乐性活动。

蒙古族传统祭祀仪式很多，如祭天、祭火、祭祖等。其中最重要、最隆重的要数敖包祭祀。敖包，蒙古语为"包"或"堆子"，选择在山顶、隘口、湖畔、路旁、滩中等特殊而易见的地方建立。内蒙古东部地区的敖包，多呈圆锥型，西部地区呈塔型。古式敖包，多数都是就地取材，用石块、柳条等堆砌而成。而现代新建敖包，其垒建形式多姿多彩，出现了砖砌敖包、水泥敖包、琉璃敖包等各式各样的敖包。

关于敖包祭祀的由来，学界观点不一。《清会典》记载："蒙古游牧交界之所，无山无河为志者，垒石为志，谓之敖包。"认为古时候，茫茫草原上天地相连，无标无志，不好辨别方向，人们便垒石成堆，当作路标和界标，由此逐渐演变为祭祀天地神、山神、路神、村落保护神等神灵的场所，这是一种说法。另一种说法认为敖包是安葬

多彩中国节

那达慕

祖先之地，关于这个由来民间有一则故事。远古的时候，蒙古人过着游牧狩猎的生活，实行的是天葬。人死后放在"勒勒车"上漫无目的地在草原上行驶。什么时候逝者从车上掉下来，那个地方就是其安身之地。由于过着逐水草而居的生活，加上草原茫茫无以找寻，人们便在安葬亲人时带上一峰驼羔，在安葬地给驼羔放血。第二年将母驼或已二岁的驼羔带上，沿大致的方向和路线去寻找。如果发现母驼或驼羔在某一处不肯前行或悲鸣，那就是安葬亲人的地点，后人就为他垒几块石头作为祭奠和标记，由此世代延传下来，便形成了敖包祭祀的习俗。还有一种说法认为敖包祭祀就是一种求雨仪式，民间祭祀者的解释较为支持这一观点。牧人认为"祭祀敖包就是为祭祀自然、山水之神。蒙古人要游牧必须依靠草原、依靠牧场。这些从哪里来？必须依靠敖包神。没有敖包神就没有雨水；没有雨水，草木就无法生长，没有了草，牧人就无法生存。因此，就定期举行敖包祭祀，祈求敖包神来护佑自然，让自然风调雨顺"。从牧人朴实的哲理中，我们可以洞见，敖包信仰伴随牧人生活而来，是游牧文化情景下产生的祭祀自然万物之神的原始崇拜和信仰。蒙古族视敖包为保护神，外出远行，凡经有敖包的地方，都要下马向敖包祭拜，献上奶制品，添加几块石头，才上路。此外，在敖包附近禁止捕鱼、打柴、伐木等行为。

在蒙古草原上有多少敖包，就有多少传说。如位于阿拉善盟额吉纳旗的"花"敖包，不是因为它所处的地方繁花似锦，而是这个名称来自天花病的"花"。相传有一位喇嘛云游此地时，正遇上了天花流行，不幸染上了此疾。该喇嘛医术精湛，不仅治好了自己，还将治疗天花的医术传授于当地的喇嘛们，让他们为当地百姓治病。人们为了纪念这位喇嘛，就建立了"花"敖包进行祭祀。又如东乌珠穆沁旗满都胡宝拉格苏木有个小山包叫萨仁巴敖包，这是由过去贝勒旗的台吉萨仁巴建立的。他认为这个小山坡像朝北趴着的狮子，利于五畜生长，所以就此建立敖包开始了祭祀。萨仁巴台吉的子孙确实也都是家境殷实，牛羊繁多，而这一带至今也水草丰美。因此，牧人们认为是得益于祖先"风水"的庇护。再如乌珠穆沁旗柴达木有个敖包叫"额吉敖包"，关于它的来源有这样的传说。从前，有一个牧马人在春天的时候不小心把马弄丢了，他骑着马在草原上四处寻觅。傍晚的时候天色昏暗，他不小心连人带马陷进了沼泽地里，越陷越深，无法挣脱。正绝望之时，突然发现眼前闪了一道绿光。牧马人朝着闪光的方向喊："救命啊！"随即他看见前方出现了一个女子，右手提着一面镜子，左手拿着带钩子的绳子。女子走过来把绳子甩给了牧马人，一会儿工夫就把人和马救上来了。牧马人非常感激她，问了姓名，并且央求他："能算算我的马在哪里吗？"她回答说："就在山的东边。"说完就不见了踪影。牧马人在她所指的地方找到了马，就认为是此地的神灵现身指点了他，从此就用奶食品祭拜此地，渐渐地建立了敖包，即额吉敖包。从那以后，据说又出现过手持镜子的人身蛇尾的女子，当地人认为那就是柴达木湖的神灵。在东乌珠穆沁旗库伦庙至今还供奉着额吉敖包神——一个头上缠着七条蛇，手里拿着镜子和钩子的女神画像。

由于每个敖包的由来和性质不同，也由于各地气候等自然条件的不同，敖包祭祀的日期、规模、形式和组织内容都有所不同。敖包种类繁多，从大的分类而言，可分为与英雄人物有关的敖包（如与成吉思汗有关的敖包）、与蒙古族圣物崇拜有关的敖包（苏勒德敖包）、旗王爷敖包（也叫诺颜敖包）、召庙敖包（与佛教有关）、部落或阿塔天神敖包（与萨满教有关）、家族敖包、家庭敖包、旅游景区的新敖包等等；从其形制而言，数量从 1~13 不等，甚至还有大型的敖包。传统的敖包祭祀有酒祭、火祭、玉祭、血祭。血祭，就是杀羊宰牛，向敖包贡献牺牲。酒祭，就是在敖包上泼洒酒水。火祭就是在敖包前燃起柴薪，将肉食、奶食、柏枝等投入火中焚烧。玉祭，就是将珠宝或硬币之类撒到敖包上。藏传佛教传入蒙古地区之后，祭敖包时一般都由喇嘛活佛们参与和主持祭祀仪式，因而以奶食、奶酒等代替了"血祭"。但至今还有个别地方仍按萨满教的传统祭祀敖包，如乌拉特中旗等地区，仍用原始的方法将公牛或公羊宰杀，

○ 喇嘛们准备的白音敖包祭品

用其皮做成皮筋缠绕敖包，将其肉焚烧的形式来祭祀敖包。此外，敖包有主黑龙、主白龙之分，黑龙敖包用红食，即肉食祭祀，白龙敖包以白食，即奶食祭祀。敖包也有层级之别，其祭祀也会不同。如乌珠穆沁旗王盖敖包属于层级高的黑龙敖包，因此用整羊来祭祀。

　　每个敖包都有固定的祭祀日期，一年只祭祀一次。其祭祀在春夏交际时段较为集中，冬祭非常少有。从祭祀者而言，一般每个家族、每个家庭、每个人都有其固定的敖包，具有唯一性和排他性。但就

145

○乌珠穆沁王盖敖包

现代而言，这种规制较为松散，一个人可能祭祀多个敖包。此外，祭祀人群中还出现了外族、外来者。在东乌珠穆沁旗，多数敖包的祭祀时间为农历五、六月，偶有四月、七月和八月的。民间说法认为农历五月为"敖包月"，从此开始了一年的祭祀活动。农历的五、六月草原进入夏季，也是大量奶食制作的时期，更是牧民一年中最为悠闲的季节。从这时起，开始祭祀敖包，娱悦敖包神灵，祈求风调雨顺，人畜兴旺。同时也要举行那达慕，进行聚会、社交、买卖等活动，达到娱神娱人的双重目的。

敖包祭祀的仪式仪程，因其规格、类型、地域、时代而有所不同。一般而言，由敖包的组织者在祭祀前一天进行修葺，悬挂新的经幡、五色绸布条，换上新鲜柳条等。祭祀当日，天刚蒙蒙亮，人们从四面八方涌向敖包。喇嘛诵经祈祷，祭祀者带来奶制品等祭品摆放在祭祀台上，绕着敖包按顺时针转三圈，祈求降福，保佑人畜两旺，并将带来的牛奶、酒、点心、糖果等祭品撒向敖包。仪式最后，人们手持哈达或奶食，顺时针挥手召唤，口中念诵"呼来，呼来"，将福分招回家。至此，祭祀结束，人们走到敖包山下平坦处的帐幔下，分享敖包"贺希格"（祭祀的整羊、奶食等），等待那达慕的开始。敖包那达慕一般有规模不等的赛马和搏克赛。

在敖包祭祀产生、延续和发展的过程中，有一点是非常明确的：敖包祭祀始终伴随着"男儿三艺"的影子，那达慕始终与敖包祭祀相伴而行。那达慕能够历久弥新，其重要的一个内在动力与敖包祭祀这一蒙古族民间信仰密切相关。民间认为那达慕本身其实就是为敖包祭祀后进行的一种娱神、媚神的仪式活动。那达慕和敖包祭祀是一体的，是一个完整祭祀过程的共同组成。当地牧民认为，蒙古族的搏克、赛马、射箭从祭祀敖包、山水之神的时代就有了，过去在敖包祭祀时才有"耐亦日"（那达慕）。

敖包的大小、敖包的影响力、敖包的所属，决定了那达慕的规模。

○白音敖包祭祀后的搏克比赛

大型的敖包，如东乌珠穆沁旗的白音敖包有 128 人的搏克赛，而小型的敖包，如西乌珠穆沁旗巴音·陶勒盖敖包则只有 32 人的搏克赛。在过去的年代，敖包祭祀仪式上的搏克、赛马以及射箭比赛，更多的是一种娱神和酬神的表演，具有神性和特殊的寓意。就"搏克的象征可以被理解为是它与古老萨满教的宇宙自然观以及游牧生活形态紧密相连，并与蒙古族信仰世界有着密切联系"。由此来看，那达慕的娱乐项目在敖包祭祀上具有神圣性，具有某种巫术的作用。通过表演，取悦众神，期望带来丰收和喜悦。

随着敖包祭祀的恢复以及人们生活水平的提高，除了极少数祭祀的小型的敖包之外，几乎所有敖包祭祀都要举行随后的那达慕。可以说，因为敖包祭祀信仰，那达慕的产生、发展和延续有了最为活跃的内在驱动力，使之活态传承至今。每年从农历四月到八月期间，各种类型的敖包那达慕交替进行，将人们带入神圣而欢乐的节日之中。

二、
庆典那达慕

庆典那达慕是较为普遍的一种那达慕类型，由各级政府组织，主要功能在于为政治、经济活动服务。1206 年成吉思汗即位时的"忽里勒台"，元代的"诈马宴"、16—17 世纪"七旗那达慕"和"十札萨克那达慕"以及内蒙古自治区成立以来的周年庆典那达慕、庆丰收那达慕、表彰类那达慕等等都属于庆典那达慕。它具有规模大、内容丰富、组织缜密、功能多样等特点，是内蒙古自治区各盟旗县以及蒙古族聚集地区政府庆典活动的重要表达方式。

我们可以从锡林郭勒盟东乌珠穆沁旗举办的历次那达慕了解到这一类型那达慕的基本样貌。1963 年为庆祝牲畜数量突破 130 万头（只）举办了全旗那达慕，为期 3 天，包括 512 名成人搏克赛、64 名蒙古象棋赛、180 匹 30 公里远程马赛；1986 年举办的庆祝东乌珠穆沁旗建旗 30 周年那达慕，历时 7 天，有 512 名成人搏克赛、128 名蒙古象棋赛、180 多匹马参赛的 30 公里远程马比赛以及接力赛等；1991 年举办东乌珠穆沁旗建旗 35 周年那达慕，有男子、女子和儿童搏克，远程赛、鞍马赛、接力赛，成人和儿童象棋赛，射箭、射击、拔河、篮球、门球等内容，在那达慕期间奖励了 500 名劳动模范；

2006 年庆祝东乌珠穆沁旗成立 50 周年那达慕，安排了 1024 名成人搏克赛、64 名女子搏克赛、128 名儿童搏克赛、远程马赛、鞍马赛、二岁马赛、走马赛、蒙古象棋、嘎拉哈比赛以及多场文艺演出，并有搏克退役和将嘎授予仪式、赛马祝赞仪式、奖励 500 名劳动模范等仪式性内容。

庆典那达慕一般需要长时间的准备和操演。如东乌珠穆沁旗旗庆 50 周年那达慕，如果将其建旗 50 周年相关活动纳入考虑的话，其筹备时间达半年以上。那达慕的前期准备除了组织层面的各种部署外，更为重要的是各类比赛的备战集训以及开幕仪式上歌舞、仪仗的排演。作为全权由政府组织和主导的大型那达慕，其筹备、组织、管理都以政府行政的名义进行。正如其他大型社会集会活动一样，为此政府也调动所有行政资源投入到整个那达慕的组织当中。

民间传统那达慕，如敖包那达慕的举行，一般而言，无需更多的准备，也无需特别的通知以及宣传。对于小型的、传统的那达慕而言，仍沿袭口耳相传的方式，传递信息。随着智能手机的普及，近年来传播方式发生了变化。微信成为最普遍最快捷的传播媒介。到了敖包那达慕那天，民众自动聚集在一起，参加祭祀以及之后的那达慕。而对于政府主办的特定主题的庆典类那达慕，宣传和前期推广是其重要环节。东乌珠穆沁旗旗庆 50 周年那达慕在召开前三个月就在旗政府网站上发布了消息，并通过《内蒙古日报》等报纸进行了反复报道，内蒙古电视台安排了"走进东乌大型开机仪式"，其六个栏目组进驻东乌珠穆沁旗进行了拍摄报道，并由内蒙古卫视对大会开幕式进行了直播。在当下，电视、广播、报纸、手机网络等现代传媒已成为外界认知那达慕的重要渠道。

庆典那达慕更是一个综合的舞台，可以囊括更多的文化因子，可征用更多的文化象征符号进行集中展演。东乌珠穆沁旗建旗 50 周年那达慕大会组织了近十种大型活动，包括"辉煌50年"大型文艺晚会、庆祝50周年军民共建文艺晚会、"50年回顾"摄影展、民族风俗实物展、"天堂草原——东乌珠穆沁"绘画展、500名劳动模范奖励大会、80岁以上耄耋老人集体寿宴、50名新生婴儿赠名仪式、50对青年集体婚礼等。开展了9种大型比赛，包括5000人长调合唱、1024名成人搏克赛、128名女子搏克赛、64名老年搏克赛、32名儿童搏克赛、60里远程马比赛、30里公马比赛、30里鞍马比赛、15里走马比赛、20里2岁马比赛以及马上拾嘎拉哈比赛等，128人弹嘎拉哈比赛、1024人扔四样比赛、256人射嘎拉哈比赛、128人球嘎拉哈比赛，256名成人蒙古象棋比赛、128名儿童蒙古象棋比赛，此外还有民族民俗及服饰展、手工艺作品展等。从整个活动安排而言，关照到了不同年龄层、不同身份者的文化需求，并突出"50"这一紧扣主题的数字。比如"50对青年集体婚礼""50名新生婴儿赠名仪式"等。为体现蒙古族敬老爱老的美好传统，邀请80岁以上的老人举办了"耄耋老人集体寿宴"。庆祝50周年，也是一次展示和宣传本地区特色文化的良机，这点从活动的安排可见一斑。如"民族服饰、用品、手工艺品展览和比赛"、"男儿三艺"、蒙古象棋、每晚的文艺演出等等，都极具地方特色。

庆典那达慕采用蒙古族和本地区特有的象征符号和传统文化元素，使得那达慕的民族特征和地域特色得以全面展现。有些仪式和仪礼也唯有在大型的庆典那达慕上才得以一见，如荣誉搏克称号授予仪式、青年搏克授予"将嘎"仪式、银嚼子白骆驼为首的"九九八十一"大赏等。

## 旅游小贴士

### 东乌珠穆沁旗

东乌珠穆沁旗地处内蒙古自治区锡林郭勒盟东北部，大兴安岭西麓，东邻兴安盟、通辽市，南连锡林浩特市、西乌旗，西接阿巴嘎旗，北与蒙古国交界，是继满洲里、二连浩特之后连接欧亚大陆桥的桥头堡。早在春秋战国时期，东胡、澹林等游牧部落便在现东乌珠穆沁旗一带活动。长期的历史发展和演变，在这块土地上孕育出灿烂的民族文化，2005 年，乌珠穆沁长调被联合国教科文组织宣布为"人类口头和非物质遗产代表作"，广袤的草原和丰富的物产，也使东乌珠穆沁旗成为全面体验蒙古族风情的上佳之地。

乌里雅斯太山景区，地处乌珠穆沁草原深处的乌里雅斯太镇以北 27 公里，坐落于风光秀丽、景色宜人、历史悠久、古老神奇的乌里雅斯太山之中，是以草原、山体、山石、民族风情、草原文化、休闲度假为主要内容的国家 3A 级旅游景区。它以优美的自然风光，神奇的历史传奇，独特的地质地貌而著称，被誉为草原上的一处异景，素有"草原盆景"之美誉。

乌拉盖草原，位于内蒙古锡林郭勒盟东北部，是世界上保存最完好的天然草原，境内有原始草原、湖泊、湿地、白桦林、芍药沟、黄花沟等独特的草原风光自然景观和布林庙、农乃庙、成吉思汗边墙、固腊卜赛汗国际敖包等历史文化遗迹，还有独特的乌珠穆沁部落蒙古族民俗风情文化。电影《狼图腾》曾在此取景，也使乌拉盖草原为更多人所知晓。

东乌珠穆沁旗属于温带大陆性气候，一年四季都可以来此旅游，尤以夏季为佳。

必游景点有：乌珠穆沁草原、乌拉盖布林圣泉、额吉淖尔盐湖、库伦庙、满都宝力格苏木。

经典旅游线路推荐：

线路一：乌里雅斯太镇（可以去参观喇嘛库仑庙和民俗博物馆）下一站—贵系斯太矿泉（观原始草原，饮矿泉）—乃林郭勒牧人度假村（观乃林河，观草原珍稀候鸟、骑马、坐勒勒车、牧羊、体验牧民游牧生活，晚可参加篝火晚会）。

线路二：自驾车线路，乌里雅斯太镇途径额仁高壁原始草原至乃林高勒牧人度假村（午餐、蒙古风味餐），至宝格达以原始森林公园进入呼伦贝尔草原。

线路三：乌里雅斯太镇（参观民俗博物馆，喇嘛库仑庙）—"牧人之家"（观看摔跤、赛马表演，骑马、穿民族服饰照相，饮马奶酒）—乌里雅斯太的景区（登山观草原，打草原高尔夫、射箭、穿民族服饰照相，参观牧人之家，晚可参加篝火晚会）—珠恩嘎达布其口岸（参观国门，界碑，中蒙会谈会晤站）。

线路四：从锡林浩特出发经过阿尔善矿泉至东乌旗额吉淖尔盐湖（观母亲湖，参加制盐工业生产线）—乌里雅斯太镇—珠恩嘎达布其口岸（参观国门，界碑）—乌里雅斯太的景区。

# 三、
## 家庭那达慕

　　家庭那达慕，是 20 世纪 90 年代以后随着牧民生活水平的提高而兴盛起来的。旧时唯有王爷和贵族才有资格和能力举办家庭那达慕，现在普通家庭也采用了那达慕这一形式，将本属于家庭内部的祝庆变成了一个公共的、开放的社区节庆。在那达慕的发展中，家庭那达慕的出现更多是缘于蒙古族审美情趣、民族习性在当代的展现。家庭那达慕的规模根据财力多少有所不同，但内容主要以搏克、赛马、蒙古象棋、嘎拉哈比赛为主，邀请社区内的人们参与其中。家庭那达慕包括老人祝寿那达慕、家庭马奶节那达慕、家庭牲畜超过千头那达慕、小儿剃发礼那达慕等等，时间一般为一至三天。

　　家庭那达慕中较为普遍的是老人寿辰宴那达慕。蒙古族以虚岁计算年龄，具有在本命年纪念，而不每年过生日的习俗。小孩到了13 岁本命年，父母要准备新马鞍，亲戚长辈还要备礼物，但不举行宴会。61 以后的本命年则要大摆宴席，举行那达慕祝寿。过去老年人的"那森巴雅尔"（祝寿）及"吉乐奥入勒乎"（纪念本命年）一般是在春节前后进行，但目前多选择在秋季，便于在户外开展那达慕的各项比赛。祝寿那达慕可分为室内和室外的两部分活动。室内活动主要以饮酒歌唱为主，室外活动主要是搏克、赛马。祝寿那达慕一开始由德高望重的长者唱诵赞词，祝赞寿星。接着儿女亲朋一个个为老人敬酒、献哈达和礼品。祝寿的礼品通常有：马、牛、绵羊或羊乌查（羊背子）、皮长袍、棉长袍、夹长袍、靴子、烟、荷包、现金等。祝寿完毕，主人家要回赠烟酒糖茶给客人。在宴席上，人们长时间的饮酒歌唱，观赏"男儿三艺"，认为"筵席长，生命就长"。

我们从东乌珠穆沁旗萨麦苏木吉仁宝拉格嘎查伊达姆扎布为其母亲吉日格楞61岁本命年举行的祝庆那达慕可以了解到整个过程。那达慕在自己家的草场举行，搭建了8座大型蒙古包，和2个作为后厨的小型蒙古包。8座蒙古包，搭在主人砖瓦房的正前方50米处，遵循了蒙古人视右手、西方为上及尊舅舅为上宾的习俗一字排开：第一家为舅爷家，第二家为主人一家（老人的大儿子，母亲跟随他们），第三家为大叔叔家，第四家为二叔叔家，第五、六家堂哥家，第七家为小儿子家，第八家为堂弟家。大儿媳，来自蓝旗，娘家母亲带着儿子、女婿还有舅舅等一行十几人专程赶来祝寿，被安置在砖瓦房里。蒙古包的西南方安置了搏克帐幔，即那达慕的主席台。各方亲属祝寿日前一天全部到达，共一百多人。那达慕的准备工作这一天也基本就绪，开始宰羊、煮茶，摆放奶食，招待各方亲戚。午后四五点的时候，进行了套马，持续一个半小时。骑手们身着蒙古袍，跨在马背上，举着套马杆，口中呐喊，呼啸而过。上百匹骏马，忽而聚拢在一起，忽而狂奔而去。宁静的草原，顷刻间沸腾热烈起来，将人们带入到了节日的欢乐之中。

祝寿的日子，是请本旗道特淖尔镇的喇嘛选定的，根据老人的生辰八字，认为农历七月十四日子时为良辰吉日。因此，老人的祝寿仪式是从凌晨开始的，可以说是通宵达旦的歌唱，天明后进入了那达慕赛马、搏克比赛中，一直持续到了下午5点才结束。

155

按照选定的良辰吉时，祝寿仪式从零点开始。蒙古包长条桌子上摆满了各色奶食，点心糖果，并摆上了仪式中不可或缺的"乌查"——羊背子，备好了奶茶、奶酒以及草原白。过寿老人身着暗红色的乌珠穆沁传统蒙古袍，头戴同色的蒙古帽，一身全新打扮，入座在蒙古包的右方。全家人以及到场的所有亲戚也都盛装出席，聚集在蒙古包里。老人等长辈坐在蒙古包的正中，其他男士坐在左侧，女士居右侧，等待仪式的开始。仪式以祝赞开场，主持人唱到："母亲是最可敬的亲人，母亲是最伟大的恩人，母亲以乳汁哺育了儿女，母

○送给吉日格楞老人的祝寿礼物

亲以双手托起了儿女；母亲将全部的爱给予了儿女，却将泪水偷偷擦去，将苦痛留给自己。母亲背着箩筐捡拾牛粪，母亲拎着奶桶屈膝挤奶，母亲吹燃了清晨的炊烟，母亲一针针将爱缝进了儿女的靴袍。操劳一生的母亲啊，今日，在您61岁的寿辰，您孝顺的儿女们，为您祝寿庆贺。请母亲入座并接受儿女亲友们的祝福吧！"祝赞开场后，最先由年长者首先为寿星送上备好的礼物，之后是儿女，亲戚，一个接着一个列队手捧礼物，祝福老人健康长寿。献礼的过程，持续

多彩中国节

那达慕

半个多小时。礼物包括绸缎、蒙古袍、马靴、内衣礼盒、衬衫、毛毯、地毯、酒、点心、牛奶、现金等。个别亲戚还带来了几头羊，几匹马。礼毕，由一位长者念诵"伊如勒"（祝颂礼赞词），并献上三首赞颂母亲的歌，由两位长者，为大家分割羊背子。随后，大家你一首我一曲轮番歌唱，期间老人的儿女为每位到场的客人敬献"老人年岁酒茶"，每个人要喝干为敬，认为可沾老人的福气。就这样，宴会持续3个多小时，人们才渐渐散去。稍事休息，已是破晓，开始准备早晨的赛马等那达慕事宜。

○吉日格楞老人祝寿那达慕儿童搏克赛

　　那达慕共有4种比赛：远程马赛、成人搏克赛、儿童搏克赛、嘎拉哈比赛。早晨六点多拉着赛马开车到达起跑点，聚齐后便开始比赛。共有28匹马参赛，全程19公里，终点为蒙古包所在地，即那达慕会场。赛马奖励了前5名，称为"酸奶五神骏"，由主持人对获奖马匹进行了祝赞。祝诵后用酸奶涂抹赛马的额头，给它赏吃奶豆腐。

　　整个那达慕最有看头的是儿童搏克，儿童搏克手们一招一式有模有样，使出浑身解数，与对手较量。观者兴致盎然，不时发出赞叹，抑或会心一笑，脸上满是喜悦和怜爱。

157

祝寿本是家庭内部的聚会和祝庆仪式，是家族、家系之间的一次大流动，目的是"为了让老人高兴，为了孝敬老人"。但通过那达慕，将内部聚会，延伸为外部性节日，辐射到周边社区，甚至更远的其他旗县。如老人所言："也就是这些'耐亦日'中彼此可以见见面，叙叙旧。以前非80岁以上的老人没有过寿的，现在大家生活好了，好多家庭都开始给老人祝寿，举行那达慕。"通过搏克、赛马等集体竞技性项目，不但让老人高兴，还让社区的人们参与其中，成为加强家族、家系间关系的有效方式。对于草原上的人们而言，短暂的夏秋季是一年中较为自由、悠闲的季节。在这样的季节，那达慕成为最适于表现和表达人们不同祝庆目的的一种形态。

另一类的家庭那达慕，主要为牧业丰收或为家庭某一特定事件举行的，比如"策格"（马奶）那达慕、马文化那达慕、"阿拉坦乌纳嘎因"（金马驹）那达慕等。乌珠穆沁旗道特淖尔镇巴彦图嘎嘎查的牧民朝鲁门擅长于调吊两岁马，从1993年起至2007年已调吊60多匹，其中40多匹马在各种那达慕中夺得了前4名。其儿女为庆祝父亲吊马取得的成绩而举行了"阿拉坦乌纳嘎因"（金马驹）那达慕。那达慕为期一天，聚集了2000多人。活动包括祝赞马匹、吊两岁马表演、打鬃仪式、两岁马比赛、套马表演、128名成人搏克比赛等。那达慕首先举行了"阿吉尔嘎·米里牙呼"，即"祝福公马"仪式。朝鲁门老人1993年调吊的2岁马现已成为公马，那达慕的第一个仪式就是祝赞了这匹马所取得的成绩以及所作出的贡献。之后，从自己和他人的马群中选择了8匹2岁马进行了祝赞，祝福马匹在比赛中取得优异的成绩。在祝赞仪式后，赛马、搏克等各项比赛相继开始。

在过去，那达慕具有神圣性和阶级性，只能在祭祀敖包、兴建寺庙等宗教信仰相关的神圣活动或王公贵族加冕、祝寿、庆典等重要场合里才能举行，老百姓不能随意举行那达慕来进行庆贺。普通人祝寿，一般没有那达慕，只在小范围内唱歌、玩嘎拉哈而已。家庭那达慕的兴盛表明，现代那达慕的民间性、娱乐性得以张扬，成为一般民众为各种祝庆目的采用的方式。比起大型的那达慕，家庭那达慕更直接，更率性，也更符合蒙古人天人合一、追求和谐的处事风格。

# 四、
# 都市那达慕

　　都市那达慕，多由因工作、学习而移居至都市的蒙古族知识阶层组织发起的。他们从蒙古族聚集区的故土进入城市、融入都市生活的同时仍然保留着对草原、对本民族文化的热爱和追求，也将蒙古族传统的文化带入了城市生活。作为城市少数族群，在都市这一多元文化的熔炉里，与其他族群的相互互动中，区分文化边界，保持族群自我特色成为都市蒙古人现实与理想的诉求。而那达慕无疑在展现蒙古民族文化个性和型塑族群认同的过程中发挥着重要作用。通过年复一年的展演，引导和创造着族群认同。这是都市那达慕最重要的功能所在。

　　都市那达慕始于 1981 年第一届北京蒙古族那达慕，以此为起点，各大城市陆续举行了那达慕，并成为一年一度的都市蒙古族的节日和盛宴。20 世纪 80 年代初，尤其在十一届三中全会以后，各民族的传统文化进一步得到重视，各民族自我展示的意识也开始高涨起来，在这一背景下产生了"在京蒙古族那达慕大会"。

第一届在京蒙古族那达慕于 1981 年的 5 月 17 日在中央民族学院操场举行，聚集了在京的蒙古族及相邻民族，如鄂温克族、鄂伦春族、达斡尔族群众达上千人。第一届在京蒙古族那达慕的成功举办，成为都市那达慕的表率，使得那达慕走出牧区，在城市举办成为可能。此后，天津、沈阳、乌鲁木齐等城市以及云南通海兴蒙乡等蒙古族聚居区也相继举行了那达慕。那达慕成为远离草原和本民族文化环境的蒙古人在融入城市主流文化的同时，寻求文化的归属感和精神的慰藉，增强民族自信心，发扬民族传统文化的媒介。

1981 年至今，都市那达慕举办的时间、空间、形式、内容不断变化，不断脱离草原传统而走向符号化的节日。其象征性更为突出，更多表现为族群边界和族群认同的符号得以存续。仅就北京的在京蒙古族那达慕来说，至 2017 年已举办 37 届。我们以草原传统那达慕为参照，可将在京蒙古族那达慕大会的发展变迁大体上分为三个阶段：第一阶段为 1981 年至 20 世纪 90 年代中期，第二阶段为 20 世纪 90 年代中后期至 2007 年，第三阶段为 2008 年至今。第一阶段，是在京蒙古族那达慕的创始期。这个阶段保留了更多传统那达慕的元素，在城市这个"想象"的舞台中，更趋近草原的时空。时间，一直延续着最初确定的 5 月中下旬；空间，在开阔、随意又可见"绿草蓝天"的大学操场；内容，仍凸现传统的搏克、射箭等那达慕项目，并因地制宜，加入歌舞、晚会以及蒙古族儿童说蒙古语等有益的活动。有的年份，如 1990 年在会场上还搭建了蒙古包。参加的人员较为固定，主要以在京蒙古族人士为主，并主要集中在北京的民族单位以及各高校的蒙古族及相邻民族的人员。这一时期，通讯并不发达，人们日常的联系还有所局限，因此，那达慕成为新老朋友聚会叙旧的最佳场合。第二阶段，是在京蒙古族那达慕变革转型期，也是传统的衰微期。在这个阶段，空间从室外向室内收缩，时间从与草原传统同步逐渐走向错位。从 20 世纪 90 年代中后期开始，因经费等所限，从室外转到了室内，主要采取聚餐、文艺演出或放映电影的形式。而学生专场举行小规模的篮球比赛或舞会等。时间上也从 5

○在京蒙古族那达慕大会入场仪式

月改在了冬季 12 月下旬，参与者，除了民族单位的人员外，还加入了企业以及在京打工者等非京籍人员，参与者范围得到了扩展。第三阶段，是在京蒙古族那达慕发展期。这一阶段，以 2008 年奥运会为契机，那达慕的空间从室内返回到室外，时间回归夏季，内容延续传统，参与者更加多元，那达慕的仪式化、符号化越发明显。以2008 年为标志，在京蒙古族那达慕恢复了每年五月中下旬在中央民族大学操场举行的传统。节日的气氛越来越浓厚，从方方面面彰显着民族特色和那达慕传统。入场仪式、集体安代舞、搏克比赛、射箭比赛、儿童会话比赛等成为固定内容，也出现了那达慕的商业活动，人们可以购买到从草原带来的黄油、奶豆腐、奶皮子等传统食品，还可以阅读蒙古语的书籍等。那达慕的参与者已经扩展到在京的蒙古族各阶层和职业者，蒙古文化班、蒙古族幼儿园、蒙古语网站等新近成立的机构和团体成为最鲜活的力量。这一阶段那达慕传统的回归，与那达慕被列入国家级非物质文化遗产名录以及国家对传统节日的倡导和重视不无关系。

从都市蒙古族那达慕本身而言，因其地域性、多元文化性、都市化，以及特定人群化而具有特殊性。对都市蒙古族来讲，在远离草原的空间，在经济社会快速转型的时代潮流中，在国际化程度越来越高的大都市里，无论那达慕的具体内容怎样变迁，无论时空怎样转换，也无论参与者社会身份如何多样，大家在文化认知上将始终一致，他们不可能舍弃"那达慕"这一节日。因为即使是想象的，这一称谓本身也使他们将自己和草原联系起来，将自己和故乡联系起来，将自己和族群血脉联系起来。即使是想象的，这样的空间和活动也依然延续着民族古老的族群信息，依然传递着曾经的历史记忆。那达慕的这一天，身着蒙古族服饰，或一家大小，或三五亲朋，从城市的四面八方循着广播里的蒙古音乐聚集到那达慕会场。大人们闲散地聊着，孩子们快乐的你追我跑。绿色的人造草坪，悠扬的马头琴，五颜六色的蒙古袍，动听悦耳的蒙古语，热烈奔放的安代舞，紧张激烈的搏克角逐……恍然间将人们带回了蓝天白云下的草原，带回了久别的故乡。以传统符号装点出的这一天，俨然成为都市蒙古族一年一度集体狂欢的盛大节日。搏克的奖励为那达慕画上圆满的句号后，个体的狂欢开始在城市蒙古族餐馆继续上演。伴着醉人的美酒，一阵阵蒙古语的欢歌笑语，回荡在城市的夜空，回荡在人们的心间，共同期待着下一届那达慕的到来。都市蒙古人的心目中，那达慕已然成为一个标志。正如一位北京蒙古族先生所言："不管怎样，城市那达慕可以提醒蒙古人自己是蒙古人，那达慕仍是我们城市蒙古人最重要的节日，谁能拒绝自己民族的节日呢？"

# 五、散居区那达慕

蒙古族的地域分布较为广泛，除了主要的聚居地之外，在西南、中部等地区有十余万散杂居的蒙古族，分布在云南省通海县，四川省成都市和凉山彝族自治州盐源、木里两县，贵州省毕节地区大方县和铜仁地区思南、石阡两县，重庆市彭水县。与彭水县毗邻的湖北省鹤峰县也有千余蒙古族人。几百年来，他们在对西南环境的适应过程中，形成了以山区农业为主的经济生活，原来的游牧文化也随之发生了变化。但他们通过家谱、墓碑、口授的方式，传承着家族的历史和作为蒙古人的执著信念。

散居区那达慕的存在和发生，对那达慕发展趋势的理解，以及对那达慕本身的文化理解都有十分重要的启示。它是在与内蒙古蒙古族同胞交往中构建的"文化传统"，但在不断的重复和表述中，已成为追忆祖先和表达思乡之情的"传统"节日，在多元文化的交往中，演变为族群边界意义上的族群认同符号。

云南省通海县兴蒙蒙古族乡位于杞麓湖畔，兴蒙乡的蒙古族自称为"蒙古瓦""蒙古勒"或"刚卓"。从民族源流上看，他们是南宋末年到元代从北方迁徙到云南的蒙古族的后裔。元宪宗二年（公元 1252 年）忽必烈领兵征大理，兵分三路，即兀良合台率西路军，忽必烈率中路军，抄合也只烈率东路军，进攻云南地区。三路军先后进入丽江地区，攻下大理城，结束大理国的统治。这是历史上大

〇云南兴蒙乡那达慕

量的蒙古族第一次进入云南，并落籍在此，远离了北方原住地。兴蒙乡蒙古族历经 760 余年的风雨洗礼，在沧海桑田的巨变中，经历了从牧民到渔民再到农民的转变，并在与各民族的融合与交流中，形成了独具特色的民族文化。

兴蒙乡那达慕始于 1981 年，它是在与北方祖居地蒙古的交往中，确立了那达慕这一"古老的传统节日"。起初每年举行一次，时间为 12 月 13 日—15 日,1993 年兴蒙乡五届三次人民代表大会决定，

每三年举行一次。那达慕由兴蒙乡政府组织,活动内容包括三圣祭典、地会表演、体育竞技等。活动中较为重点的是三圣祭典仪式,纪念成吉思汗、蒙哥、忽必烈三位祖。祭典结束,村中的蒙古族长者用三个轿子抬着三位祖先的神像,从三圣宫正大门出发,在中村、白阁、桃家嘴等村中游行,一路上,村民自发组织加入祭祖先的游行队伍。之后进入到那达慕竞技和表演之中,包括摔跤、耍龙灯、划旱船、文艺表演活动等。从活动内容来看,除了身着蒙古族服装进行的摔跤外,几乎看不到传统那达慕的影子,而更多的是反映渔业和农耕生产生活的特色活动。

# 六、
# 世界各地的那达慕

蒙古族的分布较为广泛,加之蒙古族是个喜欢游走的民族,足迹遍布世界各地。作为蒙古族的节庆,只要有蒙古人的地方就有那达慕。不同身份、不同角色、不同层级、不同地域的人们都在采纳那达慕这一节庆形态服务于自身,满足各自不同的目的,呈现出各自的特色,不断地丰富和扩展着那达慕的内涵和外延。

## （一）蒙古国那达慕

蒙古国那达慕类型也很多，有敖包那达慕、庆典那达慕等。其中，最为重要的是国家那达慕。1924 年 7 月 11 日，蒙古人民共和国成立。3 年后，蒙古人民革命的领袖苏赫巴托将军发布命令，在每年的 7 月 11 日庆祝革命胜利的同时举办传统的那达慕大会。此后，将每年的 7 月 11 日定为"蒙古国国庆日"，举行国家、爱玛格（省）和苏木三级那达慕。国家级的那达慕在首都乌兰巴托、省级那达慕在省所在地、苏木那达慕在苏木所在地举行。蒙古国那达慕的内容主要是以男子三项竞技为主，还增设其他体育项目和文艺表演以及物资交流等内容。国家那达慕由专门成立的筹备委员会组织，总理总负责，乌兰巴托市长承办。为保障国家那达慕的顺利举办，还制定有专门的法律，对那达慕各项活动做了规范。

国庆那达慕于每年的 7 月 11 日至 13 日在乌兰巴托中央体育场举行，人们身着节日盛装，不远千里赶到乌兰巴托参加比赛和庆祝活动。那达慕吸引了不少的外国游客，政府也会邀请各国使节要人参加。届时，那达慕的入场券一票难求，要排上一夜队才能买到，容纳一万五千人的中央体育场座无虚席，参加开幕式的演职人员也要超过万人。

蒙古国骑兵仪仗队将象征着战无不胜之神的"九尾白纛旗"从国家宫护送到那达慕会场后，蒙古国总统致开幕词。开幕式表演规模宏大，有阅兵式、古代军队展示、传统民族歌舞、大型健美操等。开幕式结束后，三项竞技——搏克、射箭和赛马便在不同场地展开。来自蒙古国各地的512名搏克手要一对一进行淘汰赛，最后决出冠军。数百名男女射箭手和数以千计的骏马将分别展开角逐。赛马比赛场

○蒙古国国庆那达慕搏克祭拜白纛旗（巴义尔 摄）

设在在乌兰巴托以西 40 公里的草原上，赛程为 15—30 公里，骑手都是 7—12 岁的孩子。很多人都在 7 月 12 日的早上拥向赛马场，路上的车辆排成长龙，很多人还在草原上搭起帐篷过夜。

那达慕是蒙古国最重大的节日之一，放假五天，首都乌兰巴托大批居民奔赴各地牧区，与亲朋好友一起庆祝节日，体验蒙古族传统生活方式。

### （二）其他国家的那达慕

随着蒙古人移居世界各地，那达慕也随之在当地生根发芽。日本、韩国、美国、德国是蒙古族留学或定居较多的国家，每年定期或不定期，以所在城市公园为集聚地，举办那达慕。有入场仪式、歌舞表演，以及搏克赛、蒙古特色商品。人们穿上蒙古袍，带着家人朋友，聚在一起，说说母语，叙叙家常，在异国他乡以古老的那达慕这一方式连结了彼此，构建了族群认同。如 2015 年 7 月 12 日，由"蒙

167

○美国纽约那达慕搏克比赛（永恒之火 摄）

古国驻纽约使馆"以及"纽约蒙古人协会"组织举办的第三届纽约蒙古那达慕大会，在纽约市中央著名的"中央公园"举办。那达慕项目设置了掰手腕、蒙古舞蹈、儿童木马赛、搏克比赛等多项活动。蒙古国，中国内蒙古自治区、布里亚特、卡尔梅克、图瓦、哈扎拉等国家和地区的蒙古族一同参与其间，加深了浓浓的同胞情谊。

　　在日本的蒙古人，在东京等地每年也举行那达慕。形式与美国那达慕类似，一般有搏克、蒙古象棋比赛、蒙古服饰展示、歌舞表演等内容。

○日本东京那达慕蒙古服饰展示

# Chapter Three
## Types and Distribution of Naadam

Mongolian ethnic group in China mainly live in Inner Mongolian Autonomous Region, Liaoning Province, Heilongjiang Province, the Xinjiang Uygur Autonomous Region, Qinghai Province, Hebei Province, with some concentrating or scattering in places like Gansu, Ningxia, Sichuan, Yunnan, Guizhou, Beijing and so on. The size of Mongolian habitations varies from a huge autonomous region to a small village; they spread over the country, from northeast to northwest, from the Inner Mongolia to southwest China. Beyond the border, though as the main part of Mongolia, the Mongolian ethnic group sparsely scattered in Russia, Japan, South Korea, Europe, the United States and some other Eurasian countries. The important Mongolian festival, Naadam, is diverse with openness, adaptability and integrity to meet various contexts. Each year, Mongols in different areas hold Naadam in distinct forms, like traditional Ovoo Naadam for ritual, government—organized and large—scaled celebration Naadam for politics, economics and cultures, and Naadam for tourism. Currently there are Naadam in family, city, Mongolian diaspora etc. However, no matter in which place and type, both traditional core mark the Three Games of Men and regional characteristics have achieved, developed and enriched with new era features.

## 1. Ovoo Naadam

As an essential way of gathering and entertainment, Naadam had been closely linked to the religious culture at the very beginning. When combined with ovoo ceremonies, the core system of Naadam was separated from production to cultural composition; developed from basic survival skills to spiritual pursuit and expression of religion; changed from practicability to performing and entertaining.

Mongolian ethnic group has many types of ritual, like the sacrifice for Heaven, for fire, for the progenitors of lineages and so on. One of the most important and the most grandiose rituals is ovoo ceremony. Ovoo means heap in Mongolian and is usually set at the top of mountains, mountain passes, lakeside, wayside, beach and other places that are special and easily seen. Ovoo in eastern Inner Mongolia are typically cone shaped, while tower in the west. The ovoo in old fashion were usually made of rocks, willow and other local resources. In modern times, they are rich in building styles like bricked ovoos, concrete ovoos, glazed ovoos.

The scholars cannot reach an agreement on the origin of ovoo rituals. According to Qing Hui Dian (Administrative Regulation of Qing Dynasty), "where there are no mountain or river at pasture boundaries, there are plied rocks as marks called ovoos". It tells that in ancient times, there was not anything on vast steppe to identify directions therefore stone heaps were made as road signs and landmarks, which gradually developed into sites for the worships for Gods of heaven, earth, mountain, road, village protector and so on. People holding another theory regards the ovoo as the site for burying the ancestors of Mongolian ethnic group, which is based on a folk story. In ancient times, the Mongols nomadized and hunted and they practiced celestial burial wherein a human corpse was placed on Mongolian Lele cart (Mongolian ox carts) and would settle where the body dropped. Given the immigrant nomadic life and the vast steppe, the relatives would carry a baby camel and bleed it when burying their family. And next year the two-years-old camel or its mother would be taken to find the interment site along probable routine. Where the camel refused to move or cried, there is the target place and then a few stones would serve as tribute and mark, which was passed down and developed into a custom. The third argument is that ovoo ceremony is nothing but praying for rain, which is supported by folk worshipers. Nomads believe that ovoos are sites for Nature

Eej Ovoo rituals in East Ujimqin Banner

171

God and Mountain-Water God worship ceremonies. If there are no gods, there is no rain, grass, steppe and pasture to keep their nomadic life. Thus, ovoo ceremony is practiced regularly to pray to gods for favorable nature. It can be concluded from the nomads' plain philosophy that their faith in ovoo comes along their nomadic life, which is a primitive worship and belief produced from natural gods worship in the context. Mongol ethnic group regard the ovoo as their protector. Whenever meeting an ovoo, they must worship it, offer dairy food and some rocks before carrying on their travel. In addition, fishing, gathering wood and cutting trees are strictly prohibited.

There are legends as many as ovoos on Mongolia steppe. For example, the Hua Ovoo (literally flower Ovoo) in Ejin Banner of Alxa League has its name from smallpox (Chinese pronunciation: tianhua) rather than the flowery place. The saying goes that once a Lama who happened to be infected with smallpox that broke out here. Fortunately, the Lama with medical skills not only cured himself but also imparted the treatment to locals. It is to commemorate him that the Hua Ovoo was built. And, there is a knoll called Sarenba Ovoo in Mandabulag Sumu of East Ujimqin Banner built by Taiyiji Sarenba of pre-Beile Banner. He thinks the knoll looks like a lying lion towards north which is favorable to livestock so that he built the ovoo there to practice ceremony, whose descendants were truly well off and the area have been fertile up to now. Accordingly, nomads own it to the ancestor-protected surrounding environment. Besides, there is one called Eej Ovoo in Qaidam of Ujimqin Banner. As for its origin here is a folk. Long ago in a spring, a nomad lost some horses so he rode to find them back around the steppe till the evening when he carelessly dropped into a swamp sinking down and down. Surrounded by hopelessness, suddenly a flash of green light caught his eyes. He called HELP towards the light. Then a woman appeared before him with a mirror in right hand and a rope with hooks in left hand. She came and handed the rope to the nomad. Soon he and his horse were rescued. He gratefully asked her name and pleaded her to tell him where the lost horses were. "In the east of the hill", no sooner did she reply than she disappeared. The nomad found the lost horses where she pointed. He believed she was the local god and henceforth he used dairy food to worship the site. Gradually an ovoo was built, namely Eej Ovoo. After that it was said that there once appeared a woman having a snake-like tail with mirror in her hand, who was regarded as the deity of Qaidam Lake. In Khuree Temple of East Ujimqin Banner people still enshrine Eej Ovoo—a portrait of the goddess with mirror and hook in hands.

Given the different origins, types, natural conditions, ovoo ceremony is held in different time, size, form and content. Among the great variety of types, generally, ovoos are classified into: hero-related ovoo, Genghis-related ovoo, hierolatry-related ovoo (Sülde Ovoo), Banner-Royal ovoo (Noyin Ovoo), Lamaism temple ovoo (related to Buddhism), tribe or shamanism-related ovoo, family ovoo, tourist area's ovoo, etc. In terms of shape and structure, it varies from 1 to 13 and even more. Traditionally, ovoo ceremony involves libation, offering by fire, jewelry offering, blood offering. Libation is to pour alcoholic drinks on the ovoo; offering by fire is to throw meat dairy food and cypress twigs into fire in front of the ovoo; jewelry offering is to throw jewelry or coins on the ovoo; blood offering is to offer the butchered sheep and cattle. After Tibetan Buddhism spreading into Mongolian area, ovoo ceremony is usually hosted by Lama or living Buddha, who thought blood offerings were committing sins so replaced them with diary food and wine with milk. A few areas like Urad Middle Banner still perform the ovoo rituals in the traditional way dictated by Shamanism. That is to primitively butcher bulls or rams and then use the skin to enwind the ovoo as well as burn the flesh as offering. There are two types of ovoos. The first type featuring black dragon must be worshipped with meat offering. The second type is ovoos featuring white dragon and they must be worshipped with diary food offering. What's more, ovoos differ in level as well as ceremony. For example, the higher level Wanggai Ovoo in Ujimqin Banner requires a complete ram.

Each ovoo ceremony has a fixed time, once a year, concentrating at turn from spring to summer while winter ceremony is extremely rare. In terms of the practitioner, each kin, family and individual uniquely and exclusively have a fixed ovoo. In modern times, however, the rule relatively loosened, one may worship several ovoos. Moreover, foreign ethnic groups and foreigners appeared in the ceremony. In East Ujimqin Banner the ceremony is in lunar March and June, occasionally in April, July and August. As the folklore goes, lunar May is ovoo month when folk starts ceremonies of the year. In lunar May and June, the most leisure season for nomads, steppe enters summer and a lot of dairy production is made. From then on, ovoo ceremony begins in order to please deities for favorable weather and growth in population and livestock. Meanwhile Naadam is held to facilitate gatherings, social interactions and trading, and entertain gods and human beings.

The practice procedure varies according to different sizes, types, areas and times. Normally, the ovoo organizers are in charge of the renovation which includes hanging new prayer

Sacrifices for Wanggai Ovoo in Ujimqin Banner

flags and 5 colored silk cloth strips and replacing the old willow twigs with new ones a day before the ceremony held. On that day, people from different regions gather around when it's still early in the morning. Lama reads the scripture to pray, and participants of the ritual put on the sacrifice stage some offerings like dairy products and then circle around the ovoo clockwise for 3 rounds praying for luck and protection for both people and their livestock, and also scatter their milk, wine, pastry and candies around the ovoo. In the final step of a ritual, people recite "come here, come here" with their hands holding khadag (a piece of cloth) or dairy products and waving clockwise in hope of leading good fortune to their homes. When the ritual is completed, and people walk down to the tent put up on the smooth ground at the foot of the ovoo mountain and share the entire roast lamb and dairy products waiting for the advent of Naadam. In Ovoo Naadam there will be horse-racing and Bökh games with different scales.

There is one thing for sure during the process of its origin,

175

transmission and development: ovoo ceremony has always gone along with the Three Games of Men; Naadam along ovoo ceremony. One tempertant for that Naadam remains fresh over years is bound up with ovoo ceremony, the Mongolian folk belief. They think Naadam is exactly the activity to please gods following the ovoo ceremony. They constitute an organic whole for complete ceremony procedure. Local nomads think that Bökh, horse racing and archery came into existance when people worshipped ovoos and natural gods, while Naadam only appeared with ovoo ceremony.

The size of Naadam is determined by ovoo's size, influence and owner. Large-scaled ovoos like Bayan Ovoo in East Ujim- qin, its wrestling involves 128 people, while Bökh of smaller one like Bayantolgoi Ovoo in West Ujimqin Banner involves only 32 people. In past times, Bökh, horse racing and archery in ovoo ceremonies are more of divine and special implications. "Bökh may symbolize its link with the ancient shamanism's views of the universe and nature and nomadic lifestyle, and is bound up with Mongolian religions." Therefore, the recrea- tional events of Naadam are divine in ovoo ceremonies like some witchcraft. The performance is to please gods and pray for harvest and pleasure.

With the resumption of ovoo ceremony and improvement of living standards, almost all the ovoo ceremonies are followed by Naadam. It is safe to say that the faith for ovoo ceremony acts as the most vigorous inner motivation to drive the Na- adam's origin, development, transmission and to keep its lively state. From lunar April to August, all kinds of Ovoo Naadams are held alternatively, bringing human into divine and joyful festivals.

## 2. Celebration Naadam

Celebration Naadam is a common type, which is organized by governments of all levels in order to facilitate political and economic activities. Kurultai for Genghis Khan's enthroning in 1206, Zhama Feast in Yuan Dynasty, Seven-Banner Naadam and Ten-Jasak Naadam in the 16th and 17th centuries, Naadam for anniversary, harvest, honor recognizing after the establishment of Inner Mongolian Autonomous Region, and so on, all belong to celebration Naadam. It has the features of large scale, rich contents, strict organization, multiple functions etc, which is the essential expression way of governmental celebrating throughout Inner Mongolia and Mongolian enclaves.

The profile of this kind of Naadam can be seen from previous Naadam held by East Ujimqin Banner in Xilingol League. In 1963, in order to celebrate that the number of livestock reached 1.3 million, a three-day Naadam was held, wherein 512 adults took part in Bökh, 64 in Mongolian chess and 180 horses in 30-kelemeter racing; in 1986, the seven-day Naadam to celebrate the 30th anniversary of East Ujimqin Banner was held with 512 adults taking part in Bökh, 128 in Mongolian chess, 180 horses in 30-km race and relay race; in 1991 a Naadam to celebrate the 35th anniversary of the establishing of the banner was held where there were men's, women's and children's Bökh, long-distance, saddle and relay horse race adults' and children's chess, archery, shooting, tug-of-war, basketball, gate ball etc. as well as awarding 500 model workers; in 2006, the Naadam for the 50th anniversary of East Ujimqin Banner witnessed 1,024 adults , 64 women and 128 children in each Bökh, long-distance horse race saddle horse race two-year-old horse racing and horse riding games, Mongolian chess contest, shagai contest and several performances, as well as ceremonies for wrestlers' retirement, conferring honors called "jiangga", praying and praising ritual for horse racing and awarding 500 model workers and so on.

It usually takes a long time to prepare and train for celebration Naadam. As the Naadam for the 50th anniversary of East Ujimqin Banner, considering the anniversary-related activities, it almost took over half a year. In addition to early organizational arrangements, the more important preparing is intensified training and rehearsals of dancing, songs and honor guard for opening ceremonies. Totally organized and led by governments, large-scaled Naadam is prepared, arranged and managed in the name of governments, for which they will concentrate all the administrative resources on the event just like they do for other large social gatherings.

Typically, it does not require much preparation, announcement or publicity to hold folk traditional Naadam like Ovoo

Guardians from Sülde in the Naadam for the 50th anniversary
of East Ujimqin Banner

178

Naadam. For small and traditional one, its information is still conveyed by mouth. In recent years, with the change of communication methods, Wechat has become the most common and convenient means of disseminating information. By then people will automatically converge for the ovoo ceremony and followed Naadam. And for government-hosted celebration Naadam with certain theme, publicity and early promotion are the extremely key section. The East Ujimqin Banner government had posted message three months before the Naadam was held. What is more, they had repeatedly reported it via newspaper Inner Mongolia Daily and arranged six program groups to film and report the banner of Inner Mongolia Television with a "kick-off ceremony of stepping into East Ujimqin Banner and filming". Currently, televisions, broadcasting, newspapers, network and other new media have been key channels for Naadam to be known by the external world.

Celebration Naadam is more of an integrated stage, which may hold more cultural factors and display more selected cultural symbols. On the 50th anniversary of founding East Ujimqin Banner, there were nearly 10 kinds of large activities: the large literature and art party "glory 50 years"; the literature and art party for the 50th anniversary of "Army-Mass cooperation"; the photography exhibition "look back the 50 years"; the exhibition of objects about custom; the exhibition of paintings "heavenly grassland"; awarding 500 model workers; the collective birthday banquets for seniors aged more than 80; the naming ceremony for 50 newborn infants; the group weddings for 50 young couples etc..There were nine kinds of large contests including long tune song chorus of 5000 people; 1,024 adults, 128 women, 64 seniors and 32 children in each Bökh; 30-km horse race 30-km stallion race 7.5-km pommel horse race 10-

km horse race two-year-old horse race, picking shagai on horse-back racing; 128-people flicking shagai contest, 1,024-people throwing four objects contest, 256-people shooting shagai contest, 128-people ball and shagai contest; 256 adults in Mongolian chess, 128 children in children's Mongolian chess; in addition to exhibitions of custom, costume, handicrafts etc. Throughout, the organizing considered various age group and cultural need of different identities, which also stressed the theme number 50 like "collective weddings of 50 pairs of youth", "naming ceremony for 50 newborn infants" and the like. Besides, to embody the traditional virtue of respecting the old, the host invited seniors aged over 80 to join the "collective birthday banquets for seniors". The 50th anniversary is a golden opportunity to display and publicize local culture in that all the activities, like "ethnic costume and objects, handicrafts and contests", the Three Games of Men, Mongolian chess and literature and art show, are very distinctive of local features.

Families on the floats in the Naadam for the 50th anniversary
of East Ujimqin Banner

Combined with Mongolian and local special symbols and traditional cultural elements together, celebration Naadam fully displays Naadam's ethnic and regional features. Some ceremonies and rituals can be only watched in large-scaled celebration Naadam, such as presentations of honorary wrestler, ceremonies of bestowing "jiangga" to young wrestlers, conferring nine-ninegifts like silver saddles and white camel, and so forth.

## Tips for Tourism

### East Ujimqin Banner

Extending across the west side of the Great Xing'an mountain, East Ujim—qin Banner is in the northeast of Xilingol League of the Inner Mongolia, bordering Hinggan League and Tongliao to the east, Xilinhot and West Ujimqin Banner to the south, Abag Banner to the west, and Mongolia to the north, which is one of bridgeheads connecting the Eurasian Land Bridge, after ManzhouLi and Erenhot. Back in the Spring and Autumn period and the Warring States period, Donghu people and DanLin people were already found in area round the present—day East Ujimqin Banner. And thanks to the long history and development, it gave birth to splen—did ethnic culture, ujimqin urtynduu(Long—tune folksong). is regarded as linving example of Mongolian music and was listed by UNESCO in 2005 as an intangble cultural heritage. Combined with the vast steppes and rich products, East Ujimqin Banner surely deserves the fame of picture—perfect land to experience all aspects of Mongols.

Uliyastai Mountain Scenic Area is situated in picturesque, time—honored unapproachable Uliyastai Mountain with the prominent peak at 1,050 meters above sea level. 27 km away from Uliyastai Town in the depth of the Ujimqin Steppes, which is the AAA tourist attraction (the highest level is AAAAA in China) mainly offering tourists for viewing grasslands and mountain rocks, experiencing customs and cultures, and taking a leisure holiday. The wonderful scenic spot is known as Steppe Bonsai, for its fan-tastic natural beauty, magical historic legend, unique topographical features.

As the best-preserved natural steppes over the world, the Ulagai Steppes lies in the northwest of Xilingol League of the Inner Mongolia, where there are quite a few of unique natural beauties (such as primitive steppes, lakes, birch forest, the sea of Chinese peonies or Hemerocallis fulva, etc.), cultural relics (such as Bulin Temple, Nongnai Temple, The Wall of Genghis Khan, Gulabsaihan International Ovoo, etc.), and special folklore and custom of the Mongols in Ujimqin tribe. The movie Wolf Totem was shot here and therefore made it better-known.

East Ujimqin Banner features temperate continental climate, where summer is the best time for travelling though all of the four seasons are acceptable.

Top Tourist Sites:
1. Ujimqin Steppes
2. Ulagai Bulin Holy Spring
3. Eej Nor Salt Lake
4. Khuree Temple
5. Mandubulag Sumu

Classic Tour Routes:
1. Uliyastai Town (to visit Lama Khuree Temple and Folklore Museum)—Guilestai Mineral Spring (to view primitive grassland and drink mineral spring water)—Nairingol Shepherd Resort (to view Nairin River and rare migratory birds, to ride a horse, to take Lele cart, to pasture sheep and ex-perience the shepherds' life, or to join the bonfire party in the evening)

2. Self-driving route: Uliyasitai Town—Erengobi Premitive Grassland—

Nairingol Shepherd Resort (to eat ethnic food for lunch)—Bogda primitive forest park—the Hulunbeir Steppes

3. Uliyastai Town (to visit Lama Khuree Temple and Folklore Museum)— "Home of Shepherds" (to view wrestling and horse race, to ride a horse, to take pictures in folk costumes, or to drink kumis)—Uliyasitai Scenic Area (to climb mountains and view steppes, to play golf on the steppes, to try archery, to take pictures in folk costumes, to visit Home of Shepherds, or to join bonfire party in the evening)—Zuungadabchi Port (to visit the gate of China, boundary marker and site of Sino—Mongolia Talks)

## 3. Family Naadam

Family Naadam has flourished as living standards of herdsmen have improved since 1990s. In ancient times, only His Highness and noble families were qualified and rich enough to throw family Naadam. Nowadays, ordinary families are also capable to hold family Naadam, which is now more like an open community festival instead of a celebration limited to one family. Family Naadam is the contemporary expression of Mongolian people's aesthetic tastes and habits. Though varying in scales according to financial conditions, the festival mainly comprises Bökh, horse race, Mongolian chess and shagai. People in the community are all invited to participate in the festival. Family Naadam can feature different themes, like offering birthday congratulations to elders, celebrating harvest through toasting in mare's milk, celebrating livestock's number exceeding one thousand, and memorizing a child's first haircut. It usually lasts for one to three days.

The most common one is family Naadam to offer birthday congratulations to elders. Mongols reckon their ages by nominal age and celebrate birthday only in the year of the same

183

zodiac animal with the person's year of birth. So when a child turns 13 in the year of his or her zodiac animal, parents will prepare a new saddle for the child and relatives will prepare gifts, though no banquet is on the schedule. However, a grand banquet and Naadam is a must to offer birthday congratulations to a person who is or over 61 in each and every year of his or her zodiac animal. In the past, celebrations for elders' birthdays, or "Nasenbayar" in Mongolian, and those to commemorate the year of an elder's zodiac animal, or "Jil-oruuleg", were often held around the Spring Festival. Now they're held in autumn, when the weather is more ideal for outdoor competitions. Family Naadam to offer birthday congratulations to elders comprises two parts: indoor activities and outdoor competitions. People drink and sing indoors and compete in Mongolian wrestling games or horse races outdoors. Family Naadam in honor of an elder's birthday starts with a respectable elder chanting and blessing. Then sons, daughters, relatives and friends toast and present Khadag and gifts to the elder. The usual gifts are horses, cattle, sheep, Uchi dishes (cooked sheep back), leather gowns, cotton gowns, boots, cigarettes, wallets and cash. When the birthday congratulation part is over, the hosts present guests with cigarettes, alcohols, sweets and teas in return. In the banquet, people spend a lot of time drinking, singing and watching the Three Games of Men. In their mind, the long time of a banquet signifies longevity.

In Jaranbulag gachaa, Samai sumu of East Ujimqin Banner, yidamjab held a family Naadam to celebrate the 61th birthday of his mother, Jargalang, and this offered us a good chance to experience the whole process of a family Naadam. On Yidamjab family's grassland, they established eight large yurts and added two smaller ones which served as kitchens. Right in front of the family's brick house, the eight large yurts lined 50 meters away in a row in accordance with the tradition of honoring the right, the west and the uncles in a family. Yidamjab is Jargalang's oldest son and has several uncles. From the first yurt, the nearest one to the brick house, to the eighth yurt, the furthermost one, these yurts were set up respectively for the old brother of Yidamjab's mother, Yeedamuchu himself, his father's oldest brother, his father's second old brother, a cousin older than Yidamjab, another older cousin, Jargalang's youngest son, and Yidamjab's younger cousin. The daughter-in-law of Jargalang is from Pain Blue Banner. She and her mother, brothers, sisters-in-law and uncles all came to send birthday congratulations to Jargalang and they were accommodated in the brick house. All relatives, amounting to over one hundred people, arrived in the day before the birthday. At the southwest of those yurts, Bökh yurts were also set up as the main platform of the Naadam. When preparations were almost over the host began to treat guests with mutton, tea and dairy foods. At four

The venue for Jargalang's birthday ceremony

185

or five o'clock in the afternoon, the horse roping competition began and lasted for one and a half hours. Dressing in Mongolian gowns and holding a roping bar by hand, mounted riders shouted and yelled excitedly. Over a hundred horses gathered together sometimes and soon dashed away in different directions. The exciting and tense atmosphere immediately lit up the tranquil grassland and bought people the mood of festival.

The special day to offer birthday congratulations is chosen by a Lama in Duutnuur Township, East Ujimqin Banner. Reckoning the very hour, day, month and year when Jargalang was born, the Lama thought that the time of zi, which is from 11p.m. to 1a.m., of July 14 in the lunar calendar was the most suitable timing. So Jargalang's birthday celebration began in 12 o'clock at night. Before sunrise, people sang through the night; after sunrise, horse races and Mongolian wrestling competitions started, which didn't conclude until five o'clock in the afternoon.

As advised by the Lama, the birthday ceremony started at midnight. In each yurt, there was a long table loaded with dairy foods, deserts, sweets, and an indispensable Uchi dish, milk tea, milk wine and the special liquor "Grassland White" in steppe. Dressing up in a dark red traditional gown of Ujimqin and a Mongolian hat, Jargalang, the star of the day, took her seat in the right area in the yurt. Both her family members and relatives were all dressed up and gathered in the yurt. Seniors older than Jargalang sat in the middle, other men in the left and women in the right, waiting for the celebration to begin. It started with chanting and singing by the master of ceremonies: "mother, you are the greatest and most adorable person to me in the world; you feed me on your breast milk and support me with your hands; you sacrifice for me and keep sorrows to yourself. I remember the times when you picked up cow manure with a basket on your back, when you milked the cow with knees belt, when you prepared breakfast in the early morning and when you stitched our boots and gowns. Mother, you devote your whole life for us and now, in your 61th birthday party, please let us congratulate on you and wish you longevity; now, mother, take your seat and receive our best wishes." After the chant, elders were the first to present gifts and then Jargalang's kids and then relatives. Gifts included silk, Mongolian gowns, boots, gift boxes of underwear, shirts, carpets, blankets, wines, desserts, milk, cash and so on. Some relatives even brought several goats and horses. The process of presenting gifts lasted over half an hour, and after that, an elder chanted the Irugel, a blessing poem, and sang three songs to salute mother. Then it was time for two elders to cut the whole sheep in the Uchi dish and gave out the meat to everyone. Later, people took their turns to sing. In the process, Jargalang's children toasted to each guest in alcohol or tea. They had to drink it up so that they would get luck from the aged star of the day. In this way the banquet lasted more than three hours. At dawn, people left the banquet one by one, but shortly they began to prepare for the horse race in the morning.

There were four competitions in this family Naadam: long-distance horse race, adult Bökh, children Bökh, and shagai. For the horse race, at six o'clock in the morning, people drove to the starting point of the track along with their horses. The competition started when all participants were in place. In that day, there were 28 horses racing for a 38-li ride. The race track concluded in where the yurts stood, i.e. the main platform of Naadam. The top five horses were awarded and given the name of "five excellent horses of the yogurt", and then the master of the ceremony offered his congratulations and blessings to them.

Winners of the endurance horse racing at Jargalang's birthday ceremony

After that, people rubbed yogurt on the five horses' heads and fed them on milk tofu.

Among all these competitions, the most attractive one was children Bökh. Young wrestlers tried to make every movement and posture standard and beautiful. They did all they can to topple the opponents. Inspired by those children, people sometimes applauded, sometimes smiled with understanding, all being pleased and moved by these little kids.

A birthday party for an old family member actually is a celebration and gathering within a family with the aim just to "make the elderly happy". But thanks to the Naadam festival, such a family party stretches beyond a family to neighboring communities and even to other banners and counties. The words of some old people show the popularity of such Naadam, "it's only in these 'nair' (festival) that we can meet and chat with each other. In the past you had to be over 80 to enjoy a birthday party, but now everybody lives a better life, so many families begin to hold Naadam to celebrate old people's birth-

Children waiting to join the competitions in Jargalang's birthday ceremony

days." The competitive sports in Naadam such as Bökh and horse racing can not only entertain the agedbut also connect a community and strengthen the relationships among family members. For people living on grasslands, the short summer and autumn are precious seasons with relatively more freedom and leisure. Therefore, in such beautiful days, Naadam becomes the most suitable way for people to celebrate for various purposes.

Another type of family Naadam is held for harvest or specific events, such as "tsegee" (horse milk) Naadam, horse culture Naadam and "altan unagan" (golden colt) Naadam. Qolomon, a master of horse training, is a herdsman living in Bayintug gachaa County, Duutnuur, East Ujimqin Banner. More than sixty horses have been trained by him from 1993 to 2007, among which over forty ranked in the top four in various Naadam competitions. To celebrate his achievements, Qolomon's children held an "altan unagan" (golden colt) Naadam

189

for their father. This event lasted for one day and attracted more than 2,000 people. It included horse chanting, a performance of training two-year-old colts, a horse mane cutting rite, a race of two-year-old horses, a horse lassoing performance and a Bökh game of 128 adults. The Naadam started with a rite called "ajirag miliah", which means "blessing a male horse". The two-year-old colt that Qolomon had trained in 1993 now grew into an adult male horse and the ritewas to praise its past achievements and contributions. Then the organizers chose eight two-year-old horses from the horse groups of their own family and other people's. They praised these colts as well and offered wishes to them, hoping that they can achieve excellent results in competitions. After chanting, games like horse racing and wrestling began one after another.

In the past, Naadam was sacred and exclusive for people of higher social class.Thus it could only be held on religious occasions like ovoo sacrificing rituals and celebrations for temple construction, or in important events such as aristocratic coronations, birthday parties for the elderly and grand festivals. Ordinary people, however, did not have the privilege to hold Naadam. For the masses, birthday parties could only be small-scale involving songs and shagai games with a few participants. Nowadays, however, family Naadam carrying profound folklore and much entertainment, has flourished and become a common way for everybody to celebrate for various reasons. Compared with large-scale Naadam festivals, family Naadam is more straightforward and casual, better conforming to Mongolians' pursuit for the harmony between human and nature.

## 4. Naadam in Cities

Naadam in cities is mainly held by Mongolian intellectual

class who settle in cities for work and study. Though living in cities far away from their native land inhabited by compact Mongolian communities, the intellectual class still loves their native grassland culture ardently as they are trying to integrate themselves and Mongolian culture into the urban communities. In cities, the melting pot of diverse cultures, these Mongols as a minority interact with other ethnic minorities actively. Thus clarifying cultural border and preserving ethnic identity becomes a request of the reality and their ideal. Annual Naadam festivals play an essential role in showcasing the unique Mongolian culture and shaping Mongolian ethnic identity which is exactly urban Naadam's most significant function.

Naadam in cities can be traced back to 1981, when the first Naadam festival for Mongolian people in Beijing was held and since then, Naadam festival has been celebrated in many cities annually as an important and grand festival for Mongols living in cities. In the early 1980s, especially after the Third Plenary Session of the 11th Central Committee of the Communist Party of China, the whole nation started to be on track to protect ethnic cultures, with ethnic peoples becoming more enthusiastic in showcasing their own identities. It happened around the time that the "Naadam for Mongolian People in Beijing" began to take shape.

In May 17, 1981, the first Naadam for Mongolian people in Beijing was held in the playground of Minzu University of China, attracting thousands of people, including the Mongols, Ewenks, Oroqen, Daur and other neighboring ethnic people. The success of this event proved that Naadam was not limited to pastureland geographically and could also be held in cities. Later Naadam was held successively in Tianjin, Shenyang, Urumchi and other cities and in Xingmeng Township in Tonghai, Yunnan Province, and other regions inhabited by Mongolian ethnic group. As the Mongolian people living in cities try to integrate into mainstream culture of cities, the festival serves to enhance their sense of belonging, build their confidence in their cultural identity and promote their native culture.

Naadam festival is originally a traditional festival of grassland culture, but since 1981, urban Naadam has been constantly changed in terms of time, location, form and content. Consequently, its symbolic meaning becomes so prominent that it is widely considered as a symbol of the cultural border and ethnic identity of Mongolians. Naadam involving only Mongols in Beijing has been held 37 times by 2017. Compared with the traditional Naadam in grasslands, Naadam for Mongolian people in Beijing has experienced the following three stages of development: the first stage was from 1981 to the mid 1990s, the second from the mid and late 1990s to 2007, and the third from 2008 to nowadays.

From 1981 to the mid 1990s, the Naadam for Mongolian people in Beijing was in its initial stage, when traditional elements were mostly maintained and the festival was more like that in grassland. As to when to celebrate the Naadam festival, people insisted on the mid- and late May every year. As to locations of Naadam, open playgrounds in universities where green grassland and blue sky are pleasing to eyeswere always an ideal choice. When it comes to the content, according to the local conditions, Naadam festival took in sing and dance performances, evening parties and activities in which Mongolian children spoke Mongolian language, with Bökh, archery and other traditional Naadam sports still being the highlight. In some years like 1990, yurts were also established in the venues of celebration. Participants were mainly Mongolian Beijingers, most of whom were Mongols and other neighboring minori-

Bökh in the Naadam festival for Mongolian people in Beijing

ties working in ethnic institutions or studying in colleges and universities. In this first stage, backward communication tools limited people's daily contacts, hence Naadam became the best occasion where people could reminisce with their old friends and make new friends as well.

The second stage was from the mid and late 1990s to 2007 and it witnessed great changes of Naadam for Mongolian people in Beijing and the wane of traditional Naadam festival in cities. In this stage, celebration of the festival was moved from open ground to inside space and the time to hold this festival was no longer in line with traditional grassland Naadam. From the mid and late 1990s, the festival was held inside out of limited budget and other reasons. Its contents were changed to dinner parties, art performancesand films; student session of the festival included small-scale basketball competitions or balls. Naadam was held in late December instead of May, and besides people working in ethnic institutions, participants were enlarged to people working in enterprises and migrant workers who didn't have household registrations in Beijing.

The third stage from 2008 to nowadays sees the advancement of Naadam for the Mongols in Beijing. When the Beijing Olympic Games was held in 2008, people took advantage of this event to change the venue of Naadam festival from indoorsback to outdoors and the time from winter to summer, for which more traditional elements were preserved and more participants of different backgrounds were attracted, thus making Naadam more ceremonial and symbolic. The year 2008 was exactly when the Naadam for Mongolian people in Beijing resumed the tradition of being held on the playground of the Minzu University of China in mid- and late May every year. Since then the festive mood has become stronger and the unique characteristics of Mongolian traditions have been fully displayed. Opening ceremonies, collective Andai dance, Bökh, archery, and competitions of children speaking Mongolian become indispensable components of Naadam festival. Commercial activities are also emerging during the festival, in which people can buy traditional Mongolian food such as butter, milk tofu and milk skin and read Mongolian books. All Mongolian people in Beijing from different classes and of different occupations participate in this Naadam festival and some newly established Mongolian organizations and groups such as cultural education institutions, kindergartens and websites acting as the main force. The resumption of traditional Naadam festival in this stage can be attributed to its being included in China's list of national intangible cultural heritages and the country's attention to and advocacy of traditional festivals.

Locality, diverse cultures, urbancharacters and particular participants all contribute to the distinctiveness of urban Naadam festival. Mongolians living in cities far away from grasslands face the inevitable trend of transition of socio-economic structure and the internationalization of metropolises. Yet no matter how Naadam may change in time, location and content and how participants may differ in social status, they will always keep high cultural cognition and never abandon this festival. That's because the name, "Naadam", though sometimes they can just see the festival in imagination, connects the Mongolian people in cities with steppe, their native land and their ethnic group, as the festival carries the history of Mongolian nationality. In the very day of Naadam, Mongolian people will dress up in Mongolian gowns, gather their families or friends, and then head toward the venue at the call of Mongolian songs echoing in the whole city. In the venue, you can see adults talking with others leisurely and children chasing each other happily on the man-made green grassland. The sound of morin khuur, also known as horsehead fiddle, is quite beautiful and people

Book stalls in the Naadam festival for Mongolian people in Beijing

wearing colorful Mongolian gowns are chatting energetically in Mongolian language. You can also enjoy the wild and passionate Andai dance and intense Bökh competitions. The warm

195

atmosphere makes people feel as if they were right in the steppe and their native land. It's no wonder that Naadam with strong traditional elements becomes the grandest carnival for the Mongols living in cities. When Naadam ends with Bökh winners getting their awards, people are just beginning to enjoy their personal "festival" in Mongolian restaurants. Drunken Mongols are talking and laughing, their voice echoing both in the dark sky and their minds, whispering their ardent expectation for the next Naadam. For urban Mongols, Naadam has become a symbol, which is clearly explained by a Mongolian man living in Beijing. The man once said, "Despite all the changes, urban Naadam still reminds us Mongolian people of our ethnic identity and it remains the most significant festival for us. I believe that no one will leave behind the festival of his own nation."

Three generations taking part in the Naadam festival
for Mongolian people in Beijing

## 5. Naadam in Scattered Mongolian Communities

Mongols are distributed widely all over the nation. Apart from some main compact communities, the southwest and middle China also offer residence to hundreds of thousand Mongols scattered in Tonghai County in Yunnan Province, Chengdu in Sichuan Province, Yanyuan County and Muli Tibetan Autonomous County in Liangshan Yi Autonomous Prefecture, Dafang County in Bijie City and Sinan and Shiqian Counties in Tongren City of Guizhou Province and Pengshui County in Chongqing municipal. There are also thousands of Mongols living in the Hefeng County, Hubei Province next to Pengshui County. Over the past several hundred years of adaptation to the southwestern region, Mongols have gradually adopted mountainy agriculture as the major economic source and changed their nomadic culture. But in this course, the history and beliefs of Mongols have been passed down in forms of genealogy, tombstone and dictation.

Naadam held in scattered Mongolian communities is essential for us to better understand the development tendency of Naadam and its culture. The tradition of Naadam was established in the exchange among the Mongols in Inner Mongolia. Having been held many times over the history, Naadam has been transformed to a traditional festival for people to reminisce ancestors and express love for native land and also a clearcut symbol for the minority identity of Mongols in the course of multi-cultural exchange.

The Xingmeng Mongol Ethnic Township in Tonghai, Yunnan Province neighbors to the Silu Lake, and Mongols in this village, who call themselves Mongolwa, Mongole or Khatsos, are offspring of Mongolians immigrating from the north during the late Southern Song Dynasty (1127-1279) and the Yuan Dynasty. In the second year of the reign of Emperor Xianzong (1252) of Yuan, Kublai was dispatched to conquer the Dali Kingdom in the south and his forces were divided into three.

One column led by UryankKhatai took a difficult way into the mountains of western Sichuan, Kublai himself headed south in the middle, and another column took the east road at the leadership of Chaoheyeclie. The three forces arrived in Lijiang one after another and took Dali, the capital city of the Kingdom, putting an end to the Dali Kingdom. For the first time a large amount of Mongols migrated to Yunnan Province and some settled down there, far away from their native land in the north. Since then, 760 years has past and Mongols in Xingmeng Township have turned themselves from herdsmen to fishermen and then to farmers and integrated and communicated with other ethnic groups, gradually forming their own unique Mongolian culture.

It was in the exchange between local Mongols and northern Mongols in native land that people in Xingmeng Township established the tradition of holding Naadam, which started in 1981. At first, it was held annually during December 13-15

Memorial ceremony of the Three Saints in
Xingmeng Mongol Ethnic Township

and later once in three years, a decision made by the third plenary session of the fifth People's Congress of Xingmeng Township in 1993. The government of Xingmeng Township bears
the responsibility for holding Naadam which usually includes
memorial ceremony of the Three Saints, performances, sports
items and so forth. The memorial ceremony for the Three
Saints, Kenghis Khan, Möngke Khan and Kublai Khan is one
of the most important activities in the festival. At the end of
the memorial ceremony, elders in the village will carry three
palanquins, each having a statue of one of the three Saints respectively, start from the front gate of Temple of Three Saints,
and tour around Zhongcun, Baige, Taojiazui and other villages.
As they march ahead, villagers will volunteer to join in this
parade honoring ancestors. Then they will participate in wrestling, dragon dance, land boat dance, theatrical performance
and other competitions and activities. In terms of the contents,
wrestling in which wrestlers have to dress in traditional Mongolian costumes is one of the few activities that still maintain
the flavor of traditional Naadam festival. On the contrary, most
activities carry the features of fishery and agricultural production.

## 6. Naadam Around the World

With a wide distribution and love for traveling, Mongols
have brought their footsteps to every corner of the world. As
a traditional festival, Naadam is observed in any place where
there are Mongols. People with various occupations, social
roles and different classes and regions hold Naadams to meet
their varied demands and hence endow different features to the
festival, continuously deepening its depth and broadening its
width.

## 6.1 Naadam in the State of Mongolia

In Mongolia, Naadam has various types, including Ovoo Naadam and Nair Naadam. Among all these types, the National Naadam enjoys the greatest importance. The Mongolian People's Republic was established in July 11, 1924. Three years later, Sükhbaatar, military leader of Mongolian Revolution of 1921, ordered that the nation shall celebrate Naadam festival as well as the success of the revolution in July 11, which is the origin of the national day of the Mongolia. Naadam is divided into three classes based on the Mongolian administrative divisions, namely nation, aimag (province) and sumu (village). National Naadam is held in the Mongolian capital city Ulaanbaatar, aimag Naadam in capital cities of provinces and sumu Naadam in villages. With the core being the three manly sports, Naadam also includes other sports items, theatrical performances and trading fairs. National Naadam is organized by a special committee and the mayor of Ulaanbaatar, and the general responsibility of its success falls to the Prime Minister. A special law regulating various activities in Naadam is also in place to ensure that the national Naadam runs smoothly.

National Naadam, the biggest festival of Mongolia, is held in Ulaanbaatar during the National Holiday from July 11 – 13 in the National Sports Stadium. On that occasion, people will dress up for the event and gather in Ulaanbaatar to participate in competitions and activities even if they are thousands kilometers away. It also attracts a great number of foreign visitors and ambassadors from different countries invited by the Mongolian government. As a consequence, tickets for Naadam are hard to buy. Sometimes you have to wait for a whole night to get one ticket and viewers can pack the National Sports Stadium which is able to accommodate 15,000 people. Staff in the opening ceremony alone is over ten thousand people.

First the "Nine Base White Banners" symbolizing the invincible god Sülde are taken from the National Palace to the venue under escort of the Mongolian cavalry honor guard, and after that the President makes an opening speech. Then Naadam begins with an elaborate introduction ceremony featuring military parades, exhibitions of ancient military forces, traditional singing and dancing, aerobic exercises and so forth. After the ceremony, the Three Games of Men, namely Bökh (Mongolian wrestling), horse racing, and archery, are held in different fields. Under the knockout system in Mongolian wrestling, 512 wrestlers from all over the Mongolia have to compete with one opponent in a bout until the champion is finally decided. On the other hand, hundreds of archers and thousands of horses start their fierce competitions respectively. For horse racing, the competition field is on the grassland 40 kilometers west to Ulaanbaatar and the distances usually range from 15 to 30 kilom-

The opening ceremony of the National Naadam of Mongolia

201

eters. Jockeys are children from 7 to 12 years old. People swarm to the competition field in the morning of July 12, leaving the road crowded with vehicles and the grassland dotted with tents set up for accommodations.

Naadam is one of the most significant and grand festivals in Mongolia. During the five-day holiday, a great number of residents in Ulaanbaatar go back to pasturelands to join their relatives and friends in this celebration and enjoy traditional Mongolian way of life.

### 6.2 Naadam in Other Countries

As Mongolians migrate to other countries, Naadam is also brought to and roots there. Japan, South Korea, the United States and Germany are on top of the list in terms of the number of Mongolian immigrants. People throw Naadam in city parks regularly or irregularly every year. The Naadam comprises a march-in ceremony, singing and dancing performances, Mongolian wrestling and Mongolian specialty goods. It is an occasion where people dress up in Mongolian gowns and gather

Children wood horse race during Naadam in
New York, Amercia (by Perpetual fire)

with families and friends, chatting idly in Mongolian. This special way of linking people together also helps in building ethnic identity. For example, in July 12, 2015, Mongolian Embassy in New York City and the Association of Mongols in New York co-hosted the third Annual NYC Mongols Naadam Celebration in the renowned Central Park. Activities and competitions included arm wrestling, Mongolian dances, children wood horse race, Mongolian wrestling and so forth. The brilliant event attracted Mongols from the Mongolia, Inner Mongolia Autonomous Region in China, Buryat, Kalmykia, Tyva, Hazara and other countries and regions. It has greatly enhanced the fellowship among these people.

In Japan, Naadam is held every year in Tokyo and other cities by Mongols. Much like the Naadam in the US, it features Mongolian wrestling, Mongolian chess contests, display of Mongolian costumes and song-and-dance performances.

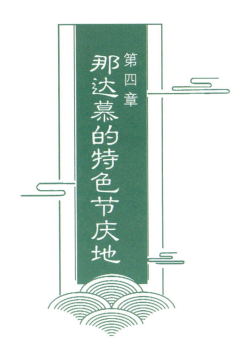

第四章
那达慕的特色节庆地

　　那达慕从古传承至今，成为蒙古族民众重要节庆活动，成为蒙古族重要的文化符号。那达慕的类型较为多样，各地那达慕除了保持那达慕的核心内容之外，不断扩展了那达慕的外延，形成了富有地方特色的那达慕。2006年那达慕被列入国家非物质文化遗产名录，内蒙古自治区锡林郭勒那达慕、青海省海西蒙古族那达慕、新疆维吾尔自治区和静县那达慕成为典型代表。此外，在京蒙古族那达慕和鄂尔多斯国际那达慕也成为近几年发展起来的独具特色的那达慕节庆地。

# 一、
## 锡林郭勒那达慕

锡林郭勒盟位于中国正北方，内蒙古自治区中部，盟府所在地为锡林浩特市。辖9旗2市1县和1个管理区，包括阿巴嘎旗、苏尼特左旗、苏尼特右旗、东乌珠穆沁旗、西乌珠穆沁旗、太仆寺旗、镶黄旗、正镶白旗、正蓝旗、锡林浩特市、二连浩特市、多伦县、乌拉盖管理区。锡林郭勒草原拥有丰富的自然资源，以其草场类型齐全、动植物种类繁多等特征而成为世界驰名的四大草原之一，境内有全国唯一被联合国教科文组织纳入国际生物圈监测体系的锡林郭勒国家级草原自然保护区。草原类型包括草甸草原、典型草原、荒漠草原、沙地草场等，是我国最具代表性和典型性的温带草原。

锡林郭勒草原是最完整地保存蒙古族传统文化的地区之一，蒙古族游牧文化中的诸多民俗事象，相对于其他地在这里保留得更为完整，更具典型性，充分展现出深厚的传统民俗文化积淀。传统的蒙古搏克、古老的吊马及赛马风俗、悠扬的长调、色彩斑斓的蒙古族服饰，无不展示着锡林郭勒蒙古族无比丰富和灿烂的民俗文化底蕴。锡林郭勒盟是蒙元文化的发祥地，素有"搏克之乡""长调之乡""中国马都"的美誉。元朝先后有7位皇帝在锡林郭勒盟正蓝旗

（侧栏）
多彩中国节

那达慕

元上都登基就位，形成了草原文化与中原文化、游牧文化与农耕文化、东方文化与西方文化交流融合的元上都文化，成为蒙元文化的核心，2012年元上都遗址成功入选《世界文化遗产名录》。

锡林郭勒的那达慕更是别具特色，不论是那达慕的类型、规模还是举办频度在内蒙古自治区都是首屈一指，每年大大小小的那达慕可达上千场。整体而言，锡林郭勒也是保持那达慕传统最完整，传承最好的地区。搏克、赛马、蒙古象棋、嘎拉哈等那达慕传统项目，具有广泛的群众基础。

作为蒙古马种的古老产地，自周、秦以来，锡林郭勒就有大量马匹源源不断地传入中原。如，唐代在北边设马市，贡马多来源于此；明、清宣化、大同等边塞重镇，每年向塞外市马定额达三四万匹，也多出于此；从辽、金、元到清代，位于锡林郭勒草原南部的察哈尔草原逐步成为了主要养马地。特别是清代，在察哈尔全境内组织蒙古族发展养马业成为了一个壮丽的景观，全国军马大多取给于此。现在，察哈尔草原虽然已不见昔日万马奔腾的壮观场面和风采，但太仆寺这一马政机关的名称，却作为地名永久地留存了下来，成为了往日锡林郭勒马业辉煌的见证。近年锡林郭勒各旗县围绕马业发展和马文化习俗的传承与弘扬，组织开展了许多在国内外影响较大、吸引世人眼球的大型马文化主题活动，如"骑着马儿过草原"旅游主题活动、800匹蒙古马挑战吉尼斯世界纪录暨阿吉乃大赛、全国马术绕桶邀请赛、锡林河国际两星级耐力赛、中国马术大赛等等，极大地丰富和发展了那达慕的赛马。

锡林郭勒也是搏克的摇篮，不论是历史上还是当下，蒙古族著名搏克多数来自这片草原。历史上有1024名群雄角逐盛会，仅在锡林郭勒一地就举办过5次。著名搏克安召、都仁扎纳、僧格、额尔敦巴雅尔、查干扎纳、哈达、巴图苏和、巴雅尔巴特等都是锡林郭勒的英雄和骄傲。锡林郭勒的搏克手们还是世界古典式摔跤、自由式摔跤、中国式摔跤的佼佼者。1956年，锡林郭勒盟5名搏克手代表内蒙古参加国家冠军选拔赛，4名搏克手在中国式摔跤上领先。2004年西乌珠穆沁旗举办的2048名搏克盛会，让蒙古族的传统搏克载入了世界吉尼斯纪录。

每年农历五月起，锡林郭勒草原沸腾起来。东、西乌珠穆沁旗、正蓝旗、苏尼特旗、阿巴嘎旗、正白旗、正黄旗等传统牧业旗县，敖包祭祀那达慕、家庭那达慕、庆典那达慕、旅游那达慕此起彼伏。甚至在隆冬，也有银冬那达慕。

○著名搏克手僧格

每年锡林郭勒各旗县举办的规模较大，富有特色的那达慕主要有：农历五月十三日锡林浩特市举办贝子庙额尔敦敖包祭祀大典及中国·锡林浩特国际游牧文化节那达慕，农历六月三日正镶白旗察哈尔查干苏力德祭祀那达慕；五至六月阿巴嘎旗成吉思宝格都山及贡扎布敖包祭祀那达慕，农历六月二十五日西乌珠穆沁旗乌珠穆沁王盖敖包祭祀那达慕，六月东乌珠穆沁旗"四季牧歌——蔚蓝的乌珠穆沁"马文化那达慕，农历五月二十五日镶黄旗举办鸿格尔敖包祭祀那达慕、农历六月一日翁贡敖包祭祀那达慕、农历五月二十五日哈音海尔瓦敖包祭祀那达慕，七月太仆寺旗举办贡宝拉格草原马奶节那达慕，阿巴嘎旗举办别力古台祭祀那达慕，农历六月十三日正镶白旗举行旗敖包公祭仪式及草原那达慕，农历六月十四日苏尼特左旗"吉鲁根巴特尔"文化敖包祭祀那达慕，7至8月苏尼特右旗王府那达慕，8月正蓝旗马奶文化节那达慕，8月东乌珠穆沁旗"绿色乌珠穆沁"草原那达慕，12月举办锡林浩特市锡林郭勒草原牧民冬季传统那达慕、正镶白旗冬季那达慕、东乌珠穆沁旗"吉祥·乌珠穆沁"——草原冰雪那达慕、正蓝旗骆驼文化节那达慕、苏尼特右旗骆驼文化节、阿巴嘎旗瑶敏·阿巴嘎冬季那达慕等。这些那达慕上，都开展传统的搏克、赛马、射箭、赛驼、蒙古象棋比赛、嘎拉哈比赛、民族服饰比赛、民族歌舞表演等丰富多彩的活动。

旅游小贴士

### 元上都遗址

元上都遗址位于锡林浩特市南面的正蓝旗上都镇东北约20公里的闪电河北岸，是元朝开国皇帝忽必烈继承蒙古汗位时确定的首都，始建于蒙古宪宗六年（1256年）， 初名"开平府"， 元朝定都北京后就把这里作为陪都，改名"上都"，又名"上京""滦京"，元朝皇帝每年夏季率领重要大臣来这里避暑和处理政务，因此将宫城建成园林式的离宫别馆。

元上都全城由宫城、皇城和外城三重城组成。元朝的十一位皇帝有六位在上都登基，这一时期的元朝，疆域辽阔、空前强盛，成为蒙古汗国的鼎盛阶段，开创了中国古代史和世界游牧民族史的新纪元。一直到元朝末年，上都始终是元朝的政治、经济、军事和文化中心。公元1358年，元上都被农民起义军攻陷并毁于战火，随着元朝的覆灭，元上都也最终逐步成为一座"拥抱着巨大文明的废墟"。

元上都南临上都河，北依龙岗山，周围是广阔的金莲川草原，形成了以宫殿遗址为中心，分层、放射状分布，既有土木为主的宫殿、庙宇建筑群，又有游牧民族传统的蒙古包式建筑的总体规划形式，是草原文化与中原农耕文化融合的杰出典范。

交通路线：

元上都遗址距正蓝旗上都镇以东20公里，从上都镇每天有三趟班车可抵达，也有出租车前往。

## 二、
## 青海省海西蒙古族那达慕

海西蒙古族藏族自治州地处青海省西部，因其地理位置位于青海湖以西而得名"海西"。蒙古族是青海世居民族之一，蒙元、明、清三个时期进入了青海，尤在明代为盛。现今生活在海西州的蒙古族大多是和硕特蒙古，是清卫拉特蒙古四部之一。海西蒙古族因长期与汉、藏、土、回、撒拉等民族杂居，相互影响和交融，形成了富有地方特色的蒙古族文化，这也突出反映在那达慕节日中。

海西蒙古族那达慕与早期青海蒙古族二十九旗的祭祀青海湖，以及协商会盟事宜关系密切。新中国成立后，在海西州各地曾陆续恢复并举办了一些小型那达慕，但是没有形成规模。直到20世纪

80 年代才真正走上复兴之路。1982 年，海西州人民政府以物资交流会的形式举办了首届"那达慕"大会。1983 年，乌兰县人民政府举办了乌兰县首届"那达慕"大会，使海西"那达慕"的发展迈上了一个新的台阶。1988 年 8 月，在都兰县巴隆草原举办了"海西州第一届'那达慕'大会"。这届"那达慕"大会举行了搏克、赛马、射箭、赛骆驼、蒙古象棋五个传统项目。1992 年 8 月，在乌兰县希里沟滩上，举办了"海西州第二届'那达慕'大会"，除了搏克、走马、跑马、射箭、赛骆驼、蒙古象棋等传统项目外，又增加了一些新的活动项目。即布格（蒙古围棋）、民歌、现代歌曲、拔河、诗歌朗诵等，从而更加丰富了那达慕的内容。2001 年 8 月，在德令哈市的戈壁草原上，举办了"海西州第三届'那达慕'大会"，比赛项目除搏克、赛马、射箭、赛骆驼、蒙古象棋外，还增加了布格、民间手工艺、服饰和蒙古包评选活动等。2005 年 7 月，在格尔木市金水河滩上，举办"海西州第四届'那达慕'大会"，在搏克、走马、跑马、射箭、赛骆驼、蒙古象棋、布格、民间手工艺等活动的基础上增加了民歌、

○海西那达慕蒙古包群落（乌席勒 摄）

现代歌曲赛、骆驼赛、书法、摄影、骏马装饰等比赛内容。2009 年 8 月，在大柴旦湖畔，举办了"海西州第五届'那达慕'大会"，有传统搏克、赛马（分走马赛和跑马赛）、射箭、还有夏特尔（蒙古象棋）赛、赛骆驼、长调比赛、布格（蒙古围棋）、骆驼赛、拔河赛。同时还举办了第七届柴达木"孟赫嘎啦"牧民文化节，增加了非物质文化遗产的参赛项目，有服饰展示、祝词、说唱、采词、诗歌、火镰点火、民间手工艺展、拉利（情歌）、都吾尔（抛石打鞭）、达罗（类似麻将）表演赛等。2013 年 8 月在都兰县巴隆乡草原举办"海西州第六届蒙古族那达慕大会暨第十一届孟赫嘎拉文化节"，包括专场文艺演出、篝火晚会和赛马、赛骆驼、搏克、射箭等传统体育及祝词、长调、说唱、拉利、服饰等文化交流项目。

每 4 年举办一次的州那达慕体现了海西蒙古族传统游牧生产与生活，同时也体现了海西州和硕特蒙古的地方特色。在整个那达慕活动中既保持了蒙古族传统的核心内容，又与海西州特定时空相适应而加入了一些不同于其他蒙古族聚居区的活动内容。如赛骆驼，突出了海西州柴达木双峰驼在蒙古族日常生活、生产中的重要地位。蒙古象棋、布格、民间手工艺比赛、歌舞演出、篝火晚会等内容，是海西蒙古族那达慕集庆祝、体育竞技、文化娱乐、经贸交流为一体的节日盛会特色。

三、
新疆和静县那达慕

　　和静县，隶属于新疆巴音郭楞蒙古自治州，位于新疆中部。
1939 年设和通县，同年 8 月改为和靖县，1965 年，改和靖县为和
静县。清乾隆三十六年（公元 1771 年），卫拉特蒙古土尔扈特部从
伏尔加河流域回归祖国后，大部分被安置在和静县，是土尔扈特蒙

○和静县那达慕赛马（确·胡热 摄）

古人主要居住地。和静县也是蒙古族《江格尔》史诗的重要流传地，蒙古族长调、刺绣、骨雕等民间艺术在当地广为流传。

和静县东归那达慕，是这一地区较为特色的那达慕类型。每年在巴音布鲁克草原上举行。不但有传统的搏克、速度赛马、走马赛、赛驼等活动，还有地方特色的民族式摔跤（且力西）、押加（大象拔河）、古吉尔牌（牛九牌）、斗鸡、斗羊等内容。同时，还有大型实景剧《东归·印象》的演出以及马头琴、托布秀尔演奏、"萨吾尔登"舞表演等。《东归·印象》主要展示土尔扈特部东归文化，生动展现东归历史，还原1771年，蒙古族土尔扈特首领渥巴锡率部回归祖国沿途历经千难万阻的过程，以及定居后土尔扈特部后裔们目前生产生活的现状。

## 旅游小贴士

### 巴音布鲁克草原

巴音布鲁克草原，蒙古语意为"富饶的泉水"，位于新疆维吾尔自治区巴音郭楞蒙古自治州和静县西北，距库尔勒市636公里，伊犁谷底东南，四周为雪山环抱，是典型的禾草草甸草原，也是天山南麓最肥美的夏牧场，新疆最重要的畜牧业基地之一。

清乾隆三十六年（1771年），土尔扈特、和硕特等蒙部，在渥巴锡的率领下，从俄国伏尔加河流域举义东归，并于1773年被安置在巴音布鲁克草原和开都河一带定居。

巴音布鲁克草原内有著名的巴音布鲁克天鹅湖和九曲十八弯等景观，景色绝美，也是摄影家们钟爱的摄影胜地。天鹅湖是亚洲最大、我国唯一的天鹅自然保护区。天鹅湖并不是一个湖泊，而是一块长 30 公里，宽约 10 公里，总面积 300 多平方公里，由众多湖泊沼泽相互连接组成的一大片水域。这里水草丰茂，气候湿爽，成为各种禽鸟理想的栖息之地。当地蒙古族牧民把天鹅视为"贞洁之鸟""美丽的天使""吉祥的象征"。

最佳游览时间：

巴音布鲁克草原景区在每年约 4 月至 10 月运营，但是草原最美的季节是 6 月初和 9 月末，而到天鹅湖去观鸟，最好的时间则在每年5 月至 10 月。

交通路线：

从乌鲁木齐乘汽车，沿乌伊公路转独库公路，驱车 460 多公里，可抵和静县。和静县离巴音布鲁克区政府 338 公里，隔日有班车往来。从区所在地租车可到达草原。

## 四、
## 在京蒙古族那达慕

北京蒙古族那达慕是一个有别于传统草原那达慕的代表，极富城市那达慕的特点。1981 年至今已举办 37 届，是北京蒙古族一年一度的节日。

在京蒙古族那达慕，是随着大批草原蒙古族学子进入首都而形成的。高考恢复后，大批蒙古族学子得以有机会来到首都北京就读，并主要集中在原中央民族学院。当时，他们看到别的民族都能过自己的传统节日，如藏族的藏历年，彝族的火把节等，1980年朝鲜族的"传统体育运动会"也得以召开。而作为人数甚多的蒙古族却在这个城市里没有本民族的节日去欢度，这种情况在多民族聚集的中央民族学院显得格外突出。为此，当时1977届的学生干部们提出倡议，将"那达慕"作为蒙古族的节日，在北京进行庆祝。第一届在京蒙古族那达慕于1981年5月17日在中央民族学院操场举行。组织全权由学生负责，即由当时中央民族学院蒙古语言文学专业学生及干训部的学员组织和协调。就活动的内容而言，那达慕传统的比赛项目搏克、射箭仍是重头戏。内蒙古体校教练带来了弓箭和弓箭手，在临时搭建的主席台前进行了表演，并组织了弓箭比赛。此外，现场自愿报名，举行了32人的传统搏克比赛。晚上还由在京的蒙古族

○在京蒙古族那达慕大会集体安代舞

演员举办了一台晚会。除了这些传统类型的活动外，针对北京的蒙古族儿童安排了蒙古语会话比赛和短跑比赛，"试图通过这一方式培养下一代的民族感情和民族认同"。

那达慕一般选择每年 5 月的某一周末在中央民族大学操场上举行，有些年份因各种原因也在室内举办。一般而言，包括开幕入场仪式，包括哈达队、在京各单位和机构代表队、搏克队、歌舞表演队等。从那达慕的过程而言，开幕仪式后，便进入各项比赛之中，搏克赛、篮球赛、排球赛以及儿童蒙古语会话与诗歌朗诵赛等依次举行。

在过去的三十余年当中，在京蒙古族那达慕大会从其参会人员、会议形式、举办场所、组织者等各个方面不断发生着变化，其在北京蒙古族中的影响也发生了相应的变化。但不论怎样变化，其核心功能并未改变，它是北京蒙古族的节日，是在京蒙古族族群认同的符号。在京蒙古族那达慕是在蒙古族进入到多元文化、多族群互动和交融的都市后，迫切需要获得自我身份的确定、重建文化归属感的情境下发生和发展的。对于京城蒙古族而言，最初，他们通过那达慕不过是在都市多元族群文化的交汇融合中，显示自己的独特存在，为自己寻找一个属于本民族的心灵庇护所，但随着年复一年的重复和不断的建构，这个"庇护所"的边界越来越清晰，越来越成为京城蒙古人族群身份的集体表达。

# 五、
# 鄂尔多斯国际那达慕

　　鄂尔多斯，位于内蒙古自治区西南部，是内蒙古自治区下辖市，辖东胜区、达拉特旗、准格尔旗、鄂托克前旗、鄂托克旗、杭锦旗、乌审旗、伊金霍洛旗。鄂尔多斯蒙古族文化与其他地区蒙古族文化之间最重要的区别是鄂尔多斯是接受成吉思汗祭祀文化影响最多最深刻的一种文化形态。成吉思汗祭祀文化渗透到了鄂尔多斯蒙古族文化的方方面面，从而对鄂尔多斯蒙古族文化个性的形成产生了巨大影响。从 13 世纪以来，鄂尔多斯蒙古族一代代传承原始宫廷文化、蒙古王朝最高祭祀仪式和蒙古民族经典民俗礼仪，并在漫长的历史中创造了以祭祀文化、宫廷文化、民俗文化为特征的独具风格的鄂尔多斯蒙古族特色文化。主要表现在以下几个方面：以成吉思汗祭典为代表的鄂尔多斯祭祀文化、以鄂尔多斯婚礼为代表的鄂尔多斯民俗礼仪文化、以宫廷"古如歌"为代表的鄂尔多斯音乐文化、以民间《筷子舞》为代表的民间舞蹈艺术、以民间祝赞词为代表的鄂尔多斯礼俗文化、以"珠拉格"（马奶节）那达慕为代表的鄂尔多斯节庆文化、以妇女头饰为代表的鄂尔多斯服饰文化等。作为文化集中展现平台的那达慕，鄂尔多斯富有特色的文化符号都有所体现。

鄂尔多斯国际那达慕大会，始于 2010 年，每 2 年一次，一般在 8 月中下旬举行。由国家体育总局、文化部、国家民族事务委员会、内蒙古自治区人民政府共同主办，鄂尔多斯市人民政府和内蒙古自治区体育局、文化厅、民族事务委员会共同承办。第一届邀请了俄罗斯、蒙古、朝鲜、韩国、日本、匈牙利、哈萨克斯坦、塔吉克斯坦、乌兹别克斯坦、吉尔吉斯斯坦等国和我国北方和草原文化相关联的黑龙江省、吉林省、辽宁省、河北省、河南省、甘肃省、青海省、宁夏回族自治区、新疆维吾尔自治区等九省区，以及港澳台地区等 20 支左右的代表团参加。项目涵盖体育、文化、经贸、旅游等多个领域。赛事包括赛马、赛驼、搏克、蒙古象棋、射箭、毽球共 6 项，还举办带有浓郁现代特色的汽车、摩托车系列比赛，以及网球、曲棍球、篮球等项目。此外，还举办了"鄂尔多斯杯"民族服饰展演、中外精品舞台剧目展演、草原那达慕音乐节，以及美术系列展、鄂尔多斯革命史展、改革开放 30 年成就展和西部大开发 10 周年成就展、中国少数民族非物质文化遗产展、鄂尔多斯青铜器国际学术研讨会暨青铜器精品展。旅游经贸活动有国际那达慕乐活营、"拥抱自然，亲吻草原"人体多米诺活动、机器人大赛及招商引资项目推荐会等。第二届鄂尔多斯国际那达慕大会的活动内容不仅囊括传统的射箭、赛马、摔跤等 14 个大项、79 个小项的比赛，还融入了户外越野挑战赛和"草原三项"表演赛等项目。与此同时，那达慕还举办汽车拉力赛、徒步穿越沙漠、国际拳击挑战赛、马术大赛等现代体育项目和非物质文化遗产展览展示、经贸洽谈等活动。

　　鄂尔多斯国际那达慕具有规模大、内容多、民族特色浓、国际化程度高等特点，是那达慕发展的一个新的类型。

## 成吉思汗陵

成吉思汗陵位于内蒙古鄂尔多斯市，是蒙古帝国第一代大汗成吉思汗的衣冠冢，位于内蒙古自治区鄂尔多斯市伊金霍洛旗草原上，距鄂尔多斯市区 40 公里。

蒙古族传统丧葬方式使成吉思汗真正的安葬之所成为千古谜团。现今的成吉思汗陵是一座衣冠冢，它曾经过多次迁移，直至 1954 年才由青海塔尔寺迁回故地伊金霍洛旗。1982 年入选第二批全国重点文物保护单位。

达尔扈特人，是蒙古族中专门为成吉思汗守陵的部落。达尔扈特是蒙古语，意思是"担负神圣使命的人"。至今为止，达尔扈特人忠诚地为成吉思汗守灵八百余年，完整地保留了 13 世纪古老的祭祀文化。祭成吉思汗陵是蒙古民族最隆重、最庄严的祭祀活动。成吉思汗祭祀一般分平日祭、月祭和季祭，都有固定的日期。专项祭奠每年举行 60 多次。祭品齐全，皆供整羊、圣酒和各种奶食品，并举行隆重的祭奠仪式。每年农历三月二十一日的春祭规模最大、最为隆重。

成吉思汗陵陵园占地约 5.5 公顷，主体由三个蒙古包式的宫殿一字排开构成。正殿正中端坐成吉思汗雕像，后殿为寝宫。原分布在鄂尔多斯各旗的成吉思汗八白宫、哈日苏勒德及其他圣物也汇集在成吉思汗陵。

成吉思汗陵是每一个蒙古人心中的圣地，是蒙古民族文化中不可或缺的组成部分，对研究蒙古民族乃至中国北方游牧民族历史文化，具有极其重要的价值。

成吉思汗陵一年四季均可前往，但以夏秋两季景色为佳。

交通路线：

前往成吉思汗陵最好通过自驾方式，或从鄂尔多斯市区和伊金霍洛镇租用当地车辆前往。

公共交通：

1.自鄂尔多斯市东胜经康巴什至成吉思汗陵旅游区的旅游专线，每日上午从东胜区鄂尔多斯广场出发，经东胜大酒店、鄂尔多斯饭店、火车站到康巴什广场后开往成陵旅游区；傍晚从成陵旅游区返回东胜。

2.在鄂尔多斯客运总站，可乘坐开往高家堡（榆林市神木县境内）的班车，途中在成陵路口下车，路口到景区大门还有约3公里，可以再换当地人的私车前往景区大门。

# Chapter Four
## Distinctive Festival Places of Naadam

Inherited from ancient times to today, Naadam has become an important festival of Mongolian people and a significant symbol of Mongolian culture. There are great varieties of Naadam, each developing their own characteristics when keeping the core contents of Naadam, thus forming the distinctive Naadam with regional specialties. In 2006, Naadam was listed as the national intangible cultural heritage. Typical examples include Xilingol Naadam in Inner Mongolia Autonomous Region, Haixi Mongolian Naadam in Qinghai Province and Hejing Naadam in Xinjiang Uygur Autonomous Region. In addition, the Mongolian Naadam in Beijing and Ordos and the Ordos international Naadam have grown as the distinctive Naadam festivals in recent years.

## 1. Xilingol Naadam

Xilingol League is situated in the central Inner Mongolian Autonomous Region, just in the north of China, Xilinhot as its league capital. Under the administration of the Xilingol League, there are 9 banners, 2 cities, 1municipality and 1 management district, including Abag Banner, Sonid Left Banner, Sonid Right Banner, East Ujimqin Banner, West Ujimqin Banner, Taibus Banner, Bordered Yellow Banner, Plain and Bordered White Banner, Plain Blue Banner, Xilinhot, Erenhot, Duolun County and Ulagai management district. The Xilingol grassland boasts abundant natural resources, ranking among the four world-renown grasslands because of its complete types of meadows and various fauna and flora. The Xilingol national grassland nature reserve is the only one that is admitted to international biosphere monitoring system by UNESCO around the country. Different varieties of grasslands can be seen here, like meadow grassland, typical grassland, desert grassland and sandy pasture. They're also the most typical and representative temperate grasslands in China.

The Xilingol grassland is one of the regions that still preserve the most complete traditional Mongolian culture. Various customs of Mongolian nomadic culture are relatively more integrated and more typical here than that of other places, which fully demonstrates the profound accumulation of traditional culture and custom. No matter the traditional Mongolian Bökh, ancient horse training and horse racing custom, or the melodious long-tune folk song and colorful Mongolian costumes, they all symbolize the rich and splendid customs and culture. Xilingol League is the birthplace of the Yuan culture and enjoys good reputations of "home to Bökh", "home to long-tune folk songs" and "horse capital of China". During the Yuan Dynasty, there were seven emperors ascending the throng successively in Xanadu, Plain Blue Banner of Xilingol League, thus the Xanadu culture, which combined grassland and central plain culture, nomadic and farming culture, eastern and western culture, came to its life and grew as the core of Mongol-Yuan culture. In 2012, the Site of Xanadu was admitted in the World Cultural Heritage List.

The Xilingol Naadam is more distinctive. Its types, scales and holding frequencies, can be ranked among the most spectacular ones in Inner Mongolia Autonomous Region. Every year, over thousands of Naadams of different scales will be held here. Generally, Xilingol is also the place where traditions of Naadam are most well-kept and complete. Traditional Naadam games, such as Bökh, horse racing, Mongolian chess and gachuha, all have a broad mass base.

Xilingol is an ancient origin place of Mongolian horses and large quantities of horses has been transported from here into central plains since the Zhou and Qin dynasties. For example, the horse market was established in northern borders of Tang Dynasty, which offered most of the horses only for emperor. In Ming and Qing dynasties, the frontier towns with an important location like Xuanhua and Datong, would buy about 30-40 thousand of horses from the northern frontier every year. All those horses were mostly from Xilingol. From Liao, Jin, Yuan to Qing Dynasty, Chahar grassland, which lies in the southern part of Xilingol grassland, gradually becomes the main horse raising place. Especially during Qing Dynasty, the horse raising industry was fully encouraged all around Chahar and turned into spectacular scenery when it supplied the most army horses in the whole country. By now, though the magnificent scene of ten thousand horses galloping together has disappeared in Chahar grassland, the name of horse administration agency Taibus, remained permanently as a place name, witnessed the glorious horse industry that once existed in Xilingol. In recent years, the banners and counties in Xilingol have organized a lot of large-scale activities in theme of horse culture that centered on the development of horse industry as well as the inheritance and expand of horse culture custom, drawing a lot of attention from both home and abroad. Activities include "riding a horse to cross the grassland" theme tourism, 800 Mongolian horses Akinal competition to challenging the Guinness World Records, national equestrian barrel racing invitational tournament, Xinlin river two-star endurance racing, Chinese equestrian competition and so on, greatly enriching and developing the horse racing of Naadam.

Xilingol is also the cradle of Bökh. Since ancient times, most of the famous Mongolian wrestlers have come from this grassland. The historic wrestling competition joined by 1,024 contestants, was held in Xilingol for 5 times. Those famous wrestlers such as Anzhao, Durengzaan, Sengge, Erdenebayar, Tsagaanzaan, Khada, Batusukh, Bayarbatu are all the hero and pride of Xilingol. In addition, wrestlers from Xilingol are also the outstanding ones in world Greece-Roman wrestling, free style wrestling and Chinese-style wrestling. In 1956, five wrestlers, as the representatives of Xilingol League, attended the national champion trials and four of them took lead in the Chinese style wrestling. In 2004, the Bökh fair held in West Ujimqin Banner with 2,048 wrestlers set the Guinness world records.

Starting from the fifth month of lunar calendar every year, the Xilingol grassland becomes hustle and bustle. In the east and west Ujimqin Banner, Plain Blue Banner, Sonid Banner,

Winter Naadam in East Ujimqin Banner (by Sarensuhe)

Abag Banner, Plain White Banner, Plain Yellow Banner and other traditional husbandry banners and counties, different types of Naadam rise as another falls, such as Ovoo Naadam, Family Naadam, Celebration Naadam, Tourism Naadam. Even in mid-winter, there will also be a Silver Winter Naadam.

Every year in banners and counties of Xilingol, distinctive Naadams are included as follows: Erdene Ovoo Sacrificing celebration of Beizi Temple in Xilinhot and Xilingol, China International Nomadic Culture Naadam held on May 13 of the lunar calendar; Chahar Tsagaan Sulde spear Naadam in Plain and Bordered White Banner on June 3 in the lunar calendar; Genghis Bogda Hills and Gonzhab Ovoo Naadamin Abag Banner during May and June; Ujimqin Wanggai Ovoo sacrificial Naadam in West Ujimqin Banner on June 25 of the lunar calendar; the horse culture Naadam with slogan "pastoral songs resounding in four seasons—the azure Ujimqin" in East Ujimqin Banner in June; Hongger Ovoo Naadam in Bordered Yellow Banner on May 25 of the lunar calendar; Orggon Ovoo Naadam in July 1 of the lunar calendar; Hayinhairwa Ovoo

227

Naadam on May 25 of the lunar calendar; Gunbolag Grassland Mare's Milk Festival Naadam by Taipu Temple Banner and in July; Bilgutei; Banner Ovoo Naadam and Grassland Naadamin Plain and Bordered White Banner on June 13 of the lunar calendar; "Julgen Bataar" culture Ovoo Naadam in Sunit Left Banner on June 14; royal palace Naadam by Sunit Right Banner during July and August; Mare's milk Festival Naadam in Plain Blue Banner in August; "Green Ujimqin" Grassland Naadam in East Ujimqin Banner in August; Traditional nomadic winter Naadam on Xilingol Grassland in Xilinhot, winter Naadamin Plain and Bordered White Banner, "Auspiciousness-Ujimqin" grassland winter Naadamin East Ujimqin Banner, Camel Culture Festival Naadam in Plain Blue Banner, Camel Culture Festival by Sunit Right Banner and Abag winter Naadam in Abag Banner in December. The various activities in those Naadams include Mongolian wrestling, horse racing, archery, camel racing, Mongolian chess games, shagai games, folk dress performances and folk song-and-dance performances.

## Tips for Tourism

### Site of Xanadu

On the northern bank of Lightning River, 20 kilometers away from the north-east Shangdu Town, lies the Site of Xanadu which is in the Plain Blue Banner, south of Xilinhot. It was the capital of Yuan Dynasty when Kublai, the empire-builder of Yuan Dynasty, inherited the throne of Khan. Xanadu was first established in the sixth year of Xianzong (1256) with the original name Kaiping. Since Beijing has become the capital of Yuan Dynasty, Kaiping was set as an alternative capital with a new name Xanadu, Shangjing or Luanjing. Each summer, the emperor of Yuan Dynasty would lead his important ministers here to spend the summer holiday and conduct

state affairs. Thus the palace in Xanadu was an imperial pavilion in the gar—
den style.

The whole city of Xanadu consisted of palace city, imperial city and outer
city. In total eleven emperors of Yuan Dynasty, there were six claimed
their throne in Xanadu. During this period, possessing vast territory and
growing unprecedentedly strong, Yuan Dynasty was at its peak stage and
started the new era of Chinese ancient history as well as world nomadic
nation history. Xanadu has been the center of politics, economics, military
and culture until the end of Yuan Dynasty. In 1358, Xanadu was captured
by peasants' revolt army and destroyed in the war. With the collapse of
Yuan Dynasty, Xanadu was gradually reduced into the ruins "embracing
the great civilization".

Surrounded by vast Jinlianchuan grassland, Xanadu borders to the Xanadu
River in south and lies beside Longgang Mountain in the north. The en—
tire site radiates from the center of ancient palace ruins in different layers,
combining the wooden palace and temple complex with the yurt—style
complex with nomadic national tradition. The Xanadu site is an outstand—
ing example that integrating grassland culture with farming culture of the
central plains.

Tour Routes:
Xanadu site is 20 kilometers east of Shangdu, Plain Blue Banner. There are
3 scheduled buses a day in Shangdu which can take you there. Taxi is also
available to take you there, the cost of which is about several dozen yuan.

## 2. Haixi Mongolian Naadam in Qinghai Province

Seated in the west of Qinghai Province, Haixi Mongolian
Tibetan Autonomous Prefecture got its name as it is in the west
bank of Qinghai Lake. Mongolian ethnic minority is one of the

permanent-residents in Qinghai Province. They immigrated to Qinghai Province during the dynasties of Yuan, Ming and Qing and went into the period of great prosperity in Ming Dynasty. Now most of the Mongolians living in Haixi belong to Hoshud Mongol, one of four Oirat Mongolian tribes. During the long period living with Han, Tibetan, Tu(or Monguor), Hui and Salar ethnic groups, Haixi Mongolians created their unique culture which is also reflected in Naadam Festivals.

Haixi Mongolian Naadam has a close relationship with Qinghai Lake Sacrificing of twenty-nine early Qinghai Mongolian banners and their alliance negotiation. After the foundation of People's Republic of China in 1949, some small Naadams reappeared at many places in Haixi Prefecture but did not form into large scale. Not until 1980s did Naadam come to its real revival. In 1982, the government of Haixi Prefecture held the first Naadam in the form of commodity fair. In 1983, the government of Ulan County sponsored the first local Naadam which marked the Naadam stepping into a new period. In August, 1988, "the First Naadam in Haixi Prefecture" was held on Balong Grassland in Dulan County, during which the Bökh, horse racing, archery, camel racing and Mongolian chess such five traditional events were contained. In August, 1992, "the Second Naadam Fair in Haixi Prefecture" on the Xiligou in Ulan County added some new events such as Mongolian go competition, folk and modern songs performance, tug of war and poetry reading, greatly enriching the Naadam. In August, 2001, except the traditional items such as Bökh, horse racing, archery, camel racing, and Mongolian chess, Mongolian go, folk crafts, dress and Mongolian yurt selection were added to "the Third Naadam Fair in Haixi Prefecture" on the Gobi grassland in Delingha. In July, 2005, folk and modern songs competition, camel racing, writing, photography and horse decoration competition appeared in "the Fourth Naadam Fair in Haixi Prefecture" on the benchland of Jinshui River in Golmud. Several years later, "the Fifth Naadam Fair in Haixi Prefecture" was held in August, 2009 beside the Da Qaidam Lake. The events included not only traditional ones such as Bökh, horse riding competition(horse walking and horse racing), archery, but also Mongolian chess, camel racing, Mongolian long-tune folk songs competition, Mongolian go, camel competition and tug of war. Meanwhile, the 7th Qaidam "Monkhgal" Herdsman's Culture Festival was held along with an intangible cultural heritage selection, dress performances, the congratulatory speech, raps, picking poetry and poems reading, lighting performance, the exhibition of folk crafts, love songs singing, rock whipping, Mongolian mahjong performance and etc. "The Sixth Naadam Fair and the Eleventh Monkhgal Culture Festival in Haixi Prefecture" was held in August, 2013 on Grassland of Balong Township, Dulan County. The events included special theatrical performance, campfire party, camel racing, Bökh, archery, the congratulatory speech, long-tune singing, rap, love song singing and dress culture exchange programs.

Held every four years, Naadam of Haixi Prefecture demonstrates not only traditional nomadic production and life but also characteristics of Haixi Prefecture and Hoshud Mongolians. The whole Naadam events not only reserved Mongolian core customs, but also absorbed some distinctive activities to match with specific conditions of Haixi, which are different from those of other Mongolian agglomeration. For example, the camel racing highlights the importance of Haixi Qaidam two-humped camel in Mongolian daily life and production. Other activities such as Mongolian chess, Mongolian go, folk

People in the Haixi Mongolian Naadam (by Wuxile)

crafts selection, song-and-dance performances, campfire parties and etc. are the features of Naadam Festival which combines celebration, sports, entertainment and economy and trade communication.

## 3. Xinjiang Hejing Naadam

Hejing County, under the administration of Bayingol Mongolian Autonomous Prefecture, is located in the central part of Xinjiang. There's a long story to tell about the name of Hejing ( 静 ) County which was originaly established as Hetong County in 1939. It changed the name into Hejing (靖) County later in August of the same year. In 1965, the name was changed again to Hejing ( 静 ) County. In the thirty-sixth year of the reign of Emperor Qianlong (1771), returning from the Volga River basin, most of the Oriat MongolianTuerhute settled in Hejing County. In addition, Hejing County also plays an important role in the spread of the Mongolian epic

Jangar. The folk arts such as Mongolian long-tune, embroidery, bone carving are widely spread among the people.

Donggui Naadam in Hejing County is distinctive in this region, held in Bayanbulak grassland every year. Events not only include traditional Bökh, horse racing, horse racing and camel racing, but also contain other events with local characteristics, such as Folk wrestling (Qielixi), Yajia (elephant tug of war), Gujir, cock game and goat game. Meanwhile, there are also different live-actions such as "East-returning and Impression", morinkhuur show, tobshur show and sauurdin show. The performance of "East-returning and Impression" mainly demonstrates the culture of Tuerhute and reflects the history of returning to the east, restoring the formidable returning process of Tuerhute led by Ubashi and the present living and production situation of their descendants since the settlement here.

## Tips for Tourism

### Bayanbulak grassland

Bayanbulak, meaning "abundant fountain" in the Mongolian language, is situated in the north—west of Hejing county, Bayanbulak Mongolian autonomous prefecture, Xinjiang Uygur Autonomous Region, with a distance of 636 kilometers from Korla. Surrounded by snowcapped mountains, Bayanbulak is typical meadow grassland in the south—east part of Ili valley. It is also one of the most fertile summer pastures in the south Tianshan Mountain and one of the most important animal husbandries in Xinjiang Uygur Autonomous Region.

In the thirty—sixth year of the reign of Emperor Qianlong(1771), led by Ubashi, the Tuerhute and the Hoxud tribes returned to the east from the Volga River basin. In 1773, they settled in the area of Bayanbulak grassland

and Kaidu River.

Inside the Bayanbulak grassland, there are the famous tourist attractions Bayanbulak Swan Lake and Eighteen Bends. Because of its spectacular scenery, it is photographers' favorite place. The Swan Lake is the biggest swan nature reserve in Asia and the only one in China. The Swan Lake is a large water area connected by quantities of lakes and swamps, with a length of 30 kilometers a width of 10 kilometers and a total area of over 300 square kilometers. It serves as an ideal home to various fowls due to its rich grassland and moist climate. In the eyes of local Mongolian herdsman, swans are the birds of purity, beautiful angel and the symbol of auspicious— ness.

Best visiting season:
Bayanbulak grassland runs from April to October every year. The most beautiful seasons of grassland are in the beginning of June and the end of September. If you want to watch the birds in Swan Lake, the best time is from May to October every year.

Tour routes:
Take a bus from Urumqi, move along the Uyi road and then divert to Duku road. Hejing County is over 460 kilometers away. Hejing County is 338 kilometers away from Bayanbulak government. Scheduled bus is avail— able every two days. Taking a jeep to the glassland from the district will cost you 400—500 yuan a day.

## 4. Beijing Mongolian Naadam

Different from the traditional grassland Naadam, Beijing Mongolian Naadam is a representative for the Urban Naadam. Since 1981, the Beijing Mongolian Naadam has been an annual festival for Beijing Mongolians and has undergone its 37th year.

The Beijing Mongolian Naadam was formed with large quantities of Mongolian students entering Beijing. After the resumption of university entrance examination, lots of Mongolian students had the chance to study in Beijing and mostly in the Minzhu university of China. At that time, other ethnic groups all had their traditional festivals, such as Tibetan new year of Tibetan people, the Torch Festival of the Yi people, and the "traditional sports meeting" of Korean people held in 1980 at the first time. As the minority with a large population in Beijing, however, the Mongolian students had no national festival to celebrate, especially in multi-ethnic Minzhu university of China. Thus, the student leaders graduated in 1977 advocated that they celebrate the Naadam as the Mongolian festival in Beijing. The first Beijing Mongolian Naadam was held in the playground of Minzhu university of China in May 17th, 1981. Students major in Mongolian Language and Literature and students from the training department took charge of the whole organization and coordination. As far as the items of event, the

Mongolian dialogue competition for children during Beijing
Mongolian Naadam festival

235

traditional Naadam games such as Bökh, archery were still the most important parts. Coaches from Mongolian sports school brought brows and arrows as well as archers. They performed in front of the shift rostrum and an archery competition was also held at that time. In addition, with 32 volunteers on site, there was also a traditional Bökh game. At that night, an evening party was organized by the Beijing Mongolian actors. Apart from those traditional events, Mongolian dialogue competition and sprint were especially arranged for Mongolian children in Beijing. "By this way we hope to cultivate the national pride and identity of the next generation."

The Beijing Mongolian Naadam normally was held on the playground of Minzu University of China at one weekend on May. In some years it may be held indoor due to different reasons. Generally speaking, the Naadam will begin with the opening ceremony, which includes the Khadag delegation, delegations of all Beijing units and agencies, Bökh delegation,

Mongolian wrestling during Beijing Mongolian Naadam festival

singing and dancing delegation. From the process of Naadam, competitions will follow the opening ceremony. Different events such as Bökh competition, basketball game, volleyball game and children's Mongolian dialogue and poetry reading will be held successively.

During the past three decades, the Beijing Mongolian Naadam has changed in different aspects such as its participants, forms, locations and organizers. For beijing Mongolians, the influence brought by it has also come to its relevant changes. However, the core function of Beijing Naadam still remains as a symbol of Beijing Mongolian identity and a festival for Beijing Mongolians. When Mongolians went into the city where exsits multi cultures and interaction of different ethnic groups, the Beijing Mongolian Naadam was generated and developed due to the demand of a certainty of identity and rebuilding the culture ascription. For the Beijing Mongolians, the Naadam festival was first served as a platform to demonstrate their unique existence and build a shelter for their very nationality. But with continuous construction year after year, the boundary of the shelter has become clearer and clearer so that it has increasingly functioned as a collective expression of Beijing Mongolian identity.

## 5. Ordos International Naadam Festival

Located in the southwest of the Inner Mongolian Autonomous Region and as one of its subdivisions, Ordos administrates Dongsheng District, Dalad Banner, Jungar Banner, Otog Front Banner, Otog Banner, Hanggin banner, Uxin Banner, Ejin Horo Banner. The most important difference between the culture of Ordos Mongolian and that of Mongolian ethnics is in other areas is that the former is influenced profoundly by the sacrificial culture of Genghis Khan. The sacrificial culture permeates every aspect of the Ordos Mongolian ethnics and has a significant impact on it. Since the 13th century, Ordos Mongolians have inherited generations of original imperial court culture, the supreme sacrifice ceremonies of the Mongol empire and classic folk customs of Mongolian ethnic groups. During the long history, the Ordos Mongolian people created its unique culture characterized by sacrifice culture, imperial court culture and folk culture which are observed in the following aspects: the Ordos sacrifice culture represented by Genghis Khan sacrifice ceremony; the folk-custom culture represented by Ordos wedding; the Ordos music culture represented by "Guru Song"; the folk dancing art represented by Chopsticks dance; the Ordos custom culture represented by the folk congratulatory speech; the Ordos festival culture represented by Mare's Milk Festival; the Ordos dress culture represented by female's headwear and etc. As a culture platform, Naadam demonstrates all the distinctive culture symbols of Ordos.

Ordos International Naadam Festival, starting in 2010, is often held in mid-to-late August every two years. It is sponsored by General Administration of Sport of China, Ministry of Culture, and State Ethnic Affairs Commission and organized by the Ordos government, the Sports Council, the Department of Culture and the Ethnic Affairs Commission of Inner Mongolian Autonomous Region. The first session of the Naadam Fair invited Russia, Mongolia, North Korea, South Korea, Japan, Hungary, Kazakhstan, Tajikistan, Uzbekistan, Kyrgyzstan and etc. Around 20 delegations from Hong Kong, Macao, Taiwan and some northern provinces such as Heilongjiang, Jilin, Liaoning, Hebei, Henan, Gansu, Qinghai, Ningxia Hui Autonomous Region and Xinjiang Uygur Autonomous Region which have relevant prairie cultures also participated in this Fair. The events covered many areas such as sports, culture, economy and trade and tourism. The activities included horse racing, camel racing, Mongolian wrestling, Mongolian chess, archery, shuttlecock and some modern activities such as automobile racing, motorbike racing, tennis, hockey ball and basketball games. In addition, there also have "Ordos Cup" national costumes show, high-quality stage drama performance from both home and abroad, grassland Naadam music festival, series art exhibitions, the exhibition of Ordos revolution, the achievements exhibition of the reform and opening-up in the past 30 years, 10th anniversary exhibition reviewing the achievements of west development, the exhibition of intangible cultural heritage and Ordos international bronze ware academic seminar and exhibition. Tourism, economic and trade activities included Naadam International Camp, Human Dominoes whose slogan is "Embrace nature and buss grassland", robot competition and investment promotion conference. The activities of the second session of the Naadam Fair covered not only 14 traditional major items such as archery, horse racing, wrestling and etc. and 79 minor items but also off-road challenge and "Grassland Triathlon" Performance. At the same time, intangible cultural heritage exhibition, economy and commerce negotiation and many modern sports such as Auto Rally, Walking through the Desert, International Boxing Challenge and Equestrian Games were held in the Naadam Fair as well.

Ordos Naadam International Festival boasts its great scale, abundant activities, distinctive national features, high degree of internationalization and other chatacteristics. It is a new type of Naadam appeared in its development course.

## Tips for Tourism

## Mausoleum of Genghis Khan

Located on the grassland of Ejin Horo Banner in Ordos, Inner Mongolia, the Mausoleum of Genghis Khan is a cenotaph of Mongolian empire's first khan Genghis Khan, with a 40 kilometers distance from the downtown area of Ordos.

Mongolian traditional funeral custom made it an eternal mystery where Genghis Khan was buried. The present Genghis Khan Mausoleum was just a cenotaph and underwent several migrations. It was not until 1954 that the cenotaph was moved back to its home Ejin Horo Banner. In 1982, the Genghis Khan Mausoleum was selected as the second batch of national key cultural relics protection units.

The Darkhard are the Mongolian tribe guarding the Genghis Khan Mausoleum. In Mongolian, Darkhard means "people shouldering sacred mission". By now, the Darkhard has loyally guarded the Genghis Khan Mausoleum for more than eight hundred years and completely saved the ancient sacrificing culture of the 13th century. Sacrificing for the Genghis Khan Mausoleum is the most solemn and sacred sacrificing event of Mongolian people, usually with regular intervals such as daily sacrificing, monthly sacrificing and seasonal sacrificing. The special memorial ceremony will be held over 60 times a year. Sacrifices such as the whole sheep, sacred wine and various dairy will be offered with grand sacrificing ceremony. Every year, the spring sacrificing on March 21 of lunar calendar is the largest and most solemn one.

The cemetery park occupies an area of 5.5 hectares. Its main body consists of three yurt-style palaces lying in line. In the middle of the main hall sits the stature of Genghis Khan. The rear court of the palace serves as the im—perial burial palace of Genghis Khan. Sacred articles such as Eight White Palaces and Harsuld distributed in Ordos are gathered in Genghis Khan Mausoleum.

As the sacred place of each Mongolian person, the Genghis Khan Mauso—leum is an indispensable part of Mongolian culture and has an unparalleled value in studying historic culture of the Mongolian and even the northern nomadic ethnic minorities in China.

The Genghis Khan Mausoleum is suitable for visit in all seasons, but the best scenery is in summer and autumn.

Tour Routes

The best way to reach here is through self—driving, or renting a local car from Ordos or Ejinhoro town.

Public Transport

1. A tour line for the tourist spot of Genghis Khan Mausoleum starts from Dongsheng district, Ordos, passes by Kangbashi, and then heads to the des—tination. The scheduled bus sets out from Ordos Square in Dongsheng dis—trict at 8 am every day, passing by Dongsheng hotel, Ordos restaurant, the train station, then arrives at Kangbashi Square, and from there the bus heads to the tourist spot. The tour line will also take you back to Dongsheng dis—trict from the tourist spot, and it's scheduled to leave at 4:30 pm.

2. At the Ordos bus station, passengers can take the scheduled bus head—ing to Gaojiabao, which lies in Shenmu, Yulin and get off at a crossing in Chenglin Road, where there is about 3 kilometers away from the tourist spot. You can take a private car of the local people's to get to the entrance of the spot, which will cost you about 15—20 yuan.

# 结 语

　　岁月的流逝，时代的发展，蒙古人的生活也在悄悄发生着变化，昔日"逐水草而居"的生活已不再是如今蒙古人典型的生活形态，千百年来形成的蒙古族文化传统与现代文明和生活方式的不断结合，使蒙古人的生活表现出更多的时代特征。但是，无论生活环境和生活方式发生怎样的变化，勤劳勇敢的蒙古人对本民族精神家园的那份守望却没有发生过一丝动摇和改变，在此过程中，以草原文化为突出特点的蒙古族文化也逐渐形成并发扬光大。

　　从某种意义上讲，那达慕就是蒙古族民族精神和文化特征的集中体现，它体现了蒙古人热爱自然，亲近自然，对自然的敬畏之心；它表达了蒙古人对祖先和历史的崇敬之情；它反映了蒙古人对美好生活的渴望和不懈追求的生活态度。

　　如同草原上的精灵一般，蒙古人在广袤的大草原上繁衍生息，发展壮大，在顺应自然规律的同时，又积极与自然抗争，向人们诠释着人与自然发展的和谐和高度统一。

　　要想真正了解蒙古人，认识蒙古族文化，那就请来到草原吧，来到那达慕吧！

# Conclusion

With time passing by and times developing, life of Mongolian people is changing without drawing any attention. The past idea of Mongolian people's primitive way of living failed to give a correct description of Mongolians' typical lifestyle nowadays. Mongolian culture and tradition formed through hundreds of years is constantly combined with modern civilization and lifestyle, contributing to more contemporary features represented in Mongolian people's life. However, no matter how living environment and lifestyles change, the industrious and courageous Mongolians have never wavered in upholding their homeland for national spirit. In this process, Mongolian culture which features grassland culture has taken hold and exerted more influence.

In a sense, Naadam is a collective representation of Mongolian national spirit and culture. It reflects Mongolian people's love, affection and reverence for nature, the respect for their ancestors and past history, as well as their strong desire and continuous pursuit of a happy life as reflected in their attitude towards life.

As the angels dwelling on the grassland, the Mongolians live and prosper on this vast grassland. They conform to the law of natural while actively struggling with natural for survival, which explain to us the harmony and high-degree unity within the development of human and nature.

To truly understand Mongolian people and learn about Mongolian culture, do come to the grassland and have a taste of Naadam.

# 附 录 Appendix

## 蒙古奶茶的制作方法
### Recipe of Mongolian Milk Tea

　　蒙古奶茶是蒙古族牧民日常生活中不可缺少的饮料，也是他们招待客人的必备良品。

　　奶茶所用的茶叶是青砖茶，因为砖茶含有丰富的维生素C、单宁、蛋白质、酸、芳香油等人体必须的营养成分。奶茶的一般做法是先将茶捣碎，放入清水锅中煮。茶水烧开之后，煮到较浓时，用漏勺捞去茶叶，之后再继续烧片刻，并边煮边用勺扬茶水，待其有所浓缩之后，再加入适量鲜牛奶，用勺扬至茶乳交融，再次开锅即成为馥郁芬芳的奶茶了。

Mongolian milk tea is an indispensible beverage in Mongolian nomads' daily life, and also an essential fancy good to treat guests.

The milk tea is made from green brick tea for it is rich in vitamin C, tannin, protein, acid, aromatic oil and other nutrient contents essential to human body. The general way to make milk tea starts with mashing tea leaves and puting them into clean water for boiling. When water is boiling and thickened, take tea leaves away with a strainer and let water continue to boil a while. In the meantime, scoop boiling water up and pour it back till it is concentrated. Then add fresh milk as appropriate and scoop it to mix it with water. When pot boils again, the water will turn into strong aromatic milk tea.

245

**原料：**

1. 牛奶 500 克

2. 砖茶 ( 也可用红茶、普洱茶代替 )25 克

3. 米 ( 蒙古炒米，也可用小米、大米代替 )30 克

4. 盐少许

5. 其他：黄油、奶皮、奶豆腐、牛肉干适量

Ingredients：

1. 500g milk

2. 25g brick tea (or black tea/ Puerh)

3. 30g rice (Mongolian stir-fried rice, or millet/ rice)

4. A little salt

5. Others: butter, clottd cream, milk tofu, dried beef in appropriate amount

## 制作步骤 /Procedures

1. 把米放入锅里干炒至深黄色，炒出米香，备用。

1.Stir-fry rice in a dry pan till rice becomes mustard-colored with rice fragrance.

2. 将砖茶切成块状，装入茶包；锅中放入约 2500 克水，放入砖茶一起煮。煮沸 2~3 分钟，至颜色深咖啡色。待煮开后用细网漏勺滤出。

2.Cut brick tea into blocks and put them into tea bag; Put 2500g water and brick tea into pot to boil for 2~3 minutes till water turns into dark brown. Take tea leaves away with a fine-mesh strainer after the water is boiled.

3. 放入米、牛奶。开锅后，再煮约 5 分钟，边煮边用勺扬茶水。放入少许盐，至米、茶、奶、盐充分融合。

3.Add rice and milk into the pot. When the tea water is boiling, heat it up for another 5 minutes during which scoop water up and pour it back. Add salt a little. Mix them till rice, tea, milk, and salt fully integrate with each other.

4.依个人口味，可加入黄油、奶皮、奶豆腐、牛肉干等，口味更佳。
4.According to personal preference, add butter, Clottd cream, Mongolian milk tofu, dried beef, etc. It will taste better.

# 丛书后记

　　上下五千年的悠久历史孕育了灿烂辉煌的中华文化。我国地域辽阔,民族众多,节庆活动丰富多彩,而如此众多的节庆活动就是一座座珍贵丰富的旅游资源宝藏。在中华民族漫长的历史长河中,春节、清明、端午、中秋等传统节日和少数民族节日,是中华民族优秀传统文化的历史积淀,是中华民族精神和情感传承的重要载体,是维系祖国统一、民族团结、文化认同、社会和谐的精神纽带,是中华民族生生不息的不竭动力。

　　春节以正月为岁首,贴门神、朝贺礼;元宵节张灯、观灯;清明节扫墓、踏青、郊游、赏牡丹;端午节赛龙舟、包粽子;上巳节祓禊;七夕节乞巧,牛郎会织女;中秋节赏月、食月饼;节日间的皮影戏、长安鼓乐;少数民族的节日赶圩、歌舞美食……这一桩桩有趣的节日习俗,是联络华人、华侨亲情、乡情、民族情的纽带,是中国非物质文化遗产的"活化石"。

　　为了传播中华民族优秀传统文化,推进中外文化交流,中国人类学民族学研究会民族节庆专业委员会与安徽人民出版社合作,继成功出版《中国节庆文化》丛书之后,再次推出《多彩中国节》丛书。为此,民族节庆专委会专门成立了编纂委员会,邀请了国际节庆协会(IFEA)主席兼首席执行官史蒂文·施迈德先生、中国文联原执行副主席冯骥才先生、第十一届全国政协民族和宗教委员会副主任周明甫先生等担任顾问,由《中外节庆网》总编辑彭新良博士担任主编,16 位知名学者组成编委会,负责丛书的组织策划、选题确定、体例拟定和作者的甄选。

出版《多彩中国节》丛书，是民族节庆专业委员会和安徽人民出版社合作的结晶。安徽人民出版社是安徽省最早的出版社，有60余年的建社历史，在对外传播方面走在全国出版社的前列；民族节庆专业委员会是我国节庆研究领域唯一的国家级社团，拥有丰富的专家资源和地方节庆资源。这套丛书的出版，实现了双方优势资源的整合。丛书的面世，若能对推动中国文化的对外传播、促进传统民族文化的传承与保护、展示中华民族的文化魅力、塑造节庆的品牌与形象有所裨益，我们将甚感欣慰。

掩卷沉思，这套丛书凝聚着诸位作者的智慧，倾注着编纂者的心血，也诠释着中华民族文化的灿烂与辉煌。在此，真诚感谢各位编委会成员、丛书作者、译者以及出版社工作人员付出的辛劳，以及各界朋友对丛书编纂工作的鼎力支持！希望各位读者对丛书多提宝贵意见，以便我们进一步完善后续作品，将更加璀璨的节庆文化呈现在世界面前。

为了向中外读者更加形象地展示各民族的节庆文化，本丛书选用了大量图片。这些图片，既有来自于丛书作者的亲自拍摄，也有的来自于民族节庆专委会图片库（由各地方节庆组织、节庆主办单位报送并授权使用），还有部分图片是由编委会从专业图片库购买，或从新闻媒体中转载。由于时间关系，无法与原作者一一取得联系，请有关作者与本书编委会联系（邮箱：pxl@jieqing365.com），我们将按相关规定支付稿酬。特此致谢。

《多彩中国节》丛书编委会

2018年3月

# Series Postscript

China has developed its splendid and profound culture during its long history of 5000 years. It has a vast territory, numerous nationalities as well as the colorful festivals. The rich festival activities have become the invaluable tourism resources. The traditional festivals, such as the Spring Festival, the Tomb-Sweeping Festival, the Dragon Boat Festival, the Mid-Autumn Festival as well as the festivals of ethnic minorities, represent the excellent traditional culture of China and have become an important carrier bearing the spirits and emotions of Chinese people, a spirit tie for the national reunification, national unity, cultural identity and social harmony, and an inexhaustible motive force for the development of Chinese nation.

The Spring Festival starts with Chinese lunar January, when people post pictures of the Door Gods and exchange gifts and wishes cheerfully. At the Lantern Festival a splendid light show is to be held and enjoyed. On the Tomb-Sweeping Festival, men and women will worship their ancestors by sweeping the tombs, going for a walk in the country and watching the peony. And then the Dragon Boat Festival witnesses a wonderful boat race and the making of zongzi. Equally interesting is the needling celebration on the Double Seventh Festival related to a touching love story of a cowboy and his fairy bride. While the Mid-Autumn Festival is characterized by moon-cake eating and moon watching. Besides all these, people can also enjoy shadow puppet shows, Chang'an drum performance, along with celebration fairs, songs and dances and delicious snacks for ethic groups. A variety of festival entertainment and celebrations have formed a bond among all Chinese, at home or abroad, and they are regarded as the "living fossil" of Chinese intangible cultural heritage.

In order to spread the excellent traditional culture of China, and promote the folk festival brand for our country, the Folk Festival Commission of the China Union of Anthropological and Ethnological Science (CUAES) has worked with the Anhui People's Publishing House to publish *The Colorful Chinese Festivals Series*. For this purpose, the Folk Festival Commission has established the editorial board of *The Colorful Chinese Festivals Series*, by inviting Mr. Steven Wood Schmader, president and CEO of the International Festival And Events Association (IFEA); Mr. Feng Jicai, former executive vice-president of China Federation of Literary and Art Circles(CFLAC); Mr. Zhou Mingfu, deputy director of the Eleventh National and Religious Committee of the CPPCC as consultants; Dr. Peng Xinliang, editor-in-chief of the Chinese and foreign Festival Website as the chief editor; and 16 famous scholars as the members to organize, plan, select and determine the topics and the authors.

This series is the product of the cooperation between the Folk Festival Commission and Anhui People's Publishing House. Anhui People's Publishing House is the first publishing house in Anhui Province, which has a history of over 60 years, and has been in the leading position in terms of foreign transmission. The Folk Festival Commission is the only organization of national level in the field of research of the Chinese festivals, which has experts and rich local festival resources. The series has integrated the advantageous resources of both parties. We will be delighted and gratified to see that the series could promote the foreign transmission of the Chinese culture, promote the inheritance and preservation of the traditional and folk cultures, express the cultural charms of China and build the festival brand and image of China.

*The Colorful Chinese Festivals Series* is bearing the wisdoms and knowledge of all of its authors and the great efforts of the editors, and explaining the splendid cultures of the Chinese nation. We hereby sincerely express our gratitude to the members of the board, the authors, the translators and the personnel in the publishing house for their great efforts and to all friends from all walks of the society for their supports. We hope you can provide your invaluable opinions for us to further promote the following works so as to show the world our excellent festival culture.

This series uses a large number of pictures in order to unfold the festive cultures in a vivid way to readers at home and abroad. Some of them are shot by the authors themselves, some of them come from the picture database of the Folk Festival Commission (contributed and authorized by the local folk festival organizations or organizers of local festival celebrations), and some of them are bought from Saitu Website or taken from the news media. Because of the limit of time, we can't contact the contributors one by one. Please don't hesitate about contacting the editorial board of this series (e-mail: pxl@jieqing365.com) if you're the contributor. We'll pay you by conforming to the state stipulations.

Editorial Committee of *The Colorful Chinese Festivals Series*
March, 2018

# 《那达慕》英文翻译人员及分工

徐伟红：负责全书统稿、译校。

夏　慧：负责第 1 章英文翻译。

郭羽嘉：负责第 2 章英文翻译。

刘紫薇：负责第 3 章英文翻译。

赵　成：负责第 4 章英文翻译。